Mythologies of Vision

Semiotics and the Human Sciences

Roberta Kevelson
General Editor

Vol. 15

PETER LANG
New York • Washington, D.C./Baltimore • Boston
Bern • Frankfurt am Main • Berlin • Vienna • Paris

Eduardo Neiva

Mythologies of Vision

Image, Culture, and Visuality

PETER LANG
New York • Washington, D.C./Baltimore • Boston
Bern • Frankfurt am Main • Berlin • Vienna • Paris

Library of Congress Cataloging-in-Publication Data

Neiva, Eduardo.
Mythologies of vision: image, culture, and visuality / Eduardo Neiva.
p. cm. — (Semiotics and the human sciences; v. 15)
Includes bibliographical references and index.
1. Image (Philosophy). 2. Semiotics and the arts. 3. Art—Philosophy. I. Title.
II. Series: Semiotics and the human sciences; vol. 15.
B105.I47N45 121'.35—dc21 98-25975
ISBN 0-8204-4184-8
ISSN 1054-8386

Die Deutsche Bibliothek-CIP-Einheitsaufnahme

Neiva, Eduardo:
Mythologies of vision: image, culture, and visuality / Eduardo Neiva.
–New York; Washington, D.C./Baltimore; Boston; Bern;
Frankfurt am Main; Berlin; Vienna; Paris: Lang.
(Semiotics and the human sciences; Vol. 15)
ISBN 0-8204-4184-8

The paper in this book meets the guidelines for permanence and durability
of the Committee on Production Guidelines for Book Longevity
of the Council of Library Resources.

Printed in the United States of America

TO PEDRO, HELOISA, AND GABRIEL

com amor

ACKNOWLEDGEMENTS

EARLIER VERSIONS of the chapters in *Mythologies of Vision* were published in *The American Journal of Semiotics* and *Semiotica*. I am grateful to Professor Richard L. Laningan, editor of *The American Journal of Semiotics*, for granting permision to reprint a modified version of the theoretical argument against conventionalist interpretation of images. I must also thank Professor Thomas A. Sebeok and Dr. Jean Umiker-Sebeok, editors of *Semiotica*, where all the other chapters were originally published. In *Semiotica*, I was lucky to have the editorial assistance of Evan P. Young and Penelope Mathiesen. I thank them for their advice and textual improvement.

With their computer skills, Lauren and Alan Skees helped me shape the manuscript and make it ready for publication.

Dana Jacobson was an attentive reader of all versions of the manuscript. I have no words to acknowledge her brilliance, generosity, kindness, and exacting criticism.

I would also like to thank my colleagues in the Communication Studies Department of the University of Alabama at Birmingham, especially Dr. Mark Hickson, III, whose comments and support were more than beneficial.

This book is dedicated, with love, to my family.

CONTENTS

INTRODUCTION

Which Semiotics of Image?

THE TASK of interpreting images is at the core of daily experience. We just have to look around to recognize the action of images. They circulate plebeian, but nimble, throughout the social environment. Images simulate situations that help us reach decisions, whether political or scientific. Personal identities spring from the pictures on driver's licenses that certify and authorize us. The intensive action of representations in daily life is reason enough to discuss the prevailing assumptions in reading images.

Recently, it has been presumed, and without great dispute, that to understand what images do, we must go beyond notions of mimetic correspondence. Not surprisingly, mimetism, the dominant conception in the Western tradition of evaluating images, could not hold its ground. The mimetic criterion for the production of images is tied to outdated historicist expectations: It indicates that representations have the exacting goal of securing a perfectly realist rendering of nature.

The wide acceptance of mimetic principles comes from the immense success of perspective as the ruling representational technique during and after the Renaissance. And, in modern times, the invention of photography is the culmination of the Western pictorial project. Nevertheless, it is difficult to believe that nowadays anyone would seriously uphold the mimetic ideal. The experience of being surrounded by proliferating images suggests that representations can refer to representations and not just to the world outside. The obsessive growth of images has driven us away from referents.

How can we accept the notion that images should match reality and be dependent upon a correspondence with nature when images have become more realistic than reality? In contrast with the traditional mimetic premise that images have something to do with either fidelity or truth, we are immersed in pictures that could not care less about the loss of referents. Currently, images are forceful, self-sufficient, and unquestioned representations. Some kind of mimetism can be found almost everywhere in daily experience—in holograms, in computerized simulations, in machines of virtual reality—while being, at the same time, almost absent from the contemporary interpretation of images. For the modern mind, images act as surrogates of reality, without being reality; rather, they are signs themselves.

In such an intellectual landscape dawns the hope that semiotics can furnish a productive interpretative tool to deal with images. Even if we accept the validity of this ambition, an important question has to be asked: What kind of semiotics should deal with the interpretation of images in an age when theory refuses all mimetic explanations? Historically, a specific type of semiotics has been offered as an alternative to the mimetic paradigm: the conventionalist interpretation of images.

Mythologies of Vision presents the conventionalist hypothesis and argues in favor of a semiotic approach to the interpretation of images free from the strictures of rigid conventionalism. My purpose herein is to reject the notion that conventions have a special priority in the understanding of images. Unqualified conventionalism fosters a deterministic conception of history and creation. That would appear to be enough to discard it as a productive theoretical option in the interpretation of images. Yet, a denser and more encompassing argument is required, mainly because conventionalism presides over a distinguished intellectual legacy, cutting across several fields of the humanities.

We have become so accustomed to conventionalist theories that they appear immune to criticism. But conventionalism employs a conceptual strategy that institutes a questionable theory of signs in its claim that images are composed of two elements, *form* and *matter*, *expression* and *content*, made into one by the powerful action of socially shared rules. Signs are more than that. During the process of writing *Mythologies of Vision*, I felt that the objections to conventionalist doctrines could and should be raised from different fronts. Therefore, in the first chapter, I develop theoretical arguments against conventionalism. Throughout the remainder of the book, I critique specific images and their conventionalist definition.

Mythologies of Vision reinstates iconicity as more than another legitimate perspective complementary to conventionalism. Iconicity is not the theoretical illusion described by zealous conventionalists such as Umberto Eco (1979) and Nelson Goodman (1968); it is at the core of a vigorous theory of signs. Semiotic analysis cannot not be restricted to identifying merely the action of conventions.

A passage in Charles Peirce's *Collected Papers* inspired *Mythologies of Vision*. Peirce therein argues that icons are necessary for the direct communication of ideas: "Every assertion must contain an icon or a set of icons, or else must contain signs whose meaning is only explainable through icons" (2. 278). So, in the first chapter of the book, my claim is that conventionalism is a belated and precarious force in the production of images. Another contention is that iconicity is clearly visible when the predatory processes of nature are considered.

The spatial gap between predator and prey can be bridged because the predator analogically anticipates the movement of its prey, while the prey tries to escape using camouflage and deception. The pursuing predator and the fleeing prey have to visualize, through analogy, each other's movements. From whatever perspective, analogy is the basic feature of the natural world. In terms of a semiotic of images, this argument redefines iconicity without resorting to mimetic assumptions. Images do not duplicate the essential traits of the world; they are creative actions and additions. Iconic signs should be seen as hypothetical exercises. Rigid conventionalist theories renounce iconicity and suffocate an important trace of visuality.

The section titled "Aberrant Images" exposes the complementary sides of conventions active in representations. The chapter "Think of Siamese Twins" begins with the consideration of how perspective became the visual canon in our pictorial tradition and the background for the display of anamorphic representations. As departures from the predominant convention in Western painting, anamorphic representation found its peak in what came to be called the Modernist adventure. After modern art, images broke away from the stricture of dominant conventions, being potentially autonomous patterns that transcend determination from the natural world. At the end of this section, the analysis of Guiseppe Arcimboldo's compositions signifies a change in the direction taken in the previous chapter, presenting how an apparently eccentric, unconventional mode of representation is made into a tamed representational parlor game.

The starting point of the last part of the book, "Extreme Visions," is an evaluation of psychoanalytic explanations of Marcel Duchamp's works. "Tell me what you see, Rrose Sélavy" is a stand against deterministic Freudian interpretations. The individualistic and unconventional gestures that have outlined Duchamp's mutant productions cannot be reduced to psychological symptoms. They are cultural manifestations of a public nature, not the expression of biographical drives. The chapter "The Photographic Paradox" completes the circle. As progenies of Renaissance perspective, photographs have been made into social operators. Through photographs, reality is reduced to representations. Visuality bestows legitimacy to a reality that is made into signs, subverting the mimetic ideal of natural correspondence.

The essays in the middle of *Mythologies of Vision* reflect my concerns regarding the action of conventionalist doctrines over historical and cultural approaches to images. The chapters under "Uncommon Interpretations" examine historical viewpoints, without having to tread the familiar ground of traditional art history. The idea of visual culture, formulated in Norman Bryson's, Keith Moxey's, and Michael Ann Holly's anthology *Visual Culture*, is the most exciting contemporary alternative to the *status quo* in historical interpretations. When commenting on *Visual Culture*, I was interested in the theoretical grapple around conventionalist principles put forward by thinkers on image at work in disparate fields of study. My conclusion is that there is a price to be paid for the reduction of culture to the action of conventions: The dynamics and contradictions of living historical experience are altogether lost. The essay on Heidegger illustrates how an attempt at reforming historical conceptions fails if conventionalist assumptions are left untouched. Heidegger tried to dispose of the notion of history dictated by metaphysics, only to fall under the spell of another force: the chimera that language embraces history and Being.

The intention in *Mythologies of Vision* was not just to undermine conventionalism but to demonstrate that, in a truly productive theory of images, there is more than the dichotomy between mimesis and conventions. Mimetism and conventionalism are intellectual solutions presenting different replies to the same problem; yet, they deal with precisely the same elements. Both views surmise the existence of distinct attributes—*form* and *content*, *mind* and *matter*, *conceptual* and *corporeal* elements—fastened to one another by a third ingredient, a mode of relation, effective enough to bridge the gap. Mimetism alleges that similarity is what links matter and form, whereas conventionalism professes that a rule joins what is disparate; they are the extremes of a long-standing legacy.

Mythologies of Vision asserts that images are not subservient copies of either nature or conventions. Images are additions emanating from a fundamentally creative agency. This redefinition of visuality is a step toward producing a theory of images qualified to overcome the distinction of *mind* and *matter* active in conventionalist doctrines afflicting the contemporary interpretations of images.

Instead of pointing out theoretical affinities that would be noticed anyway, this introduction hints at a method of reading the book: The reader should detect how concepts echo from chapter to chapter. The actual process of reading the book and recognizing the polyphonic recurrence of themes discloses that, through the adoption of a semiotic standpoint, conceptual boundaries are torn apart.

CHAPTER 1

Against Conventionalism

CONVENTIONALISM is the most consistently accepted theoretical paradigm in the historical interpretation of images. It may be countered that theoretical doctrines based upon conventionalism are not identical, that significant differences set them apart,[1] and that it is reductionism to put them all in the same basket. However, all conventionalist outlooks, with dissimilar intentions and results, partake in a common belief: Generating rules are the clue to the understanding of examined messages.

Conventionalism helped perpetuate a distorted and fragmented theory of signs, professing that messages are composed of dissimilar elements—one, material, the other, mental—inextricably made into one: the effect of rules shared conventionally. A specific conception of sign production then came to the theoretical foreground, discriminating any other possible type of sign as a mere aftermath of conventions.[2]

Even the staunch critic of conventionalist doctrines sees why conventionalism is an attractive if dogmatic paradigm. Conventionalism accounts for the communicative efficacy of messages: Images are semantically powerful because their program of production is shared by their makers and consumers.

Looking at the pictorial creations of an age, we inevitably distinguish a twinkle of unity in different visual solutions. Images participate in a heritage of

---

[1] See Hirsch Jr. (1983) for a comment on contemporary conventionalist trends. He shows it to be a theoretical option of authors as diverse as Heidegger, Foucault, Kuhn, Feyerabend, and the post-Saussurian structuralists in France.

[2] In a critique of iconism, Eco (1976:197) maintains that a sign-function is exclusively "the correlation between an expression and a content based on a conventionally established code (a system of correlational rules)." Eco is aware that the legitimate existence of iconicity would falsify his discriminating definition of images.

visual patterns continuously and serially transformed. And these connected series allow the interpretation of visual constructions. Two modalities of time are intensely at work: the present accounts for the actual visual solution, and the past, that is, the unfolding of the connected series, creates step by step the experience of history.

That images are historical cannot be disputed. Reading and interpreting images result from the attempt to place the visual configuration inside the unifying system that produced it at a specific moment. Here, history is clearly defined as an anthropological enterprise (Argan 1991: 16). The temporal dimension that offers the clue for the interpretation of images has everything to with culture and cannot be restricted to the chronological sequencing of natural time (Panofsky 1975: 224). Cultural undercurrents define the historical life of images.

Iconology claims that images are historical legacies. Conceptual and cognitive expressions, images are part of the present that produced them. To interpret an image requires the reconstruction of lost pieces of evidence (Gombrich 1975: 16). The methodological clue is to recognize similarities among images, and furthermore, to establish bonds of pictures to literary, philosophical and scientific texts, or whatever qualifies as relevant. In opposition to Panofsky's (1975: 199) recurrent stress on hierarchical norms that would furnish the foundations of lofty artistic creation, it is possible to conclude that, fundamentally, all forms of expression are equivalent. "High art" easily receives the influx of images that may be judged as "low art."

Images are the offspring of formulas repeating themselves endlessly. Pictures are laden with culture. Panofsky's iconological method is itself a criticism of images as the expression of individual mastery. Images embody collective cultural conceptions. The style of an image conveys a complete cultural view, symptomatic of a given period.

For that reason, iconology depends so much on the concept of *Kunstwollen*, which indicates the existence of a set or a field of forces operating within visual patterns. This field of forces organizes images according to collective cognitive models that shape the expressive possibilities of images. If that is the method of interpreting images, Gombrich asserts that the object of iconology is not the constituted symbols but the institutions that created them (Gombrich 1975: 21).

An image, according to iconology, is a document that is discerned in relationto its appropriate cultural order (Calabrese 1987:27). The communicative power of an image arises directly from socially allotted conventions. Peaches, on a fifteenth-century Flemish picture, can be more than peaches; they personify veracity (Panofsky 1970: 54). The painted object conveys allegorical meaning. Panofsky discerns the allegory in peaches through reference to Cesare Ripa's *Iconologia* (1611) that codified among so many other images the moral and ethical attributes of this fruit. Panofsky's reliance on Ripa's *Iconologia* does more than decipher an image; it regards images as emblematic illustrations of a text.[3]

The aim of historical interpretations is limited to the revelation of cognitive codes and rules bonding an image to the totality of culture.[4] Michael Ann Holly (1984: 186) puts it succinctly: A system of rules determines the basic presence of a work of art. Culture, acting as a kind of guide to historical existence, is an *a priori* molding of the activities of individual image makers.

A price is to be paid for such a conventionalist interpretation. Images lose their individual traces. They grow as a part of a vast and contradictory metaphysical construction. Even Panofsky's first critics perceived the problem. In the monumental *Early Netherlandish Painting*, Panofsky (1953) formulated an astounding contention: Only a shallow analysis could qualify Jan Van Eyck's paintings as minute realistic representations. Van Eycks's naturalism hides intricate symbolic references conducting theological conceptions. The theological conceptions are what we have to probe if we want to grasp the

---

[3] A recent analysis of Panofsky's iconological method comes to a similar conclusion. According to Holly (1996: 162), the outcome of Panofsky's conception of meaning as finality is "to discover texts or systems of textuality that precede and thereby absorb the images."

[4] In his most complete methodological declaration, Panofsky (1962: 3–31) suggests that the interpretation of images moves through three complementary levels, identified as preiconographic, iconographic, and iconological. The preiconographic description of an image allows the identification of what is at once visible in a picture. The iconographic level of interpretation discriminates the strictly conventional nature of an image. In Panofsky's famous example—a person greets another in the street raising the hand and taking off his hat—whoever is greeted has to know that this is an intended gesture of politeness. The codes, the conventions of politeness, shared by both persons meeting in the street, will determine the meaning of what is happening. But when talking about iconological meaning, we must refer to something unconscious and unintended, precipitate by force of cultural values, deeper codes, that present and articulate history. In all levels, codes and conventions are acting.

meaning of Van Eyck's paintings. Beyond the detailed depiction of a bourgeois setting, Van Eyck's paintings harbor religious meanings awaiting to be set free.

After Panofsky's interpretation, Van Eyck's paintings could no longer be considered uncompromising naturalist compositions: The paintings were supposed to serve as instruments for preaching. The famous picture of Giovanni Arnolfini and Jeanne Cenani (1434) was a sermon, a portrait, and a marriage certificate. Is there any other explanation for the inscription in the picture: "Johannes de Eyck fuit huit" (Jan Van Eyck was here)?

Panofsky examines other details of the portrait, presumably bearing symbolic images. He claims that the Arnolfinis are not in a simple hall. They are in their nuptial chamber. In the chamber, the mirrors are the symbolic expression of purity, and the dog in front of the couple is a codified image of marital fidelity. Peaches, the indication of honesty, blush on a windowsill. Panofsky (1953: 205) talks about a symbolic program materialized in the picture, merging portraiture and narrative, sacred and profane art. The symbolic texture of an image is never to be dismissed. The haunting minutia of Van Eyck's pictures are religious signs. Panofsky argues that it does not matter whether Van Eyck's contemporaries were capable of recognizing the occult meanings of those images. In *Perspective as a Symbolic Form*, Panofsky (1975) made a similar avowal: Unconscious rules unify a variety of intellectual productions, cutting across philosophy, art, science, literature, and religion.

For Otto Pächt (1956), the unconscious nature of the symbolic program is its main problem. Hidden symbols in an image are incompatible with the finality and purpose of creation. If Panofsky's claim were right, the *Arnolfini Marriage* would be understood simultaneously as a rational structure and an irrational construction: "Each [interpretation] is based on a different notion of artistic creation (the one implying a rational, the other an irrational structure), and each claims it can seize the very essence of the artistic phenomenon and grasp it in its totality" (Pächt 1956: 276).

Thus, the confusion was inevitable. The sophisticated, complex and allegorical intention of Van Eyck's paintings may be just a projection of Panofsky's.

Kantian Premises

The problem in Panofsky's methods extends beyond Pächt's criticism. The recognition of contradictory forces, rational and irrational, in Panofsky's interpretation is not bothersome.[5] The problem with Panofsky's iconology is epistemic.

The Panofskian association of history and culture is based on Kant's conception of historical movement as a balance between a finalist drive and contractualism. Understood as a sound form of knowledge, art history draws from Kant's arguments the thought that artistic creation is no longer tied to the desire to represent nature mimetically. This indicates a collapse of the most persistent dogma in the humanistic tradition, specifically the soldered conjunction of mimesis as an aesthetical principle and the expression of beauty. With Kant, the faculty of knowing nature and the judgment of art are drastically separated from one another. Conventions are the explanation of images. Historians aim at unveiling conventions which are the rules and the cognitive codes that culture creates.

If the prevalence given to conventions were true, any art product would be extremely resistant to novelty and creation. Being so influenced by Kantian contractualist conceptions, Panofsky reduced images to the subservient role of illustrating texts.

Experience, Sign, and History

To arrive at a theory of images that does not balk at the variety of historical experience and avoids determinism, we must first acknowledge that all modes of signs are possibilities. Signs follow three modes of possibility: a may-be, a can-be, and a would-be (Peirce 1909 [1976]: 868). A representation classifiable as a may-be is a more abstract hypothesis than a factual possibility deemed a can-be. And a would-be is a nonfulfilled conditionality. Three basic relations operate in signs: triadic relations of comparisons that dwell on pure possibility; triadic relations of performance that are extracted from the existential nature of

---

[5] See Moxey (1995) for another indication of contradictory forces in Panofsky's iconography. Moxey suggests that Panofsky's use of earlier discussions on perspective in a latter work, such as *Early Netherlandish Painting*, represents the Panofskian desire to conciliate an art conspicuously mimetic with the unveiling of "hidden symbolisms." For Moxey (1995: 783), the attempt is an ideological strategy, aiming at naturalizing historical interpretations, as well as a logical impossibility: "The new concept of hidden symbolism is both symbolic, because it is naturalistic, and naturalistic, because symbolic."

factual events; and triadic relations of thought participating in the nature of laws lived as conventions. Thus, conventions are not everything.

The triadic model denies duality. It stands in contradistinction to the conventionalist model that postulates an *a priori* system of rules fusing two radically diverse elements: one intelligible, the other sensible. The triadic model creates the condition for refusing *a priori* assumptions: The triadic model posits an interminable interaction (Fisch 1986: 318). It is sheer action among signs, or to use Peirce's terminology derived from the Epicurean philosopher, Philodemus, *semiosis* As long as historical experience accumulates, semiosis is infinite.

Signs, according to this conception, are more than the mere actualization of conventions. They are activities and processes. In Peircean semiotics, conventions do little more than indicate possibilities. The notion of semiosis conjures up a historical point of view, directly related to the legacy of visual patterns that iconology suggests. History and semiotics are contiguous theoretical fields.

Before Convention, Beyond Mimesis

An exhaustive semiotic of images must begin by considering the workings of the nature. Events in the natural world generate images. Sprawled over the surface of things, image writes the natural prose of physical events. The dry boughs of a tree project tortured shadows over a crumbling wall. The paws of a stray dog are imprinted in fresh cement. Shadows and paw prints are images: What is distinctive about these natural images is their absence of symbolic value; they do not descend from conventions; they are physical happenings. And, as signs, they have to be called indices, for an index necessarily springs from "an existential relation" (Peirce 1931: 2.283).

Indices are forms extending in a continuous space. The degree of material similarity to an event, as in the case of a projected shadow or the imprint of a paw, is the consequence of isomorphic congruences between models and indices. What looks like correspondence or imitation is just reversibility. Because indices are directly imprinted from their models, if the model is altered, fading away, or through the alteration of a surrounding medium, such as light, then the image is changed: "The image has no permanence; it disappears if the model disappears" (Thom 1983a: 263). That a difference exists between shadows constantly changing as the day glides by and the marks left by the walking dog over wet concrete must be recognized. The permanence of indicies, their plasticity (Thom 1983a: 263), depends upon the inherent degree of the medium's reception. The generative model is maintained.

Human beings have the plasticity of memory, the biological capacity of keeping as a sign what was traced indexically over the retina and the visual cortex. The natural world is doubled. What happened is somehow retained. The mind collects indices and reinterprets them as visual patterns that analogically refer to natural events. Analogy is not the capturing of an essential property of the world, pristine and perfect, because the perceptual system is neutral and transparent to nature. An icon may not convey at all a sensuous relation of likeness to its object. What happens is more subtle than that.

The central nervous system designates a place that simulates iconically the position of an organism facing another. Apparently, it is a model of radical otherness: *same* as opposed to *other*. But, in reality, the principle at work in this situation is fundamentally analogical: The active mind contemplates and addresses an external object, creating its cognitive *analogon*. The most fundamental image of life is expressed in predation: "The hungry predator is its prey" (Thom 1983a: 125). As a result, what seems different is a process ruled by analogy in which one organism lives the role of predator, and another of prey. Bodily reactions are triggered under the guise of a capture when the predator analogically anticipates the movement of the prey. Thom (1983a: 273) describes the process as a diverse interaction: soon after the first impulse to attack, the predator looses its initial identification with what is trying to capture and hence becomes itself again, a predator radically different from the pursued prey.

The displacement of the predator precedes and enables the emergence of identity, thus granting the conditions for naming and associating conventional tags to the world. Naming is not an exclusive faculty of human languages. Sebeok (1981) argued forcefully that geese, swans, ducks, birds of prey, and crows recognize the distinctive visual traits of individuals belonging to their group. In the natural world, naming comes through several sensorial channels or a combination of them. Naming allows animals to become individuals. Names are part of their personality (Sebeok 1986: 82). The process is not different from what happens among human beings: The name is an important tool in distinguishing *self* and *other*.

Prior to the strictures of conventions, and a precondition to them, biological existence demands that organisms stir in a state of mutual coordination. The conceivable reactions of each organism to another can be attack, flight, defense, or paralyzation. Hence "the essential function of the nervous system is to provide a simulating model of external processes to the organism" (Thom 1975a: 74). Organisms recognize and locate continuous forms in space. From the animal world, human beings inherited elementary modes of coordination: avoidance and group gathering, springing from predatory spacing, notwithstanding the human ability to attenuate violence and predation.

Iconic images are hypotheses that simulate the natural world. Iconicity is a fundamental faculty for living organisms. In iconic images, the logical processes of figuring possibilities and the materiality of indices are fused. It is the same fusion that, according to linguistics, integrates phonic matter and concept, codifying them, fastening *the sensible* to *the intelligible.*

The symbolic order ultimately emerges in the crossroads of the sensible and the intelligible. Conventions have to be a latter stage in the constitution of signs. This becomes clear after considering how icons, indices, and symbols relate to present, past, and future.

Indices are fated to be ruled by the past tense; being causal effects of physical events, and, in their singularity, indices are sentenced to disappear. Indices bear the impermanence of the natural world, where everything flows, and subsequently ceases to exist. On the other hand, icons are ruled by the present, by a special kind of presentness: They are available for recollection. The permanence of an icon depends upon the plasticity or competence of the actual mind. Products of conventions, symbols are free from the material constraints of the natural world: They are characteristically social. For that reason, historical studies tend to give precedence to symbolic conventions. Yet, to grasp the flow of history, there must be more than the endless transformation of the present into the past, more than the destiny of icons and indices.[6] History is always written from the standpoint of the future. The past is transformed into conventions and remains in the future. The historical permanence of facts results from the relative stability of conventions.[7]

---

[6] See Peirce's remark in the Collected Papers (4.448): "An icon has such being as belongs to past experience. It exists only as an image in the mind. An index has the being of present existence. The being of a symbol consists in the real fact that something will be experienced if certain conditions are satisfied, namely, it will influence the thought and conduct of its interpreter." History exclusively based upon symbols and conventions turns easily into a deterministic construction.

[7] Thom (1983: 16) clearly defines stability: "A process (P) is structurally stable if a small reaction, if a small variation in initial conditions led to a process (P') isomorphic to

Symbols are determined by each specific human group that produced them. In its conventional arbitrariness, the symbolic experience suppresses the impermanence of physical experience, driving us away from the alluring ferocity of the material world. The material aspect of the symbol is discarded, forcing us to face its conceptualization.

To conclude that iconic images depend upon a represented referent is unjustifiable. Since mirrors and paw prints are indexical, they are effects of causality; but how can we deny that images in mirrors and paw prints bear a one-to-one mimetic correspondence to their models? The ground is fertile for misconceptions. Umberto Eco can hastily infer that the experience of mirrors is a condition for iconic representation. Human beings would have produced drawings "to achieve without mirrors what mirrors allow them to achieve" (Eco 1994: 210). The problem with Eco's interpretation is that it does not consider that causal duplication of reality is indexical, for it depends completely on the referent actually existing within the visual range of mirrors. Another referent in front of the mirror will produce another image. Contrary to what Eco insists, mirrors are not absolute icons; if anything, they are absolute indices.

Do iconic images aspire to be as faithful as mirrors? The question is misleading. Even though indexical, plane mirrors are the supreme mimetic accomplishment. For what reason around 1435 would Leon Battista Alberti advise, in *Della pittura*, the use of mirrors as corrective guides to painted images? At the peak of the *Quattrocento* enchantment with mimetic illusionism, Alberti (1973: 83) wrote: "It is marvelous how every weakness in a painting is so evidently deformed in the mirror. Therefore, things taken from nature are corrected with a mirror." Strict and perfect mimesis is never purely iconic; it is consistently indexical.

Under the observer's gaze, the analogical nature of an icon succeeds from its own internal order. If we were to present a diagram about the evolution of signs, the following iconic representation would suffice: indices → icons → symbols. The graphic configuration does not duplicate an existing thing in the outside world, and neither is the arrow in the diagram conventional.[8]

(P)." The configuration of iconic images is structurally stable in relation to conventional rules that eventually will grant their possibilities.

[8] Not long ago, I was driving with a five-year-old child. We stopped at the traffic light. It was a light with three signals: a red light, a yellow light, and a green arrow pointing upwards. The arrow lit up and the child asked me: "Are we suppose to go up?

Of course, the words "indices," "icons," and "symbols" are conventional signs; but the visual pattern does not mirror events in the outside world. An icon, being a First, "has its being or peculiarity within itself" (Peirce 1992: 299). It is meaningful in virtue of its qualities. As such, it is a shorthand of itself, a possibility opened up by its very arrangement. An icon is an abbreviation of what it could state if the sign configuration were a proposition. Hence, for iconic images, the truth-value of its representation, a property given by correspondence to an external reference, is an aftereffect without a major import to the nature of the icon itself.

At this point, we must discriminate between mimetic correspondence and the cognitive analogon that iconicity produces. Mimesis may be viewed as an assumption rooted in what Bryson (1983) called "the natural attitude," or the idealized goal of accomplishing an "essential copy" of reality. In that sense, mimesis is the direct outcome of perceptualist ideologies. However, the cognitive analogon, that is any icon, does not emanate from the illusion of a direct access between consciousness and the external world. The iconic process is altogether disparate from a naive conception of mimesis, where a direct correspondence, a point-to-point imitation, prevails.

Iconicity does not display the straightforward bond between a sign and a natural object or event. An analogon is a sign action, aiming at simulation. Now consider this alteration in the previous diagram: indices ← icons ← symbols. It does not develop from indices to symbols, but from symbols to indices. A different sign arrangement confers another sense upon the iconic representation.

Iconic analogy is a complex kind of representation. Through analogy a form can substitute for another: "The concept of 'substitution' involves that of purpose" (Peirce 1931: 2.275). Icons are approximate surrogates of other signs. And this proxy is possible when similar purposes and functions can be attributed to different images.

An icon replaces another and, only after this internal semiotic exchange, the actual mind where the alteration occurs is lead in the direction of the external

---

Are we going to fly?" He was literally following the iconic visual information. At this moment, no conventional force, capable of suppressing the iconic disposition of the green arrow, was at work; however evident it may have been to the child that colors and signs in traffic lights are more than just colors and signs: They are codified instructions to be followed.

world. That is why Gombrich (1993: 69) formulates an interesting asymmetric paradox: Perhaps the world may never look like an image, but an image may be made to look like the world. In an approximate and partial manner, an image can act as if it were another thing. It is not a subservient copy, but the outcome of "a particular act of the will whereby we cause an image, an icon, to be associated, in a peculiarly strenuous way, with an object represented to us by an index" (Peirce 1931: 2.435). The basic operative foundation of images is iconic and definitely preconventional.

The flaw of conventionalist doctrines goes far beyond the interpretation of images. When conventions serve as the starting point of analytic methodologies, they lead to circular arguments. As early as 1762, Jean-Jacques Rosseau glimpsed at this logical trap, but immediately shut it down. In *Sur le contract social*, Rousseau (1978) drew a neat line separating nature from conventions. According to Rousseau's argument, necessity rules nature, whereas freedom and consciousness, typical of human association, are responsible for conventions. Reason and will, not force, are the foundations of the social pact. Arguing against proponents of despotism that considered subjugation and tyrannies to be based on natural rights, Rousseau asserts that despotism is sustained not by force alone; it depends on a mode of political deliberation. Whether despotic or the expression of a collective will (*la volonté générale*), social life is an outgrowth of conventions. For Rousseau's political theory, society is a pact, a convention, always derived from other conventions.

The endless reference to conventions is not to be mistaken for a vindication of conventionalism. Quine (1969) imagined that conventions are established when an agreement is reached by a board of syndics meeting at a table, using a system of conventions: language. A prior convention is always necessary to settle the issue at hand. It is a situation of constant recursion.

Conventionalism precludes a fundamental insight about sign production. Meaning cannot be solely obtained in reference to an abstract set of conventions that antedates and rules the use of signs. Even when conventionalism manages to be purged of teleological presumptions, it still is deterministic and content-oriented. The uncompromising reliance on conventionalism is an impoverished theoretical decision.

PART 1

Aberrant Images

CHAPTER 2

Think of Siamese Twins
Perspective and Anamorphosis

HOWEVER ARCHAIC this may seem, we should start any discussion about perspective as systems of signs with Plato. We can see in Plato's cosmology several traits of what would much later be considered a semiotic problem. The world around us—chairs, birds, trees and men—is an image, a representation of the divine and true order. The perceived world is a sign.

The image is a step in the process of gaining knowledge. There is the object, then its name; then the definition and the representation that entails knowledge and understanding. This is a gradual process towards light. The word *circle* names the circle, defined as a result of the idea of equidistance of the circumference from its center of the circle. It can be drawn with a pair of compasses and understood as the conceptual form called circle.

A relationship of imitation *(mimesis)* governs eery single stage describe above. The object, the name, the definition, and the image designed represent the idea of circle, an objective, truthful, unchanging and therefore perfect *form*. Consequently, the nature of knowledge is imitative. When Plato talks about imitation, he does not mean that the representation is a slavish, therefore good and faithful copy of the original form. Far from it, something has been added to this form. Here lies the precise problem of images as sources of knowledge. Images are steps away from the truthful and perfect form. We should bear in mind that Truth is the logical pattern through which images ought to be assessed. Only Truth can allow the selection, exclusion, and even condemnation of images as foundations of knowledge.

It is a truism that we cannot fully understand Plato's condemnation of representative arts without some insight into his cosmological interpretation of the world. Imitation does not restrict itself to the arts; it rules whole universe, human, natural or divine.

It is possible to recognize three hierarchical levels in the universe: forms, senses, and *simulacra*. The intellectual forms are perfect, unchanging, and eternal, with no contradiction; the senses, in their multiplicity, copy and deform the ideal model. The copies of copies, simulacra, are a multiple manifestation, mutable, and extremely false, like the reflections of moonlight that create unstable and incorporeal images on the waters of lakes or on the surfaces of mirrors.

A carpenter makes up several chairs imitating their conceptual model, the form of the object. A painter who represents a chair on a canvas does it as someone observing the chair; he does not represent the *form* of that chair. He copies what is already a copy; he produces a simulacrum that is irretrievably far from the truth. The painter imitates not what is, but what seems to be; not the truth but a fantasm (McKeon 1952: 152).

Only the *form* is true. Whatever we experience through our senses is imitation, worlds away from the truth. Music, painting and dance are imitations;[1] painters, as producers of contradictory, false and deceitful images, should be crowned with laurels and expelled from social life.

Moral Judgement and Perspective

Plato's moral philosophy presumed an identity between Virtue, Beauty and the Truth. He, therefore, upheld a moral stand as far as representations went. The more imitations we have, the more suspicious we should be. In *The Laws*, Plato dreams of some form of pictorial social control; images ought to be produced according to ethical criteria. He defends censorship and admires the rigid pictorial canon of Egyptian painting, whose main characteristic is to avoid depiction of whatever is transitory. This is the only way to aspire to eternity. In Egypt the paintings and the reliefs were the same for thousands of years; the same pictorial rules were followed by all Egyptian painters.

Perspective horrified Plato. He consider it immoral that a painter would correct the proportions of reality, adapting them to the conditions of eyesight. Perspective represents just an aspect of reality, and a false one at that: the point of view of a spectator. Perspective is sheer appearance, mere illusion, resulting from the conscious intention of deceiving, in which painters, sculptors and architects are perversely engaged.

---

[1] Barker (1984) gathers an exhaustive collection of passages in Plato's writings where music is discussed. In the same work, one can find a thorough presentation of musical sources, from Homer to Plutarch, from Pythagoras to Aristides Quintilian. Nothing but a thesaurus of quotes would allows us today to retrieve ancient Greek musical experience.

It is unfair to reduce the question of perspective to a strict moral point of view. Perspective is a visual solution for this dilemma; should we represent objects as they are or as they are seen? If we choose to represent objects from their actual relationships, then it is mandatory that the spectator should be put out of the pictorial scene. Plato preferred objectivity and permanence over solutions that created representations following a subjective point of view. The viewer is always deceived; he thinks that he sees the objects as they are, not knowing that they are represented as they appear to be.

There is only one way of avoiding the illusion of appearance: through representation made according to fixed and measured proportions, without any regard to what we see. Truth cannot suffer any correction. The point of view of the spectator must be avoided.

Plato understood that when we face an image there is the possible threat of an illusion, the danger of believing that what is in front of our eyes is a criterion of evidence. When an image is presented as certain and true; this can only be the source of a serious mistake. Images designed according to perspective, for example, are committed to transitoriness for they are constructed from the point of view of a subject. Only concept and form are permanent; images cannot represent *forms*.

Plato's arguments have failed miserably. Techniques of *trompe l'oeil* have flourished and have enchanted generations ever since his dissension. Pliny (23–79 A.D.) tells us in his *Naturalis historia* that to win a competition of dexterity in painting, Zeuxis finishes a cluster of grapes so perfectly that birds would come to peck it. Responding to the challenge, Parrhasius paints a curtain so perfect that Zeuxis himself asks to have the curtain drawn so that the picture could be displayed. Yet there is no painting underneath; the curtain is the painting. Surely the painter of curtains won; he had duped more than just birds; he deceived a fellow-artist. In any case, the story reveals that image making is essentially a technical affair, whose objective is to replicate reality. Is there any better reason for Norman Bryson (1983: 1) to consider this story the central anecdote summing up "the essence of working assumptions in Western painting?"

It is curious that Pliny stresses not an error of observation imputable to the birds or, if it were the case, to human beings but a feeling of wonder and enchantment with the painter's technical dexterity. Illusion seduces and satisfies when we see image and reality merging.

Several centuries later, from 1400 onward, the painters of the Italian Renaissance started to construe their works following techniques of perspective.

Plato's haranguing against perspective is solemnly left behind. Vasari says that Paolo Ucello (1396–1475) stayed at home days on end examining the mysteries of perspective; when his wife called him to sleep, he would say: What a marvelous thing is perspective.

To paint in perspective was not enough. Perspective was also an intellectual adventure, as we can surmise if we consider the many volumes written by artists on perspective: Alberti's *Della pittura*, Piero della Francesca's *De prospectiva pingendi* and Leonardo's *Trattato della pittura*, for example. The painter should draw the scene as though he were in front of a window. The vision, monocular and immobile, should dwell in the depths of space.

Erwin Panofsky (1975: 78) stressed that perspective is more than just a technique; it is a symbolic form that identifies an intellectual content with a sensorial way of representation. There have been different visual solutions as far as perspective goes. Perspective is not a transposition of a supposedly eternal mode of seeing to a canvas or a paper; it is a historical construct.

Perspective does not represent the conditions of sight; it represents the representation of visual conditions. There is a significant difference between what is commonly perceived and what is represented as perspective in a flat surface. Images appear in perspective because we, as viewers, have inferred it through a visual judgment.

Perspective is a simultaneous translation of things into images. The idiom of this technique can be summed up as a metrical problem; distances should diminish or not in respect to what is seen by a cyclopic and immobile viewer. Besides producing this adjustment, the loss of contour of opaque objects and the chromatic use of bluish tints fading away would represent farther distance. Historically, perspective is a Renaissance answer to medieval questions concerning the nature of signs; Huzinga (1973: 439) suggests that it follows a trend typical of the spirit of the Late Middle Ages, in the sense that it develops representations aspiring to the most complete and finished sensorial form. The meticulous enumeration of the world ought to be present. Those paintings were made with the firm intention of reaching such a degree of similarity to the represented objects that to deceive the viewer can only be one of the features of the show. The real thing, however, is not just to cheat our sight; a very careful strategy of representation is worked out, putting the eyesight and the understanding in an open, face-to-face, conflict.

Contemporary Visions of Perspective

An important interpretation of perspective as a form of knowledge is Pierre Francastel's work (1905–1970), which would fall into the general label of sociology of art. Particularly original in Francastel is his idea that it is not enough to take the work of art as a mere pretext to recognize social categories or ideological interests. The work of art cannot be seen as a mere reproductive agent of the conditions of perception. Works of art participate in other systems of signification; they are not just a joint venture of the hand and the eye. The knowledge implied by an image also entails some form of deciphering. According to Francastel (1967: 9), this is the task of the sociology of art. Works of art should be seen as texts that do require historical and technical understanding.

Paintings demand interpretations of the same intellectual status as some other modes of knowledge recognized in academia. To interpret a work of art is another way of performing it. There cannot be rigid separation between the technical and the artistic features of a work of art. Technique and art shape the world. Therefore, it is incorrect to restrict ourselves to the exclusive examination of paintings and sculptures. Francastel's interpretation of Renaissance art springs from his assessment of what could be considered a technical problem: How the architect Fillipo Brunelleschi (1377–1446) managed to raise up the cupola of the Santa Maria dei Fiori's cathedral.

Brunelleschi breaks with old methods of construction that belong to medieval masonry and also brings about a new conception of space as something homogeneous, infinite that could be expressed by mathematical and geometrical devices. The cupola could then be raised up with no traditional beams, thanks to calculation. Brunelleschi's solution entails a concept of space conceived as fully mathematical.

Mathematical relationships pervade every single thing in the world. We can now speak of an unified conception of the world. Light is another element that goes across all entities in a landscape, unifying them. Perspective is possible as an artistic and technical solution because space is thought of a something homogeneous and measurable. This is a figurative unity, more than just an optical fact. The conception that inspired Renaissance painters was reached step by step; there was no absolute visual unity among the artists engaged in the use of perspective techniques. The system of a completely unified perspective was suggested by Leon Battista Alberti, but it was only a theory, to which the great majority of Renaissance painters did not comply.

Piero della Francesca, another painter and theoretician concerned with geometry and perspective, would narrate in the same pictorial space several successive episodes according to the medieval visual mode. Again, this is another argument for those who would say that during the Renaissance it was feasible to recognize several visual solutions that were originally from the Middle Ages (Huizinga 1973: 434).

The device of unifying the pictorial scene , in a single and open space, would take some time to prevail. Slowly, steps were taken in the direction of a complete system of perspective, where the fixed point of fugue would establish the locus of the viewer. Only then we can speak of something new and revolutionary in visual terms; the viewer and pictorial world were then related in the form of a system that is logical, precise, and mathematical (White 1972: 120).

The scientific revolution that begins in the seventeenth century interpreted nature with a nomenclature akin to perspective. Nature is a book written with the alphabet of geometry, with circles, triangles and squares. Even more important than what the common sense and Aristotelian physics could assert is the revelation of a new order in the universe. And this new order postulates an infinite universe ruled, in Heavens and earth, by universal, unified, and homogeneous laws. Science is mathematical and so is nature (Koyré 1973: 170).

Science thinks that the world, symbolized by perspective, is infinite and organized from the point of view of an observer. Galileo Galilei criticized the Aristotelian theories of movement and impetus. According to Galileo, movement is not a property of bodies; it reveals itself in relation to an observer. A body can only move in relation to a state of rest; and movement is perfectly apprehended by numbers.

By the time of Isaac Newton, science had produced a picture of the world that could be described as solid, cold, colorless, silent and dead (Burt 1954: 239). Any immediate quality perceived by human beings was merely a curious effect, something minor in relation to the infinite machine of the world, which is obviously bigger than anything else.

We should remember that Alberti's *Della pittura* was written in 1463; Galileo would be born in 1564, and in 1632 he would write the *Dialogo sopra i due massime sistemi del mondo*. In fact, there are two centuries separating the painters' theoretical discussion on perspective and the emergence of modern physical science; we must take this into account. There is no calm and uninterrupted straight line going from artistic perspective to science. The scientific spirit tried to revamp rigid geometrical perspective. It also provided intellectual arguments against mannerism, which prevailed as a pictorial style in the Late Renaissance. Galileo himself would consider mannerism as a standpoint that could only give birth to illusions and mistakes. Galileo expressed a special aversion for ellipsis; he would say it, when assessing Johannes Kepler's (1571–1630) astronomical system. For Galileo, Kepler's was a mannerist astronomy (Koyré 1973: 283).

Galileo was no dilettante as far as aesthetical discussions went; he was in fact a fierce critic of anamorphic art and its obsession with aberrations. He repudiated its labyrinths of lines, its strict concern with discovering hallucinatory and chimerical forms, rivers, clouds, beaches in minute or micro visual details (Koyré 1973: 278). With anamorphic art, everything went berserk. A new world revealed itself, and it was irrational, threatening and phantasmagorical. Anamorphic art would force on us another mode of contemplation. Anamorphic pictures were made from a distorted single angle, undoing classical perspective's visual interpretation, which had shown everything frontally and at eye level. Moreover, anamorphic art engendered a cult for aberrations; it implied that classical perspective was not a precise tool for representing the world: In short, traditional perspective was a lie (Baltrušaitis 1969: 69).

Anamorphosis

One of Jurgis Baltrušaitis's major publications, *Anamorphoses* (translated into English as *Anamorphic Art*), was a rare systematic attempt at dealing with the theme of deformed perspective. Reading this book, we notice that anamorphic art is more than a crack on the classic Western manner of depicting reality. For a semiotic of images, anamorphic art can be seen as a historical attempt to project visual forms according to an extreme internal logic of visuality, with as little regard as possible for reference. Visual forms fed upon themselves. The distorting effect is monstrous and magical. In it, there is a severe separation between reality and appearance. Appearance triumphs; there is no trace left of the antique and up to now considered natural way of seeing, even if we can barely recognize a tenuous and perverse correspondence with reality.

It is certain that from Plato's point of view anamorphic art could only be the living proof that if we reach for false similitude, we will end up with sheer phantasmagoria; we would fall into an abyss of simulacra, we would be driven into madness. The greater the autonomy of images, the more we will have to face the possibility and threat of illusion.

It is also true that we can now see a radical attribute of images in operation: the possibility of taking the logical trait of iconicity to an extreme. The image is therefore hypothesis; it present itself as a conjectural representation. There is really no way to abide constantly by mimetic canons. It is quite ironic that precisely at the height of the Age of Science, at the peak of the scientific achievements of the seventeenth century, we see the spreading of a social crave for the visionary possibilities of images, derived from the rational form of representation that is perspective. It is much better to think that anamorphism was then working as antidote.

If images are so independent from their referents, then we will experiment an uncontrollable flux of representations. Everything flows, and as a sign of this fact, there is no grid that allows us to recognize a stable order in this world. *Le monde est fou*. What could be a Garden of Eden would harbor fugitive visions of plants and trees transforming themselves into animals, thanks to the active force of representations that projects worlds and undoes them (Baltrušaitis 1969: 81). Anamorphic representation insinuates that matter is in itself fragile, contrary to our previous belief that had it was constant and unchanging.

When the relationship of an image and its referent is mimetic, the ground of the representation works like a mirror; it serenely gives back whatever was represented to the eyes. The mirror is an idealized metaphor of mimetic relationships. Mirrors were exacting representations for the purposes intended by classical representation. We can see in mirrors a term to term correspondence of the representation and its referent. Mirrors are faithful and submissive; their truth-value derives directly from such bondage. The image should interfere as least as possible in the traces of represented things. Referents rule images.

When such general principle do not apply, we have chaos. Visual forms wrap upon themselves in a crazed whirlwind. Illusion spreads itself through the surface of the world. Life can only be a nightmare, a freewheeling and monstrously frightening dream that brings about disorder and anguish. The world is a hell of mirrors.

Mannerist painters have also used mirrors, but those mirrors are convulsed surfaces. Hocke (1974: 15) mentions that in his opinion mannerist style in the visual arts started with a painting by Francesco Mazzola, known as Il Parmigianino (1503–1540), *Self-portrait in Front of a Convex Mirror*, but the difference was that, in this case, perspective does not serve us with a faithful and serene representation. Distorted by a convex mirror, the painted hands are just enormous and oddly out of proportion. We experience a strong sense of strangeness. The mirror, which in the past was a warranty of calm and fidelity, now expresses the rebellious autonomy of images, in themselves indices of the world's tenebrous labyrinth.

Aberrations

All this background should be present in our minds, if we have any design on understanding Baltrušaitis's *Aberrations*. Its starting point is perspective which was so closely analyzed in *Anamorphic Art*. Now the argument leads us towards an aberrant and deformed world. We are no longer facing depraved representations; the world is in itself depraved. This world that was seen as logical by classical perspective is under the pressure of the dark forces of desire, passion, and irrational imagination. Perplexed, we can then ask: Why is the world like this? Is it the whole world or just deformed irruptions here and there? Does a monstrous morphology rules reality as such? It is as though we are faced with projections of forces threatening whatever was felt beforehand as ordered and stable. If the world is unstable, we are in the midst of a catastrophe. Aberration should be taken in two senses: as a moral trace and as an optical phenomenon that reveals to us a subverted and transfigured nature.

No realm is free from aberration. The human face, the mineral world, the architectural constructions, and even the idealized paradises that were natural gardens are under the influence of aberrant action. Nature is a totality where we can figure the emergence of subtle alterations that are not commonly perceived. Those nascent shapes are ruled by a hallucinating syntax, an ever changing mirage, a constellation of forms that shift like a kaleidoscope.

The sacred becomes beastly. Jean-Paul Sartre looks like a goggle-eyed fish, Charles de Gaulle has the profile of a coon-hound. And over several pictures of human beings similar to animals, in 1950, the French magazine *France-Soir* wrote that those images were the proof that men do not (just) descend from apes. Who of us is the billy-goat, and who is coyote ugly? Baltrušaitis tries then to demonstrate that this is more than a contemporary joke for contemporary people. If we knew, we could recognize an ancient tradition, not immediately obvious to us.

Our present is never alone; the ghosts of the past follows us in our ignorance. At first, the ancient treatises of physiognomies of authors such as

Pseudo-Aristotle, Polemon, Adamantius and Pseudo-Apuleius would just say that human features express character: Strength is signalled by bushy hair, posture, and hard abdomen; timidity can be inferred from the opposite traces: soft hair, lack of strong muscles, and squinting eyes (Baltrušaitis 1989: 2). It is inevitable that gradually the mere recognition of proliferating similitude would bring about disquieting and bizarre revelations. How can we read correctly the signatures of the world? If the world is such a semiotic process, what rule warranties our interpretations?

The indices are here under our gaze, but those apparent forms may be misleading, like a capricious swirl permeating each object to the point of indiscrimination. It is not enough to postulate that microcosm and macrocosm are crossed by the process of similitude. The theories of interpretation at the end of the sixteenth century arose to a crisis like this, as we can appreciate while reading Michel de Montaigne's (1533–1592) lines in his essay on experience, where he implies that what is left to him is the interlacing of doubts; reason and experience had acquired several forms that. It is impossible to choose from. Can anything be similar to anything else? If that is true, then we have a problem; knowledge stems from analogy and contemplation, but the act of contemplating could weave an indiscriminate web of similitude. All things were potentially similar to each other and everything should be possible: every interpretation, any solution. Knowledge would be a mess.

It is a real pity that Baltrušaitis does not try to treat this semiotic problem, now presented through the guise of iconicity and its truth-value. Historical knowledge is just enough for him. Several knots are restored; why bother?

Morphology and history would provide different answers to the same question. Reading the second chapter of *Aberrations* on pictorial stones, it is feasible to envisage that what appeared to be restricted to the production of similitude is in fact something to do with a secret morphology in action in the entrails of the earth. Traces of a whole world can be viewed in the veins of pictorial stones; those are not harmonic lines but signs of the disconcert of the world. Each slab of marble or agate is flooded by marks imprinting the turbulent action of cosmic forces. In them, we can envisage both realistic scenes and the anticipation of modern aesthetic movements; we could also be "at the heart of the world of visionaries, the surrealists, a supernatural, disturbed world brusquely revealed in an actuality of nature" (Baltrušaitis 1989: 100). At this moment, historical exactness melts away, but even so Baltrušaitis is not disposed to pursue a rigorous morphological framework. Morphology is for him nothing more than an adjective.

Attribution of sense to referential elements is another problem glossed over by Baltrušaitis. As in animal physiognomics, the recognition of scenes in pictorial stones results from the action of signs completing what is given to perception. Drawn lines could be added as visual aids to the configuration of forms already present in the stones. Painted landscapes could perfect the suggestion offered by the wondrous rocks. The circle is unbroken. Hypothesis are overlaid on forms; and the configuration of images offered by those forms are working hypothesis, guide-lines, as if it were, for the viewer.

This is certainly a historically defined obsession. It is typical of sixteenth-century authors to face the task of classifying the apparition of figures over stones as a revelation of the secret life of minerals. When Athanase Kircher (1602–1680), author of *Ars magna lucis et umbra* (1642), suggests that nature is a geometrician and an optician who uses all the laws of perspective, a painter (Baltrušaitis 1989: 73), he is giving to nature the status of a conscious organism at work over those mineral forms. Nevertheless, we should be suspicious of such enthusiastic outburst; the very same Kircher gives chemical tips so to produce those spectacular forms. We might be dealing with an interesting chapter in the history of fakery. Fakery is another semiotic question passed over out by Baltrušaitis in favor of a historical wavering.

Natural Images, Gardens, and Landscapes

Men *like* animals, stones *like* landscapes, gothic vaults *like* arboreal interlacing, gardens *like* lands of illusion: What may be seen as metaphorical relation gradually turns into a concrete form of reality. The semantic operator *like* is no longer an indicative of mere possibility. The possible is in fact actual. Images do not merely indicate just possible worlds, they are turned into actualities. Referents are reshaped according to the suggestions of images. Nature is consciously made into a fantastic construction. Now, we are way behind the sheer discovery of surprising identities in what was given to our sight.

Representations act over natural accidents in order to make them what they are not. Bushes are clipped to reshape the foliage. Leaves are turned into palaces as a counterpart of gothic masonry imitating arboreal forms. Autonomous representations are taken to an extreme point: Referential nature is suppressed.

So, the eighteenth-century gardens are made into fairylands, bustling with excitement, containing mysterious humor. Natural events are a pantomime of signs. Reflections prevail over representations that, in their turn, induce other reflections. The world is a vast *camera obscura*. Baltrušaitis (1989: 43) mentions grottos in eighteenth-century gardens built up with optical devices that create visionary perspectives. Anything goes. We will find traces of remote eras in an eighteenth-century garden: Chinese pagoda, Greek column, Egyptian tomb, Bedouin tent, pyramids, Dutch windmill, you name it. Illusion spreads all throughout nature. Everything is transfigured to the point of painters not being lead to face nature as something there, present for our gaze as a pure phenomenon. To look at nature could even require a special instrument as *Claude's mirror*, in reference to Claude Lorrain, that functioned as a camera obscura, a kind of catoptrical grotto (Baltrušaitis 1989: 157).

It is surprising how traditional conceptions are subverted. Referents are now to be seen from the point of view of their representation. If that is so, what is the point of distinguishing representations from referents?

This is a question left untouched in Baltrušaitis's work because his choice to confine himself to an immensely erudite narrative makes him stop at limits that could only be transposed with some other conceptual framework. The diptych *Anamorphic Art and Aberrations* is a very useful work with enormous merit and brilliance in so far as it reestablishes historical binds that were fogged for and unperceived by our contemporary eyes. Nevertheless, such strictly narrative approach leads to an endless multiplication of connectives. We are tempted to ask for something more. We need an answer, even if provisional, to a question such as this: How can iconicity, as a logical trace of images, lead to the creation of autonomous worlds and therefore to the enthrallment that is illusion?

Let us forget for a moment that referents can be attributed to images. We will take images in their most immediate plasticity. At this point, an image can only be a semiotic configuration of material elements. A paint brush barely touches a piece of paper. A point remains; it is an expression of absolute concision. We can think of the point as the limit between silence and words, for when we represent a sentence graphically, at the end of the phrase and after the point, comes silence. The dead light of a star, the single ring of a doorbell, a stone hitting a windshield, a drop of water flowing from a tap could also be points. Wassily Kandinsky (1866–1944) would ask himself if a point an produce a whole visual work. Yes, it can, as long as the point is related to another visual element: point and plane together, for example. The conjuction of point and plane is the most basic pictorial configuration (Kandinsky 1970: 45).

Paul Klee (1973: 34) does consider what happens when a drop of ink hits a flat surface like a sheet of paper. The point will be made into a spot, a revelation of a set of forces hidden inside the point. This set of forces could be seen as a group of lines emerging from the very center of the dot. Time has now mingled with what it was pure space. The point was moving and has transformed itself into lines. A line walks through the page; it is a track left by a moving point. The direction of a line crossing a blank page splits the plane in two. Different but consistent reactions will emerge from different forms of splitting, from brisk obtuse angles or all-encompassing circles. We do not have here any convention at work, it is more of a *pregnance*, an intrinsic property tied to the formal order of a figure (Thom 1983a: 266).

We have up to now presumed that images will necessarily occur over flat and blank surfaces; but, in historical terms, representations first occurred on the irregular walls of caves. The piece of paper is a latter ground that idealizes images. The flat surface offers to images some very precise formal possibilities that will determine what images should look like.

The plane works as a continuous and neutral surface that will allow the image disparate resources. Over such a blank surface there will be projected lines and elements. These elements are mere possibilities of representation; representation as such will be completed only after the viewer's recognition of the represented referent. Creation is no longer a painter's task. The artist needs the viewer as a cohort in the magic circle of creation (Gombrich 1971: 254). Such new point of departure emerges from the semiotic possibilities of the surface over which the images will be projected. More than twenty years ago, Meyer Schapiro (1969) demonstrated convincingly that the historical unfolding of representative forms is intermingled with the semiotic possibilities of non-mimetic elements.

An argument for this idea can be developed if we acknowledge that only after the semiotic constitution of an all-receptive and autonomous plane over which images will be sketched, can we have a projection that intends to be three-dimensional. Flat and blank surfaces, non-mimetic elements, and the mental faculty of the viewer are connected into the same withinness. Perspective is an appeal to imagination. The deformities of perspective representation, which bothered Plato so much, demands that the viewer rebuilds, in his own mind, the represented object.

As important as anything that happen over the actual surface of the canvas, or paper, is really the frame, another non-mimetic element, without whichthere could beno three-dimensional depth. Is it fair to discount that semiotic element in the constitution of visual configurations? To produce an image from a small block of marble is not the same thing as to extract it from a 10-meter cube. The resulting representation will be big not thanks to any convention but through its material property. Schapiro (1969: 235) considers representations which predate the development of perspective, and concludes that in the archaic arts one finds the trend of subordinating the physical magnitude of represented objects to values that are not physical or visible. For Schapiro, this is not the result of conventions. The archaic artist was certainly aware of the differences in size, separating human figures from big buildings, but he represented human figures disproportionally bigger. The same representational choice is made when one uses linguistic superlatives to qualify intangibles such as love, passion, and wisdom as greatest, highest, etc.

If we follow such a line of thought, images depend only upon themselves, with no referent to subordinate them to. This was a lesson of earlier times that conventional conception of images came to forget. Images can postulate visibility in its most material terms, not just depending upon the represented referent but being what it is. Images the create the most firm kind of existence. It is there, under our gaze, and such presence makes everything possible as far as image representation goes, even if the referent cannot exist as such in the material world. As far as images are concerned, the truth-value of the external referent is of minor importance.

To imitate something is not the main task of images; in images there is no contradiction, just the presence of semiotic forms unified under the attention of whoever contemplates them. The aftermath of classical perspective was therefore the predominance of the autonomy of images. History came to terms with morphology. So, it should be no great surprise that eccentric images would become tamed displays of conventional solutions. Giuseppe Arcimboldo's paintings emerge. They fulfill this promise.

CHAPTER 3

Poses, Onions, and Noses
Arcimboldo's Merry Eccentricities

THE PORTRAITS are stiff. Giuseppe Arcimboldo (1529–1593) drew them mostly in profile. The paintings show uncommon assemblages; heads made of flowers, fruits, bodies and snatches of landscapes cheat us out of the sense of reality.

The subjects are about to retch. The world got stuck in their throats and they had to regurgitate it all over their bodies (Maiorino 1991: 59). The image is aptly grotesque. It could be the central metaphor in *The Portrait of Eccentricity*, Giancarlo Maiorino's (1991) interpretation of Arcimboldo's works.

Any attempt to describe an Arcimboldo painting will fail. They are mainly made to be seen. How should we deal with compositions so strange? Each picture is a portrait and an antiportrait (Maiorino 1991: 81). The manner of expression is excessive. Faced with those paintings, we are doomed to experience an endless becoming to the point of being unbearable.

The judgment of Arcimboldo's importance has fluctuated. The *Allgemeines Lexicon der Bildenden Künstler* restricts itself to a historical account of his life. Arcimboldo ended as Palatine Count, a nobility title given him, in 1591, by Rudolf II. In fact, Arcimboldo was highly exalted in his day. Peter and Linda Murray, however, in their *Dictionary of Arts and Artists*, see no reason for enthusiasm; they argue that Arcimboldo was much overrated in his own day (and now). The Surrealists claimed him as one of their predecessors. When Erwin Panofsky (1985: 91) considered the unfolding of the Platonic concept of *Idea* as a driving theme in the theory of art, Arcimboldo deserved just a footnote.

Arcimboldo's *tête composées* were no more than an oddity. For Panofsky, they deserved to be quoted as an illustration of Gregorio Comanini's allegorical recommendations. *The Autumn* allegories are to be made out of fruits; *Flora* with flowers. If a human profile is composed of animals, the cheek will be inevitably an elephant. The cheek is where shame shows itself. Elephants were thought to be shameful animals; so says the *Physiologus*, a Greek bestiary very popular during the Middle Ages, that presented Christian allegories with moral purposes. Pliny also defined the elephant as a chaste and shy animal, for it copulated away from anyone's sight. The form of a wolf should hide an eye. A tuft of wolf's hair is aphrodisiac. Love reveals itself in a gaze (Brion 1961: 147). The analogy is perfect.

Now, Maiorino tells us that Arcimboldo can be seen as a landmark. With Arcimboldo, we are forced to stare at the orchids of autonomous imagination. There is no quiet on the art front. We are always getting used to what it is new.

The fate of the modern artist is to create independently. There is no set of rules to follow or by which to judge his works. Novelty is the key word. This is our a method of composition and a standard of praise. But it is was not always like that. Giorgio Vasari's comment about Mannerism, *una molta assoluta perfezione*, suggests that perfection is a continuous goal, never to be fully reached by one artist. How could one really attain a much more than absolute perfection? If hyperbole is a pattern of judgment, why can it not be a stylistic trace? The ground is fertile for conjunction, hybridism, and exaggeration. Arcimboldo's paintings are, from then on, more than acceptable; they are the symptom of a coming era. Extravagance will become the dominant vogue.

The Notion of Pictorial Invention

Considering Vasari's ideas, Lionello Venturi (1964) mentioned that artists are capable of knowledge and art. This capacity implies making with knowledge. An artist's lack of objectivity will condemn him to make artificial products. Freedom is the artist's burden. He has to face his own free will under the threat of producing capricci, extravagant products of his fancy (Venturi 1964: 116). Imitation vanishes as an aesthetic norm. If we disregard the outside world as a pattern to be imitated, we are left with the masters's tour-de-force action. For Vasari, the model is Michelangelo's *maniera*, Michealangelo's style of painting.

We are on the threshold of an aesthetic revolution. A new style is recognized as more important than a conformity to models. Mimetic representation is far less decisive than the actual performance of the artist. Composition and style are the real values that will sanctify a work of art.

Was it always that? Michael Baxandall (1991) showed that in fifteenth-century Italy the definition of what constituted a picture was the result of commercial contracts. The client commissioned the painting. It was considered his right to demand that the execution of the work followed specifications. Art was defined as a business transaction ruled by legal contracts, rather than an aesthetic performance.

The conditions of the painting were established beforehand. The contract had to be respected. It determined details concerning the size of the painting and the materials—silver, gold, ultramarine blue—to be used. Some clients paid by the square foot painted. On the part of the artist, the time spent over the work was included in the final price.

One contract stated that Domenico Ghirlandaio (1449–1494) should hand over a panel on the *Adoration of the Magi* to the Friar Bernardo Domenico di Francesco, prior of the hospital Spedalle degli Innocenti (Baxandall 1991: 17). The document mentioned the price to be paid and the deadline of the artist. Ghirlandaio shall make the panel with good material, following a design previously approved by the Friar. The painting is to be accomplished by Ghirlandaio himself, with his own hands.

From 1410 to 1490, the details of such contracts varied. There was a growing interest in the actual execution of the painting. The skill of the artist was being considered more and more valuable. The artist's execution was more important than the materials used in the work. Of everything that could settle the market value of a painting, the dexterity of the artist was the main element. By 1450, prices of paintings could be different. A painter would not charge the same price if a painting was done with the assistance of apprentices (Baxandall 1991: 28).

The seeds of individualism, competition, and also of extravagance are planted. There was a close connection between the commercial procedures that ruled the art world, the aesthetic role played by the artist's accomplishment (no longer the themes, the functions or the materials of paintings) and the existential values that were cherished by artists in their daily lives. Leonardo (1452–1519) and Albrecht Dürer (1471–1528) were their own patrons. They did what they pleased. For both, freedom of action was very much prized (Levey 1967: 79).

Thus we are nearer the idea of Art for its own sake. Painting was seen less and less for its educational and instructional utility (Levey 1967: 79–107). Masaccio (1401–apr.1428) had already abandoned the medieval system of visual composition that followed the stricture of a narrative text (Lyotard 1971: 198). Human figures were presented against the view of a landscape. A *veduta* was opened in the surface of the painting, and this meant that images were a result of autonomous composition. Invention soon came to be valued more highly than imitation of a model offered by Nature. Later, Giovanni Bellini

(1430–1516), considered a forgotten inventor of landscape (Francastel 1967: 289), painted those views as detailed fragments, parts of a whole. In a painting, the overall pattern of composition was the prominent element. Bellini was not observing or faithfully representing Nature; he was composing a picture.

The emphasis on composition is a sign of individualism (Francastel 1967: 290). Art was seen as an immanent creation, an effect of the artist's *ingegno*. Invention is then a synonym of Art. Pleasure, fantasy, and whim will be judged as positive aesthetic values that define what is, in fact, artistic.

Landscape gradually spread itself from the corners of compositions to the foreground. Was this just the result of the natural exhaustion of religious themes as the main narrative trait in pictures? Could art be reduced to offering a edifying message? Alberti said that paintings should have an *istoria*, but an *istoria* is more than a mere illustration of a theme. It is a superior appeal to the intellect (Alberti 1973: 48). A visual address, the *istoria* acts upon the viewer expressing the formal composition of a painting.

Composition became the main stylistic device in pictures. Performance defined art. Nothing was more important than style, not even precious materials. Alberti complained of artists to use too much gold. "There is more admiration and praise for painters who imitates the rays of gold with colors" (Alberti 1973: 85). Leonardo (1976: 48) claimed there was a special value in the depiction of landscapes, rivers, valleys, woods, and ravines. The contemplation of landscape paintings justify the status of painting as a poetic expression akin to music.

A poem is like a picture; some are more pleasant the nearer you stand; others are best represented from farther away. Those are Horace's words in *Ars Poetica*. When Leonardo compares painting to poetry, he revives an analogy made by Aristotle (Rhetoric 3.125 and 1414a7–14). For Aristotle, political oratory is similar to the painted depiction of a scene. The larger the audience, the further removed should be the point of view. On the other hand, forensic style required a more detailed speech; the scene and the audience are nearer (Trimp 1973). The connection of politics and persuasion, present in Aristotle, is lost. Leonardo is saying that painting and poetry have pleasure and enthrallment in common. In painting, there is no greater instruction than contemplating the formal expression of a scene.

Landscape representations turn painting upside down. They are a revolutionary invention in Western Art (Gombrich 1990: 141–160). Their appearance is innocent. The represented scene is viewed from the distance, as if it were under absolute control. Landscapes are free from the traditional requirement of illustrating proverbs, scenes, or verses from the Scriptures. They are a new artistic genre.

The view is no longer a detail presented through a window in the background of a room. The window took over the entire room. We should learn how to face the world as if through a window. The window is the frame that isolates the landscape, imprisoning it inside the painting (Roger 1991: 17). The traditional rapport between the window and the scene is reversed. Now we have a simultaneous experience of recoil and proximity (Simon 1991: 43). Landscape depiction is a fresh chapter in the history of representations. Its main trace is the blending of part and whole. Landscape paintings are produced a single point of view: the spectator's gaze.

Individualism is a requirement for the painter and the public. Concerning the commerce of art, this means greater autonomy for the artist who does not follow the demands of patrons. The artist now paints for a faceless market that responds to his personal whims. He hopes to sell his paintings, but he does not have to work under orders.

Painting becomes a private experience ruled strictly by the senses. Decorative art thrived in this climate of search for pleasure. "The decorative arts were no longer employed in the service of the Church and the Prince, but helped to make a prosperous citizen's environment agreeable and indeed artistic" (Levey 1967: 92). Gilded lampstands, inkwells in arabesque and miniature statues, signs of withinness, shine through decorated houses. *Withinness* is a concept that was gradually achieved in painting and then applied to the public performance of stage scenery (Kernodle 1944). Looking at history, we find many clues to interpret Arcimboldo. He was part of an era where invention and not mimesis prevailed as an artistic principle.

Yet *The Portrait of Eccentricity* departs from historical contexts. This is my regret about Giancarlo Maiorino's book. Reading it, we learn very little about Arcimboldo himself. Checking the bibliographical references, we find rich clues that were left intact.

Introducing Arcimboldo

We stumble on biographical findings. Giuseppe Arcimboldo was born in Milan, a member of an illustrious but impoverished patrician family. The duchy of Milan was at the time ruled by Hapsburg power; Milan was a province of the Spanish Empire. There are no records of Arcimboldo's early days. Probably, his father, Biaggio Arcimboldo, a painter himself, introduced young Giuseppe to the tricks of the trade. A receipt of June 7, 1551 mentions Arcimboldo's name and his stipend for working in the Duomo of Milan.

As an artist that grew up in Northern Italy, coming from Lombardy, Arcimboldo was trained in the mastery of chiacoscuro effects. He also relied on extreme realistic detail as a pictorial resource (Chastel 1972: 295). Arcimboldo is a follower of Bernardino Luini (apr. 1481–1532), his father's teacher.

Some of Arcimboldo's surviving paintings would qualify him as nothing more than a slave to conventions. That is the case of his portrait of Maximilian II and his family which was highly praised by Giovanni Paolo Lomazzo. The whole Imperial family is represented, each gazing in a different direction. Nothing is free from scrutiny; a network of gaze is woven. As the ruler, Maximilian will not face the beholder. His gesture is precise and pedantic. Both hands—one thrust in the right-hand pocket of his pants, the other holding the sword—aim at an indistinct intersection, on the floor. This is the tone of the picture; the consort is dancing together. The Queen Mother and the elder infant glimpse at the viewers, who are facing them. The second son gapes at Maximilian, and the baby in the basket looks, lovingly, at his Mother. There is nothing out of place; even the family pet dog is there. Everyone poses in a luxurious scenery of velvet curtains and marble tiles.

Under the indirect influence of Luini and with his father, Biaggio, Arcimboldo learnt how to make use of caricatures. Caricature was a tradition sprung from Leonardo that many Milanese pictorial workshops taught to their apprentices. Arcimboldo found this training useful in his later years, when he painted his composed heads.

In 1562, Arcimboldo was appointed to the Court Painter of Ferdinand I. His destiny was similar to many artists or thinkers of his time. Arcimboldo would live as a protegé of princes. He was active in the Courts of Ferdinand I's successors: Maximilian II and Rudolf II. His duties comprised more than just painting the Court. Arcimboldo designed coat of arms, besides creating and organizing the divertissement of the Court, the tournaments and stage shows.[1] He acted as adviser and curator of the Hapsburg Imperial Collection: the *Wunderkämmer*.

---

[1] Leonardo also served for twenty years as a master of ceremonies and organizer of Ludovico Sforza's spectacles and feasts in Milan.

Eccentricity and Conventions in Wonderworks

How can a master of convention be considered a prominent guide of eccentricity? All of Arcimboldo's surroundings follow the conventional pattern of his age. Arcimboldo was a Catholic who served sovereigns that were followers of the strictest Catholic Orthodoxy (Sanchez 1986). Such was the case with Ferdinand I, son of Philip, the Fair, and Joan of Castille. Ferdinand was brought up in the Iberian Peninsula, tutored by the very rigid values of Cardinal Juan Martinez Siliceo.

Under Maximilian II's rule, the sanctimonious ideas that prevailed with Ferdinand fell out of fashion. Maximilian praised tolerance. He ascended to the throne in 1564 and reigned up to 1576. Arcimboldo followed the new vogue of audacity. In 1563, he painted the first composed head. Everyone was delighted with this allegory of summer. He was the Court's Official Painter. Arcimboldo knew how to please; the next ruler, Rudolf II, did not remove Arcimboldo from his privileged position in the Court. In fact, Arcimboldo was the favorite painter of both Maximilian and Rudolf.

Rudolf's mother, Maria, was the sister of Philip II, a staunch bigot, who thought of himself as the Defender of the Faith. Maria approved of sending Rudolf away to Madrid, where he would receive a rigorous education. The family wanted to prepare Rudolf to become the Austrian heir to the Spanish throne.

In Madrid, Rudolf meets the glowing splendor of Philip's Court. Sensuousness was what struck Rudolf most. He was charmed by the efforts of erecting the Escorial Museum, under Philip's orders. For Rudolf, it must have been quite an experience; the new environment was a glittering blend of different intellectual fashions that left its imprint on him. Orthodoxy and esoterism: Philip, the Defender of the Catholic faith, thrived on alchemy, and astrological predictions, and showed a special flair for the occult and hermetic doctrines. There was no demarcation or any clear-cut rank. All fitted together. Togetherness united what was common and what was rare and unique. The very mixture must in itself have been wondrous.

In the cupboards of Rudolf's collection, one could find painted Indian quills and pottery; Egyptian shards; bells, whistles and other uninteresting objects; a painting by Arcimboldo depicting half of a cake eaten by a catfish; satyrs side by side with paintings by Tintoretto, Titian, Grimmet, Terniers, Francken, Flores and Arcimboldo's *The Four Seasons*; a large nude with wild boar; Leonardo's original portrait of a lady. And, again, Arcimboldo: faces made with birds, roasted meats, fruits; opaline medallion-cameos; landscape paintings; Lot and his wife by Bosch; a map (we cannot tell what it refers to); musical instruments; another Arcimboldo's portrait made of birds. And more: mandragore's roots that suggested tortured bodies, shells from South Seas beaches, tarantulas, mysterious fossils, scorpions, siamese twins, freaks of natures showing six paws, stuffed dragons, counterfeited basilisks and mermaids, sold to Rudolf by charlatans at high prices. Those were some of the objects listed in the inventory of His Majesty Treasury and Art Gallery in Prague.

The Hapsburg Collection existed under the utmost material rule of contiguity. Nothing is affected by an exchange value. Everything is just what it is. The result is accumulation. The inevitable effect is storage, without systematic order. If there is no evident classificatory logic, just the sense of occurrence; we are left with assemblage. There can be no possible frame of reference. The material world is its own expression.

Arcimboldo's eccentric paintings portray the larger world embodied in the Hapsburg Collection. The principle of extreme accumulation also presides in the design of the composed heads. One could even say that Arcimboldo's work is an encyclopedic introduction to the museum (Alfons 1987: 79).

A composed head by Arcimboldo is a weird conglomeration of objects familiar to the beholder. They are and are not human faces. We gape in wonder, as if going through the *Wunderkämmer* as in the *Wunderkämmer*, we experience diversity and lack of harmony. Nevertheless, all is joined in a larger whole where every single object shines.

Arcimboldo is, to the smallest detail, a person of his time. Is he prey to convention? How could a Court Painter avoid this? How could one say that is Arcimboldo the smirking Prince of Eccentricity?

Assessing Arcimboldo

A significant dispute around Arcimboldo is whether or not his work is a visionary antecipation of Surrealistic movement which followed centuries later. An anachronistic trap is open, and some authors fall into it.

Marcel Brion (1961) saw Arcimboldo's composition as the expression of a philosophical point of view. What is the point in painting portraits with the tools that the models used in their trade? Was Arcimboldo trying to make a timeless statement about the human condition? It is just too poor to restrict oneself to recognizing Wolfgang Lazaius, scholar and antiquarian of Rudolf II, in a pile of painted books. It is a trivial affair to see Johan Ulrich Zasius, manager of Rudolf II's finances, in The Jurist. The Hapsburg Court enjoyed those recognitions, but Brion (1961) says that we should go further than that.

Arcimboldo's portraits declare that Man is annihilated by what he does (Brion 1961: 144). Man's true identity is crashed by the labors society imposes upon him. The composed heads are portraits of inauthenticity. There is some charm in this interpretation, but it is certainly far-fetched. Arcimboldo's time did not know ideas based upon alienation. They give to Arcimboldo a social sense, alien to the spirit of his age and to himself as an acolyte of Princes. It is hard to image those noblemen crying for the loss of their human essences. They were parasites indulging in the pleasures of court life.

Arcimboldo was far from being a heroic rebel, laughing at the expenses of a philistine court that could not understand the implications of what he was doing. Arcimboldo's eccentricity was merely predictable. It belonged to the very center of the world he tried so hard to please.

Arcimboldo cannot be seen as a solitary crank. A conscious adept of the Mannerism prevailing in his lifetime[2] (Hocke 1974: 246), Arcimboldo was the master of tamed eccentricity. He lived and worked in Rudolf II's Prague. We must remember that Prague, the Mannerist city, was the convergence of all accepted oddities in Europe.

Let us go straight to the point. Arcimboldo was a jester. He did nothing but parlor games. It is tempting to dismiss Arcimboldo completely as a merely frolicsome artist; or, else, Arcimboldo was a smart visualizer. In his still life compositions, he turned the painting upside down and one could find hidden human forms. Was this only a cocky demonstration of his ability to compose visual forms with little or no depth?

Arcimboldo laid pictorial signs to provoke a response. This response could not be named an orientation, because the composition in itself was peculiar and altogether novel. The overall effect is puzzling. Looking at those paintings we discover something that we should know, but which was not taught to us. We

---

[2] On the other hand, Pontus Hulten (1987) repudiates the idea of Arcimboldo being a Mannerist. In fact, Arcimboldo should be understood as an anti-Mannerist. His pictorial conception of the world, in which all beings are equally revered and put at the same level of importance, is the very opposite of the artificial, academic and graceless presentation of the Universe created by the Mannerists (Hulten 1987: 31).

see it revealed to us at the very moment of viewing. Arcimboldo's paintings can easily be regarded as perverse and frightening forms of instruction.

Barthes has a different point of view. For him, Arcimboldo is no extravagant. His paintings are always on the fringe of common sense, at the verge of being a proverb (Barthes 1984b: 116). There is eccentricity but his audience can accept it as such.

The pictorial compositions obey a rule of smoothness. The images are illustration of statements. To be literal is a warranty of effective communication. The audience rejoices on obviously literal compositions. Herod? Spread over the face one will see the bodies of children that are about to be slain. Water? Then, all that is actually related to aquatic life: pearls, crab, turtle, octopus, oyster, lobster, and coral reefs.

Arcimboldo's paintings are deceiving possibilities, with no direct link to reality. The *têtes composées* are metaphors and fantasies. Possibility rules. Artistic forms cannot be judged in relation to standards of truth. Arcimboldo's allegories embody the Horatian tradition of *ut pictura poesis* (a painting is like a poem). They are the outcome of the Renaissance idea that defined painting as a pleasure. In those pictures reality plays no dominant part.

Time has changed the condition for the appreciation of Arcimboldo's allegories. The members of the Rudolf II's court are dead. We would have to peruse through history books in search for old icons to find the similarities between the paintings and whoever they depicted. For us, the visual experience of those paintings is restricted to the elements combined in the overall design. As there is no actual and rigid designation, we are bound to experience a fluid combination. There are no exterior referents enticing us to recognition. We are left with a combination of signs, so much like a syntactic process. That is certainly why Barthes (1984b: 117) has the impression that Arcimboldo's composed heads were written. For him, Arcimboldo moves from play to Rhetoric: The next step goes from magic to wisdom.

Barthes's shadow hangs majestically over Maiorino's book. There is a direct connection between the way Maiorino organizes *The Portrait of Eccentricity* and Barthes's interpretation of Arcimboldo. *The Portrait of Eccentricity* is conceived as an interdisciplinary effort, conjoining an artistic-historian, Giorgio Vasari, a theoricist, Giorgio Comanini and a painter, Giuseppe Arcimboldo. Three references: Two of them are directly rhetoricians and the third is a painter. We should not conclude that Arcimboldo is buried under a theoretical apparatus different from the one prevailing in his own work: For Maiorino, Vasari, Comanini and Arcimboldo have the same status of rhetoricians.

At first sight, Rhetoric is the appropriate tool to deal with Arcimboldo's oeuvre. Rhetoric is concerned with seductive persuasion, with adulation of an audience. Its main concept is not factual truth but verisimilitude, therefore what a specific audience admits as possible truth. Maiorino (1991: 136) points out that even better than Aristotle, a rhetorician like Quintilian foresaw the possibility that rhetoric could foster the construction of an autonomous world. This possible world is presented as a linguistic construct, resulting from permutational resources. Metaphors and allegories refer to possible worlds.

Possibility emerges from what actuality furnishes, under the order of a new combination. There is a connection between possibility and recombination. The formal principles of recombination are limited to a restricted set, but the resulting possibilities are multiplied to infinitely. It is easy to identify in this logical postulate the same working principle of any language experience; we have a restricted set of formal rules which makes its acquisition feasible and economical, and out of which an infinitude of sentences may be made.

The different qualities of actuality are recomposed by combination. We start with a version of the actual existing world and end up with another. This is what rhetorical constructions like metaphors do. Metaphors, allegories, and Arcimboldo's paintings name what is possible.

With a rhetorical apparatus, it is feasible to suggest that visuality only depends upon itself. The key concept is no longer mimetic representation but verisimilitude, understood as the mere possibility of being truthful.

A painting, like Arcimboldo's *The Librarian*, is a synecdoche. The part, books, represented the whole: both the librarian and the very library (Maiorino 1991: 46). It is not actual, but it is possible.

Before Maiorino, Barthes was not the first to postulate the existence of rhetorical devices on visual configurations. Again, it could be the ut pictura poesis idea. Let us compare painting and verbal objects. Much to our surprise, we find that this has been tried many times before.

Margarita Levisi (1968) showed a close connection between the Spanish poet Francisco Quevedo (1580–1648) and a painter like Giuseppe Arcimboldo. The same taste for caricature was shared by Quevedo and Arcimboldo. Born fifty years later, it is fair to presume that Quevedo was influenced by Arcimboldo.[3]

---

[3] Margarita Levisi cannot establish without doubt whether Quevedo knew

Image and Text in Arcimboldo

Visually, a caricature is a measure of disquiet; it is a shift from the part to the whole. Linguistically, synecdoche is similar instance of such flow from part to whole. Are we right to assume that synecdoche is an element of visuality? Or does the visual configuration precedes the rhetorical trope?

In perceptual terms, we see something if we can single out what is essential from any accidental trace. Identity comes to the fore. How can we really single out what is a constant trace if we are always under the erosion of everflowing time? Over the years, do I see myself as one or many faces? My face is changing all the time, but I assume that my face is a constant configuration skipping all changes.

Why doesn't change take over? Similarity is a fusion, resulting from an act of perception. We are always building up the fusion of dissimilar configurations. Order is therefore made up. Gombrich (1972: 29) would say that a mask is laid upon a changing face. We resist disorder. Constancy is seductive. Without the mask, there is no distinction between the appearance of human beings. My caricature can loom up as more real than the reflection of my own face spread over a mirror. Any face is on a compound head.

It is a mistake to draw conclusions about images under the assumption of a forced analogy between linguistic and non-verbal forms. The analogy of images and texts is a metaphor. It is a vague approximation.

Barthes relies too heavily on a conventionalist conception of representation. How can one disregard that convention is a latter stage in the generation of images? Images can postulate visuality in its most material terms, not depending upon rules or even represented referents, but being what it is.

Arcimbolo's allegories. Quevedo should have known at least the *Allegory of the Hunter*, composed of wild beasts, for Rudolf II sent it as a gift to his cousin Philip II of Spain (Levisi 1968: 221). Quevedo could have read also Comanini's description of this painting. Arcimboldo's original pictures or even copies were perhaps to be found by Quevedo in one of his trips to Milan, the city where Giuseppe was born. This influence could have also come about through cultural coincidences (Levisi 1968:235). Anyway, in his moral satires, Quevedo appeals to the same compositional resources as Arcimboldo—namely composing a totality out of independent parts. The final product was an artifice joining unnatural and surprising elements in an analogical connection.

The limits of the analogy between verbal language and images can be glimpsed in Hubert Damisch's exploration of Charles Lebrun's (1619–1690) physiognomics. Damisch (1980) considers the representation of human faces a semiotic operation. He presumes that it is feasible to isolate a physiognomic system, as a result of combinatorial possibilities.

And then we bump into a difficult question. Can the composition of a facial expression be reduced to a closed set of distinctive traits, as if it were a phonological system? The notion of code is merely an extension of the central concept of langue. It simply does not work in the analysis of facial expressions. Twitches are distinctive ripples on a human face; but they cannot be reduced to a system organized by distinctive traces (Damisch 1980: 124). There are no intermediate elements. Therefore, the configuration of a face is not arbitrary. Faces are the direct product of passion. A human expression comes directly from muscular contraction. They are indices or, if you wish, tokens, at this stage free from codified or symbolic mediation.

The only comparison to be made with linguistics is to consider those facial movements as an alphabet. The facial movements are a series of meaningless strokes, like the letters before the action of a conventional rule. The drawing should be referred to actual faces, and the faces addressed to those masks, in a constant process of trial and error. The unceasing remission certifies that this conjectural representation is not an artless product of rigid convention. It is a product of creation on the part of the artist, and recognition from whoever sees the drawing. The relation between conventions and caricatures is quite subtle. One does not predate the other.

Conventions can act as guides to icons. The trial and error process of producing an image can be frozen into a rule to be followed. Nevertheless, the diagram configuration is primarily a sensorial conjunction offered as a hypothesis that could be understood as if it were a rule. The critique of iconism is a pseudo-problem. Icons, indices and symbols are in constant process of semiotic interaction. Surely, indices and iconic representations have different natures. We could never believe that cause and effect relations have the same nature as the conjecture inspired by indices, not even if one admits that this conjecture was spawn, as an abductive link, by the material conditions. Furthermore, there is really no thought without conventional resources.

Barthes's abstract conception of code debars him from examining detailed historical context. Convention is a historical product, but Barthes's conception of history and society is too far away from any concrete situation.

Neither Barthes nor Maiorino can dispel the immense confusion around what has been called Mannerism. Perhaps, we should listen to Gombrich. He suspects there is no Mannerism. Most likely we will only find Mannerist works (Gombrich 1990: 129).

We should tackle tangible visual solutions in actual pictures. Under the general name Mannerism, we encounter a enigmatic variety of artistic objects. *Maniera* suggest manner which, in its turn, implies style and individualistic expression, signatures of an interior might. Maniera and *capriccio* are closely related.

Argan (1986: 265) mentions that capriccio had a precise meaning in Arcimboldo's contemporary critical terminology. Arcimboldo's *capricci* expressed an individualistic contradiction of a rule. These paintings are responsible for an inversion of beauty. In fact, the paintings do not refute the rule, but confirm it. Those capricci confront us with the beauty of the irrational monstrosity. What one calls Mannerism is a belated tag, imposed upon existing works. This does not completely invalidate the tag, but reveals its precariousness.

Could creative imagination supersede nature? That is not an easy question. What is the status of nature in the project of creating a perfect world? We have to probe a heart-rending ambiguity. For Mannerists, Michelangelo is a model to be overcome. Such reverence brings about the threat of decadence, a direct result of imitating the unsurpassable Master; and as movement toward perfection is continuous, there is no firm coherence in the idea of Mannerism as a pictorial school. Frequently, but most specifically in the case of Mannerism, stylistic coherence is a posterior attribution of historians.

To find solace under the garb of Mannerism is a perilous affair. The emphasis on an abstract idea of code leads Maiorino to expect that the object of visual analysis can be reduced to a grammatical knowledge (Maiorino 1991: 53). Grammar is a metaphorical expectation. When history is at work, there is more deviance than the supposition of a grammar can support.

History Tells

The pictorial production of Arcimboldo belongs to an age where individual eccentricity is converted into the grotesque. All this springs from a novel conception of singularity that was sketched out very slowly. In every picture by Arcimboldo, what is whole and what is part appears with no hierarchy. Arcimboldo's composed heads give raise to feelings of contradiction, paradox and bizarrerie. Where did this came from? Perhaps history can tell us. The sense of amazement, of maraviglia, was already present in the metaphysics of microcosm that was so dear to the alchemists festering Rudolf II's Court, and earlier to a philosopher like Nicholas of Cusa (1401–1464), and, in another way, to the naturalistic genius of Paracelsus (1493–1541), as Marcel Brion (1961: 156) pointed out. Himself an influence over alchemists and astronomers, Nicholas of Cusa defined existence as synthesis. It was a lesson learnt from Saint Augustine's discussion on Time. In his *Confessions*, Augustine mentioned the impact he felt on hearing Saint Ambrose say: The letter kills, the spirit vivifies. Letter and spirit are radically opposite. Speech, as expression of the letter, is an exploration in time. Speech is a series of thoughts in search for revelation. It is not where Truth resides. On the other hand, intuition guides the spirit as a unity. Intuition is timeless; it is not subject to change. Only intuition is truthful. Intuition and memory are revealed in a flash. The experience is one of sacred permanence that does not eliminate itself, as Time does.

How can one say that Time branches out in three boughs: present, past and future? Time is three. It is composed of present of what is past, present of present things, present of what is to come. Three kinds of Time come to one's mind: remembrance present of things past, present vision of things present, and present hope of future things. The present transfigures itself into three courses, but the only unity is the present one of memory. The present is a neighbor to eternity. What appeared contrary is, in fact, appeased.

Everything is One. Eternity precedes all changes (Duhem 1959: 208). Nicholas of Cusa is talking about what he calls the absolute maximum. He mentions the possibility of a unity without contradictions, where everything coincides. Knowledge springs from the acknowledgement of one's own ignorance. Part and whole are in a relation of total convergence. The One is both an act and the potency of all entities. Everything is co-eternal (Duhem 1959: 273).

There are no irreducible contraries. All rests in conciliation. Each object is in the universe. The universe is in each object (Duhem 1959: 289). Every object is a microcosm constituted like its macrocosm.

Nicholas de Cusa's influence will reach people ranging from Leonardo da Vinci (Duhem 1959: 336) to Johannes Kepler. As we know, Kepler lived, like Arcimboldo, under Rudolf II's protection. Nicholas of Cusas's metaphysics of microcosm can be traced to the idea of nature prevailing during the sixteenth century. This is a major emphasis on Arcimboldo's paintings. In them, we can see the alchemist's idea of nature as a living force. For alchemists all beings merge with each other. Kepler himself holds the principle of classical animism (Koyré 1973: 286). The sun is supposed to have a motrix soul. This soul is responsible for both the solar movement and the creation of a magnetic force that attracts other planets and makes them move around the sun.

Philosophically, Arcimboldo's composed heads are optimistic gnosis. They express the belief that the same divine force gathers up on all there is in this world. Matter is impregnated with the divine. The earth lives and moves with a divine force (Yates 1971: 22). Any occurrence in the world is alive and related in a network of correspondences. Whatever happens in the part is also present in the whole. Both universe and man, as macrocosm and microcosm, refer to the same ocean of life. All the alchemists's gnosis presume that the universe is ruled by an organicist dynamism. The world is in a constant process of transformation. The world is rooted upon an undetermined raw material. The primal matter undergoes evolution and transforms itself in search of perfection and organization (Koyré 1971b: 109). Matter lives and changes.

All beings are created from a vital matter. The same processes are at work in every sphere of the universe. Man is the microcosm where the secrets and the wonders of macrocosm are repeated. Analogy determines the process of knowing.

A World of Symmetries

From the metaphysics of macro and microcosms, it is inferred that the world is expressed as similitude wrapped upon similitude up to infinity (Foucault 1966: 33). The surest mean to reach an understanding of the world is to establish analogical relations. The path goes from what is known to what is still unknown. Knowledge rises from identification with its object. Knowledge comes with sympathy and sympathy emerges from analogy. Only the similar can know its similar (Koyré 1971b: 86).

Paracelsus's writings and medical teachings fit into this image of the universe. Whatever we see as a visual manifestation of the world offers a clue to its intelligibility. To attain knowledge we have to read what is displayed on the surface of the world. The world is covered with ciphered signatures. The investigation of corporeal signatures allows knowledge. The origin of knowledge lies at a deeper level than what immediately we see. The whole world is a signature of the Creator, the visible body of an invisible spirit (Koyré

1971b: 85). The universe is a reproduction and an analogical reflection of the initial structure of its whole.

Paracelsus's conception of illness is directly related to the metaphysics of microcosm. Illness has no cause in itself; it comes from external causes. There is a direct analogical correspondence relating Man, as microcosm, to macrocosm. Salt, sulphur and mercury correspond to the soul, the spirit and the body of Man. Each specific ailment demands the restoration of a lost balance. The patient must be observed carefully. Once the problem is identified, the remedy will be inferred by analogy. The doctor will then know what substance is to be prescribed. Daily observation and practice are of much use (Paracelso 1973: 68). Bearing in mind both the condition of the patient and the structure of the universe, the cure will be revealed as if it were a ciphered expression.

Man is not separate from nature. The human heart can be seen as the sun of the body. The action of the heart and the sun are similar. Moon and brain are equivalent; that is why we call mental disorders, lunacy (Paracelso 1973: 108). Analogy identifies the causes of disfunction; the cure is also determined by analogy. The drugs shall be prepared according to the principle of similitude: similia similibus curantur.

Analogy and similitude are key concepts for the understanding of the mental ambiance prevalent in the sixteenth century. However mystical it may have been, this Age of Similitude demanded an empirical approach to knowledge. The act of knowing was to be disclosed by the interpretation of the world. The world offered to the inquisitive mind a network of analogical clues. Knowledge rises from contemplation.

Now we must face a thorny question. It is just too easy to establish analogical relations. Analogy does contrive connections, but it does not work as a normative principle capable of sorting out what it produced.Similitude is an endless linkage of assimilation. With similitude as a cognitive guide, we are left in the midst of a whirlwind. The knowing mind will have to meet an accumulation of inferences. Analogy leads to infinite addition (Foucault 1966: 45). Arcimboldo's paintings are a visual expression of those intellectual choices and dilemmas. His composed heads are not really eccentric. They fit exactly into the center of the Age in which they were accomplished.

This Age has absorbed what could be otherwise eccentricity to the point of becoming an aesthetic convention. Historical assessment shows that Arcimboldo is in the mainstream. Why are his pictures labeled grotesque? According to Maiorino, there was a shift of values that set Mannerists like Arcimboldo away from Renaissance cannons. The parts of Arcimboldo's pictures are made under the regulation of mimetic techniques. The whole of the composition infuses us with an intense sense of strangeness. We are in the confines of the grotesque. Naturalistic representation is a means out of which grotesque images grow as an end in itself. Eccentricity is an epistemological standpoint (Maiorino 1991: 119).Takento its perverse extreme, like Arcimboldo does, analogy breeds the grotesque.

From now on, we shall be speaking of morphological unfoldings. We will leave history behind. Formal properties are timeless and forego historical contextualization. Morphology subtends history. It is history's duty to catch up with the dynamics of form. But, in their turn, forms become an expression of concrete human relations and historical contingencies.

Analogy is form-generating. It is a sparkle that denies distance. It is like discovering the bonds of a sea wave in the crown of a tree. Or, if we wish, hearing in a wuthering breeze the slashed rumor of liquid leaves. Is it the sea, or is it the tree? It is something new. Different events are combined. The result is a conjunction of being and non-being. We are left with a blend of possibility and actuality.

Analogy follows the principle of proportion. There is analogy when out of four terms, the second one is related to the first, in the same proportions as the fourth is related to the third (Aristotle 1966: 92). Then, a transformation can be worked out. The fourth term can be a substitute for the second, and the second can be exchanged for the fourth. We are left with a compound expression, resulting from analogy. This is the analogical working principles of a metaphor:

$$\frac{a}{b} :: \frac{c}{d} \qquad \frac{\text{dawn}}{\text{night}} :: \frac{\text{infancy}}{\text{old age}}$$

This can produce expressions like 'old age is the night and infancy the dawn of life.'

We find a sharper definition of analogy in Aristotle's metaphysical discussion on existence and being. The continuity of existence is reinstated by analogy; and with it, the sense of an intimate unity that presides the diversity of experience. Much later Paul Valéry (1957) defined analogy as a generating aptitude that combines, agglutinate and, therefore, allows perception.

In *Metaphysics* Δ 6,1016a/25–30, Aristotle says that all beings are one, for the genera, subjected to differences, are one. Horse, men and dog are a unity; all of them are said to be animals (Aristotle 1974: 264). The very model of proportion suggests the possible union of all occurrences. Proportion, as a numerical expression, puts together different categories. Through analogy, unity shines. Comparing and blending qualities, analogy generates representations. The possible will become actual. Analogy plays a major role in inventing (Perelman and Olbrecht-Tyteca 1989: 589). Forms are intertwined layer upon layer. More than awe, laughter is the method for unravelling the threat of terrifying indefiniteness. We glimpse the blooming of grotesque forms, an effect of surface, a unique germination like individual singular laughter (Bakhtin 1984: 67). We laugh at tragicomedy. Fear is left behind.

Referents are powerless to handle the swirling action of analogy. Analogy has no commitment to the outside world. Contemplation is on the brink of an abyss, from which aberrations will spring. Nothing is certain; perception is only just an unstable bundle of sensations. The grotesque is ready to take over, subrogating our previous exposure to a moored world.

How can one outline the grotesque? The graceful and the soothing lay side by side with repugnant and disruptive forms. Uncommon shapes are mixed (Kayser 1986: 117). Morphological elements cohabit without prescribed logical order. The absurd irrupts and induces to the gates of the grotesque. Analogy is life-giving.

Analogy and Life

At this point, we should remember some of Pavlov's experiments. Pavlov pours a weakly acidic solution into a dog's mouth; the animal reacts by briskly moving its head. Abundant saliva runs into the dog's mouth; the acid is washed out. The dog's mucus is purified. In another experiment, before the acid is placed in its mouth, the animal is subjected to a repetitive sound. When the dog hears the noise again, it joggles its head and produces the abundance of saliva (Pavlov 1974: 202–203).

It is not necessary to insist upon Pavlov's notion of conditioned reflex. Body and brain are distinct configurations joined in analogy. If an organism is not skilled in connecting what is different through analogy, it will wane.

Organisms live under the spell of novel stimulation. Those stimulations must be bound to previous ones. A living organism searches for analogies. It must join stimulations and connect them to previous inhibitions. Analogical association brings to life the reaction of the organism.

When a dog is hurt, one of its reactions is to lick the wound. Once again the dog appeals to saliva. There are no curative properties in saliva, but its liquid functions as an analogical operator. It is soothing to evoke water that dissolved food and stopped hunger, whose gastric irritation interrupted an integrated physical state. As if it were a remedy, licking evokes healing. Saliva restores the continuity severed by the bruise.

Reading Waddington (1962), we can see that analogy and biological development come hand in hand. Embryos are alike. Similarity guides the history of the development of an animal. The evolution of the species is inscribed in the body of each animal. When an animal develops, the new stage retains similar traces of previous ones. Analogy conducts the evolutionary history of biological development.

Analogy is also imprinted in the symmetrical organization of my body. I look at my own hands. They are alike. Are they really? To my understanding, those hands are undistinguishable. My understanding cannot grasp the distinction of one hand in relation to another. Nevertheless there is a merciless fact. The left glove will not fit into the right hand. Left and right hand are not equal as my understanding could tell.

According to Immanuel Kant (1959a), this is the same case as with ears and images on a mirror. They are symmetrical and incompatible pairs. One cannot substitute the other (Kant 1959a: 55). They are not wholly identical. It is their existence as sensible phenomena that qualifies each hand as a singular and distinct entity. Yet there is something more than my understanding. Kant would call this sensible intuition. It reveals the existence of an organizing element, previous to any singular event. There is an independent support, a whole where each symmetrical part can occur. The support is an all-encompassing space present in all objects.

If we think about symmetry, as a formal unfolding of analogy, we can see the beginning of what could be named order. Representation and experience, order and change are outlined mutually. Order is diffused over nature. Our daily experience of natural life says that reality is a succession of non-chaotic and stable forms (Thom 1975b: 1). The duality of forms expressed by symmetry can be discerned in such different domains as crystallography, chemistry and genetics. Life and symmetry are intermingled. Biologists recognize in nature pairs as that of phenotype and genotype, or of nature and nurture. Those pairs are in "some way bound up with the distinction between discrete and continuous" (Weyl 1952: 127). As substrate, space is a continuity where discrete events will follow.

Form predates experience. Symmetry is part of *a prior* order at hand everywhere and always. In the end, symmetry is a logical postulate that underlies our representations. Usually two elements are at work in a symmetrical arrangement. Symmetry can be either an expression of a coinciding formal and geometrical relation, or a biological configuration distributing our members over a central axis. The axis crosses the external parts of our bodies. It is also present in the symmetrical structure of the dorsal spine and the brain.

As a spatial transformation, symmetry must have been apprehended when we first looked at mirrors. Mirrors absorb reflection. They harbor symmetry inside them, as if symmetry were a representation of something deeper, of whithinness. Mirrors register faithfully everything. In addition, mirrors present autonomous images; they are closed upon themselves. A primitive revelation of symmetry occurred in refections flashed by ponds and lakes that doubled the sky and also laid it at our feet. This experience defined sameness. After it, one could recognize a face reflected on a sheet of water as one's own.

Space reveals itself as underlying symmetry, and symmetry can be defined as reflexive transformation that preserves the structure of space. With Hermann Wyel (1952), we learn that symmetry is automorphic. The starting point of all symmetrical configuration must be bilateral. Bilateral symmetry comes from a simple transformation. A point in space unfolds onto itself, generating, as in a mirror, a reflection that is its image. We now have identity, transformation of formal properties and inversion.

As it turns out, symmetry is a congruence of spatial parts. Similitude grows in symmetry. Symmetry unfolds in a mirror-image effect. Similitude, symmetry, and mirror-image effects bring about the possibility of a generation of forms. The patterns are reflected, rotated and translated over an axis. Images are made according to a basic morphology invented from bilateral symmetry. Bilateral symmetry will be figured out as the ground for correct proportion. The idea is one of order, perfection, balance and beauty. Whole and part are perfectly integrated. Beauty is bound up with symmetry.

Symmetry Across Cultures

That is why we can find formal aesthetic recurrences creeping up in different cultures so distant from each other. Claude Lévi-Strauss

(1968: 245–268) called those symmetrical solutions split representations. It is baffling to see them happening in different places such as Northwest Coast of America, China, Siberia, New Zealand, India and Persia; and also over entirely distinct periods: eighteenth and nineteenth centuries for Alaska, the first and second millennia B.C. for China, the pre-historic era for the Amur period and a timespan stretching from the fourteenth to the eighteenth century in New Zealand (Lévi-Strauss 1968: 246). None of the obvious reasons account for that coincidence. Common origin, cultural contacts, diffusionist hypothesis are weak motives for explaining the strong sense of affinity to be seen in those formal solutions.

The split representation depicts individuals in symmetrical profile. The knowledge of what is a face predominates over how we see it. The design shows a highly elaborate symmetry with asymmetrical details. The constant technique of split representation does not suffer the pressures of historical or formal evolution, Lévi-Strauss concludes in his analysis of Caduveo facial painting that "over regular faces, painting is laid as dislocated form, ruled by systematic asymmetry. The effect is one of strangeness and eccentricity. Usual faces are under the action of an artifice. The facial painting does not represent an image of a deformed face. It actually deforms a real face" (Lévi-Strauss 1968: 255).

We can see split representation as an emblem of the society that made it up. In a very concrete way, society is inscribed over the painted body. Nevertheless, before being a social instrument, those representations are sign patterns with formal stability. It is due to the internal connection of signs that stability came about. In a first instance, there is a thought about morphological properties of signs. Then, the resulting pattern will be appropriated by social life.

Themes and contents are offsprings of formal arrangements. Bilateral symmetry is the basis out of which never-ending combinations sprout. A potential infinite emerges under an aspect of order. It is therefore possible to say the existence of nature's codex of symmetry (Weyl 1952: 60).

Along Infinity

Little by little symmetry will lead to infinity. The very idea of cosmic harmony is feasible through a reflection on symmetry. Part of Arcimboldo's intellectual background was the stir caused by Copernican cosmology. The key to the mathematical proportion inherent in nature is the supposition that the world is a wonderful symmetry. The planets were organized in a standard pattern of measurement. They revolved around the Sun. Kepler was then free to infer his heliocentric theory. The a priori order of cosmos is deemed symmetrical. There is a total unity in the world; This is the first law of the universe (Hallyn 1987: 98).

The idea, claimed by Aristotelian theories, of a closed world with different laws for lunar and sublunar regions no longer holds. The critique of Aristotle's astronomy implied the conception of an infinite universe, with the same laws on all realms. The cosmos is about to be destroyed and the universe is to be considered as undefined and infinite (Koyré 1986). The medieval conceptions that outlined the world as limited (Lovejoy 1964: 101) started to change. Nevertheless, Copernicus did not take a stand to defend clearly the idea of an infinite world. His overall image of the world is finite.

Even Kepler refuted the doctrine that presumed an infinite universe. A statement about the infinitude of the universe could only be metaphysical. If the universe is wholly geometrical, there cannot be Infinity. All entities are geometrical and therefore limited and finite.

Influenced by Copernicus and trying to reinterpret Copernican theories according to Hermetic principles, Giordano Bruno (1548–1600) was outspoken about an infinite universe. The number of worlds and their extension had to be infinite. This conclusion is both an expression of plenitude and a direct logical conclusion from the limitless power of the Creator's Mind. For Bruno, infinity is a certainty and not a problem (Michel 1962: 177).

Getting to Prague in 1588, and well after Arcimboldo's allegories were enjoyed by everyone, Giordano Bruno joined Rudolf II's Court. Bruno mingled with astrologers, alchemists (Yates 1964: 313) and probably with Tycho Brahe, Kepler and Arcimboldo.[4] There was no job for Bruno at Rudolf's Court. So he moved out. Nevertheless, it is fair to assume that Bruno's enthusiastic defense of Infinity did circulate in Prague, reaching Arcimboldo. Anyway, Arcimboldo was surrounded by this intellectual climate. The theories of the plurality of solar systems, and of inhabited planets, of the infinity of the numbers of the stars and the infinite extent of the universe in space (Lovejoy 1964: 155) were common

---

[4] Bruno presumed a motive for the exceptional role to be played by the artist's fantasia and ingegno. It was his opinion that there are as many artistic rules as there are artists (Panofsky 1985: 67). Bruno's conception could be a cosmologic and aesthetic justification for Arcimboldo's paintings.

topics for an educated person by the beginning of the sixteenth century.

Bruno dedicated to Rudolf II his *Articuli adversus mathematicos*, condemning the mathematical interpretation of the world, and in confrontation with the future tendency to be expressed by Galileo in The Assayer. Bruno disagreed with the idea that The Great Book of Nature is written in a special language, with the alphabet of triangles, circles, and other geometrical figures; without these characters, one will stray into a dark labyrinth[5] (Galilei 1973: 159). Infinity existed without of a mathematical framework. The result could only be disappointing.

There is a lack of definition in Bruno's conception of Infinity. It is either senseless or hypothetical, more of an ineffable and negative concept with a tendency to self-contradiction (Lovejoy 1964: 120). An infinite entity cannot be, otherwise it could only be finite. Infinity is naturally unattainable.

Infinity is, therefore, a suspicion. We arrive at it after recognizing in serial counting the possibility of adding one more number. Even so, counting is insufficient to define actual infinity. The discussion on infinity derives from what is clearly bounded and appear finite. Infinity evolves from numbers expressing the circumscription of a limited set.

A set is considered finite if it has the equivalent numbers in a one-to-one correspondence. The equivalence is exact and refers to finitude. The collection of fingers on my hands is finite; it is in a symmetrical one-to-one correspondence.

George Cantor (1845–1918) noticed that this bi-univocal correspondence could help define both finite and infinite sets. Infinity was referred to a symmetrical framework. Cantor (1963: 112) imagined two ordered aggregates similar to each other in bi-univocal correspondence. Any two elements of one set are equally ranked as two elements of the other set. The sets are equivalent if each element of one set is perfectly paired to another element of the other set. In mathematical terms these sets have the same power or cardinality. The

---

[5] Panofsky (1954) observed that Galileo abhorred Mannerism, allegories, and anamorphosis. The ongoing changes in anamorphic representations ought to be disciplined by basic geometric shapes. Galileo ignored Kepler's rectification of Copernicus's statement that the orbits of planets were circular. Only a Mannerist turn of mind responded to Kepler's notion that the orbits were elliptical. The ellipse is an anamorphic circle.

solution proposed by Cantor was befitting for both finite and infinite sets. Theformal elements of Cantor's thought are pairing, analogy and symmetry. With them, infinity will be outlined.

If we put together two sets—N=(1,2,3...) being the set of all natural numbers and E=(2,4,6...) the set of natural even numbers—we can thus extract a generating relationship between those sets as the one of n corresponding to 2n. The even set of natural numbers is not smaller than the whole series of natural numbers. Each set of numbers is in a one-to-one correspondence. They are countably infinite, or denumerable in Cantor's terminology.

Symmetrical pairing processes produce the discovery that even numbers, which were supposed to be just a part of the whole of natural numbers, are also infinite. Infinity is not framed to the adding of natural numbers that suffer a potential addition leading to a never-ending serial chain. Hahn (1956: 1596) sums up the problem stating that all pairs of natural numbers are denumberably infinite. So, a set is infinite when it contains as a part another collection with as many elements as the whole. The part could be excised and we would still have an infinite collection of terms.

This does not define infinity through counting. Infinity comes from symmetrical and serial arrangement. Can we reduce this process to a doubling operation? If the one-to-one duplicity is possible, we must presume that the other way round is also feasible. As halving is another kind of pairing, we can go on halving and halving infinitely.

Infinity can be usually inferred from the presumed existence of an extended continuum. On the other hand, the continuum is propitious to an infinite division (Weyl 1963: 38). The infinite subdivision designate the infinitely small. So, infinity is both never-ending and an expression of infinite subdivisions. The subdivision enunciates something considered infinitely less than, and also limited, precise and caught by algebraic operations.

This is more than going through the linear series of natural numbers (1,2,3...). Fractions are discovered as a result of concrete acts of measuring. An entire number is laid upon an event of the world. Measuring brings about the segmentation of the numerical line.

The impossibility of considering the continuum as rigid being finds its most concise expression in Zeno's paradox (Wyel 1963: 41). Partial fractions do not add up to a synthetic whole made of an infinite number of elements. Movement is inconceivable. The existence of the continuum as an integral whole is denied. Infinity carries the weight of attracting folly to an otherwise plain reality.

Nothing is safe. The Mannerist threat is at large and, as if to proof all this, labyrinths lurk in straight lines.

The Maze as Imago Mundi

We are now reaching an important point. Maze-making is the mythic key to Mannerist transgression (Maiorino 1991: 142). The maze is the inevitable conclusion, the confluence of themes of analogy, symmetry and infinity.

The experience of seeing an Arcimboldo painting could be reviewed under the sign of the labyrinth. We look at the details of the portraits. Is it an eye or a fish? Do we recognize a human mouth in a shark? Is the bonfire a hair piece? Identity fluctuates. Should we defy anachronism and then see the grotesque Minotaur, preying on the center of the maze, as an Arcimboldesque composition? The labyrinthine traits in Arcimboldo's paintings conduct our eyes which wander through clues disposed to deceive. As a maker who could claim the invention of the merry-go-round, among other devices, Arcimboldo pursued the image of Daedalus. Daedalus is more than just the designer who plotted the labyrinth. He is the original portrait of eccentricity.

Before Arcimboldo, Leonardo da Vinci tried to live up to the role of the major inventor. All of Leonardo's rationality was prefigured by Daedalus. A maze is a construction in the form of a cave. It could also work as the layout of a ritual dance (Santarcangeli 1977: 255). There is nothing irrational in a labyrinth. It is an excessively rational construction: a monstrous building made to house a monstrous being.

Marcel Brion (1959) demonstrated that Leonardo saw himself as some sort of Daedalus. In 1485, after the irruption of a plague, Leonardo proposes to Ludovico Sforza an ambitious plan for rebuilding Milan. As though possessing the rational thread at the hands of Ariadne, Leonardo tries to undo the labyrinthine urban model that prevailed in medieval cities.

Vasari described Leonardo's fascination in drawing interlacing that would fill up a circle. Leonardo was then decomposing the maze into the basic forms of circles and spirals. Mazes spring from the impossibility of movement produced by circles. Within the spiral, the wanderer shall be under the illusion that he is moving. Spirals trace never-ending ways, with no visible reach. The endless repetition of crossways in a labyrinth creates the image of infinity.

A labyrinth is generous with symmetries. Nothing disturbs more than the risk of simultaneous chaos and order. A lake that we were looking at reveals changing forms at its bottom. Always in groups of three, caustic lines in a triple cuspid junction break up the otherwise tranquil waters (Berry and Nye 1977). An endless symmetrical constellation branches out, dancing in the depths of the seas or in river beds. The phenomenon repeats itself in the cracks of dry lands.The world insinuates its own labyrinths. A labyrinth stages a secret and perverse harmony, symmetrically disguised. The wanderer is lost. This infinite journey can only be a condemnation. Knots and interlacing are means to draw an infernal route.

The linear character of these compositions is a reenactment of the feasible solution to get out of the labyrinth. There is one way of escaping from a maze. We have to follow all the corridors and their folds. We will move to and fro (Rosenstiehl 1988: 264). The wanderer must rebuild the whole of the maze in his mind. If he forgets his way, he will be wrecked. To advance and then to go back is the rule that allows the wanderer to recompose his very steps. The coming and going is like rolling and unrolling a continuous thread.

A labyrinth is a primeval image of knowing. The first movement on the part of the wanderer constitutes the hypothesis that his steps backward will test. A global knowledge of the labyrinth is deduced from local checkups. The continuous thread offers itself as a solution for the deceiving knots that structure the labyrinth. The three steps to undo a labyrinth should be easily identified as abduction, induction and deduction.

Arcimboldo could have been acquainted with Leonardo's interlacing. Albrecht Dürer had turned Leonardo's compositions into engravings. And Dürer himself was a household name in Hapsburg circles, for he had been appointed in 1512 Court Painter of Maximilian I. Rudolf II was one of Dürer's admirers.

Brion argues that Leonardo's labyrinths were significant tasks. It had to be so in an artist that followed the *Quattrocento* ethos of searching for a complete unity in everything he did. Marcel Brion (1952) observed that the interlacing lead to a center. In the center was written *Leonardus Vinci Accademia*.

Before dealing with meaning of this inscription, we must inquire what is a center in a labyrinth. The center holds the mystery of a labyrinth. The center is an *imago mundi*.

Mircea Eliade (1952: 67) says that rites of initiation are homologous to the penetration of a labyrinth. We have reasons to look anxiously for the center. We crave Serenity and Paradise. The *imago mundi* shelters the totality we lost. Everything should be there, in an analogical correspondence, like a microcosm. The ordeal of reaching the center will be rewarded. At first, we find the exposure of a fearful secret. The beastly creature is the expression of otherness;

a strange composition resulting from a deviant conception. The Minotaur is both the opposition and the complement of Mankind.

In the dark cave, the Beast is thirsty for light (Santarcangeli 1974: 300). As for us, we will be freed from darkness with darkness. When we find the center we experience the lost unity that was ours before the Fall. The swirling vertigo of Icarus falling is akin to a labyrinth (Durand 1969: 133). In a body a labyrinth can be woven. There, one suffers punishment. Labyrinths are microcosms of Sin.

Why should Leonardo write *Leonardus Vinci Accademia* in the center of an interlaced labyrinth? Brion (1952: 20) finds it difficult to decide whether or not this *Accademia* did exist as an organized institution. He even doubts that Leonardo himself engraved the inscription. The etching was made by someone right-handed; Leonardo was left-handed. Was this a joking metaphor for a rite of initiation? The wanderer who crossed this labyrinth could then claim to be a member of an invisible society. There are other questions. If Leonardo did not etch the inscription, who did? One of his followers? Or was this a joke, a pun on Leonardo's name? Vinci calls to one's mind the word vinco that stands for the interlacing in a basket-work. Vinci means to connect, to lace, as an equivalent for vincoli, knots (Brion 1952: 21).

Leonardo's interwoven labyrinths provide a metaphorical representation for the ordeals of the soul. After crossing the contradictory interlacing of the sensual world, the soul attains salvation (Brion 1952). In this case, the labyrinth represents the paths of our wrongdoing before reaching the center. The labyrinth yields repulsion and attraction.

If we look at the very center of Leonardo's interlacing, we discover a baptismal fount. After baptism, the lost unity shall be recovered. Flesh and soul, the profane and the sacred are reunited. The name of Leonardo at the center of the labyrinth indicates that he will find there a place to contemplate himself. (Brion 1952: 31) The earlier medieval interpretation of the labyrinth as an expression of the mystery of the world is completely changed. Contrary to what medieval conceptions would state, the center if the labyrinth is not Heaven, or Jerusalem or *Civitas Dei* (Santarcangelli 1974: 3282). After the Renaissance, at the center of the maze rests a personal name, indicative of an individual destiny. The dramatic wandering of the soul aspiring for salvation is toned down. Salvation turns out to be a personal drama.

By the sixteenth century, the labyrinth is no longer a tenebrous experience. It is a garden where grotesque forms shine as decorations. In Arcimboldo's time, the labyrinth is transformed into a worldly game. Harmony and disorder play against each other. In this infinite match, only personal skill matters. Individualism blooms. Arcimboldo's allegories are merry labyrinths where frivolous eccentricity dances.

PART 2

Uncommon Interpretations

CHAPTER 4

Remembrance, Like Rembrandt, Is Dark But Festive

THE BELLS are tolling. They call for the wake of art history, and the funeral rites were rehearsed by practitioners of the field. The upheaval in the history of art has arisen slowly but surely. In some quarters there is an assumption that the traditional historical interpretation of art is under a non-too-soon identity crisis.

As an intellectual project, art history suffers radical redefinitions. A disturbing sign that in the history of art no one seems to be sure of anything is the fact that nowadays even the corpus of Rembrandt paintings cannot be firmly anchored in their attribution. Remember, we are not talking of a secondary painter but of one of the most representative figures in art, from whom it irradiates the fundamental cultural topics unfurled in all spheres of Western heritage (Bal 1991). Embarrassment lurks at every corner of art history, up until recently a placid field of studies, the serene guardian of canonic works to be worshipped in the altars of high culture.

At the threshold of *Visual Culture*, an exciting anthology, masterfully edited by Norman Bryson, Michael Ann Holly, and Keith Moxey, we stumble on a tough statement very typical of this intellectual climate, which also defines with precision the experience of reading the contributions to the volume: "The essays in this collection could be considered as contributions to the history of images, rather than to a history of art" (Bryson, Holly, and Moxey 1994: xvi). In general, a healthy sense of perplexity, and rage flows through the pages of the book. But we cannot help wondering how a discipline considered by Erwin Panofsky (1955: 2) as the embodiment of the high ideals of the humanities, namely "the dignity of man, based on the insistence of human values (rationality and freedom) and the acceptance of human limitations (fallibility and frailty)," could come to such a bedeviling impasse?

Certainly too much was taken for granted. Panofsky's thrilling promise of an iconological interpretation of images became the stifling recognition of themes and motives, and little else. Questions that appealed to contemporary life either were forgotten or omitted as though they meant nothing. Race, gender, class, and all the political dimensions of art production were dismissed with a gesture implying futility. Under the excuse of historical objectivity, reactionary options ruled art history, both in method and in its election of objects.

The craft of traditional art history always required the establishment of a cannon hedged and contextualized by temporal boundaries. History of art was the inventory of a tradition and an act of judgment. Under what conditions was the artwork produced? What makes it representative of a precise moment in Western culture? Art was always presumed as already defined, given, and recognizable without doubt.

The authors contributing to *Visual Culture* are at odds with the mainstream of art history. The vitality of each essay in this collection stems from the critical examination of the principles of art making and their effects beyond the closed boundaries of historical and artistic contexts. Minute care is taken to avoid the snares hidden by unscrutinized theories. Every piece in *Visual Culture* has more than the courage to come to the edge of an abyss, and then face the threat of contributing to undoing what tradition tendered secure and comforting. Bryson, Holly, and Moxey demand change and transformation in a discipline so inbred and impervious to novelty.

Far from being a source of solace, history is now argued in its very foundations. Are historical narratives possible? Can we accept causal historical explanations? Do we retrieve history? Such problems may be unsettling and difficult to accept, but there is no way out of them: "The historian can never come to grips with historical events, for these are mediated by the opaque medium of language" (Moxey 1994a: 59). It is a mistake to suppose that art and history are a prioris sheltered in worlds of their own that eventually come together under the soothing tag of art history. Living history, not to be impoverished as mere historical inventory, is effective action. So Holly contends that "historical artifacts, particularly visual ones, are themselves always laboring, more or less successfully, to systematize their own historical accounts, as signs producing signs" (Holly 1994: 361).

Signs and language are considerations that now come to the foreground. There is hope that semiotic perspectives will bring the necessary changes in the nature of historical interpretation. The status of "painting as sign" (Bryson 1988b: xvii) is understood as the alternative to classic theories whose archival intentions stagnated art history.

The lesson is clear. There is no stability as art history naïvely claimed. The disciplinary frontiers separating fields of investigation are blurred: We should not separate visuality and poetics (Bryson 1988a). Nothing is given, not even the category of context that used to be the undisputed cornerstone of historical interpretations dealing with art.

But how could it be so, knowing, after Podro (1982), that context was the tightrope on which the historical approach to art had to balance itself? The demand for contextualization was an option resulting from the evaluation of the interpretative advantages of taking a context-bound stand against formalistic and idealistic assessments of art as irreducible to anything else. History of art would collapse if it disregarded painstaking contextualization. The editors of *Visual Culture* offer us another brand of history.

History Is All Remorse

The consequences of Bryson's (1992) driving the stake into contextualization are likely to be liberating. There should be no point in defining a historical approach from the strictures of contexts. Contexts are not just peacefully waiting for historical redemption: They are produced by history, being endlessly made and remade. This insight forces us to admit that contexts are always attached to the actual present of historical interpretation.

Contexts are more than beacons committed to help in the unselfish search for historical truths. In its traditional mode, history is an impossibility, nothing more than a tottering expectation. We cannot easily uphold the idea that contexts are an unchanging presence preceding art making, as one wishes that effects follow a given cause. Or as a mirror silently engulfs any object plunging in it. Now a new batch of authors and disciplines historically unaligned are called to contribute to the task of interpreting images. Barthes, Lacan, Bakhtin, Foucault, Culler, Derrida, Freud, Heidegger, Wittgenstein, Saussure, Merleau-Ponty, Fassbinder mingle comfortably with Wölfflin, Burckhardt, Panofsky, Gombrich, and Svetlana Alpers.

If the context is a real totality, its boundaries transcend the time limits of when the image was produced. There is good reason for including the present. Each interpretation reinvents history. Links are forged and context is therefore larger than past occurrence. Context has "infinite extendibility" (Bryson 1992: 39). The present is an inevitable force changing a past that could never be pristine.

In theoretical terms, that means a drastic shift, a turn from the traditional dominance of the author generating images to our contemporary reception. Time's arrow points to a reversed direction, from today to an unredeemable past. The works of art are "constituted by different viewers in different ways at different times and places" (Bal and Bryson 1991: 179). No time dimension is stable. Heraclitus and poets, like Jorge Luis Borges, knew all too well: Time is an indivisible river. Why should the interpreter aspire to a positive but untenable objectivity? A line is drawn separating old historians from new critical thinkers: "Historians coolly analyze; critics are passionately engaged" (Holly 1990: 373). Without context restricting our interpretations, we must look for an alternative to the prevalent theories of image: the perceptualist and economist approaches to visual configurations.

Perceptualism contextualized images according to the relation between the maker and the natural world. In Gombrich's *Art and Illusion* (1960) we find the most complete and influential statement of this conception. Perceptualism casts weight upon the procedures of the image maker, the formulator of visual hypothesis, launched either by an interpretation of traditional solutions or by attempts to convey the perceptual pattern of the outside world. The core of the artistic enterprise is consequently mimetic, its method is trial and error. The artist makes a schema and matches it to what is given to him as the maker, through tradition or other forms of contemplation, that is to say, looking at the natural surroundings. Gombrich considered the perceptualist account as a condition for the historical interpretation of images. The schema is an effect of history. The transformations and corrections in a visual pattern indicate the overall stylistic unity, the ruptures and the rebirths of an art model. The historicity of images is identifiable if we consider their perceptual nature. The historical flow starts from visual solutions having a certain degree of permanence, either as a visual nomenclature or as the analogical bond of image to reality.

There are serious objections to perceptualist theories. Bryson could call them the pinnacle of gullibility. The "natural attitude" of perceptualism admits uncritically the possibility of an essential copy of reality, resulting from the belief that there is a direct access of the consciousness to the actual world (Bryson 1983: 31). Perceptualism forgets other forces striving in the creation of images. The history of images should also be the narrative of discontinuities, showing the action of power structures, and revealing the social interests in the production, circulation, and interdiction of visual patterns. The social history of images should deal with conflagration and strife rather than illustrating the perceptualist conception of visuality as a net thrown to an inert world. To stick to the mere rendering of perceptual conditions does not assist us in deciphering the social strategies of image production. Perceptualism has to be towed away so that we can see the social inventing itself through its representations. We are now heading toward a richer theory of images, attentive to the ties between "the image and power" (Bryson 1991: 63).

It is undeniable that the economist approach faces what perceptualism left out. An economist interpretation starts recognizing that social forces are present in image making. Power relationships are an integral part of the visual schema; and, by extension, the visual schema should be conceived as a power device. If such is the case, the social aspect should always be there in our interpretations of art. But how can we pin down the vectors of social power? Obviously, granting that consciousness is an ingredient of an overall social process strong enough to determine our cultural notions. There are forces outside consciousness exerting pressure over what is produced by the human mind.

Marxist economism ends up placing art as an upper institutional stratum directly dependent upon an economic basis of which it is an expression. Economism acknowledges the productive nature of sociability, and defines image making as a subordinate activity to an economic base. It had to be so, for "the base is the more important concept to look at if we are to understand the realities of cultural process" (Williams 1973: 5). That is precisely the problem with economicist theories, ranging from vulgar Marxism to the Gramscian revaluation of cultural hegemony as an instrument of class conflicts, themselves related to economic struggles in social life. As a consequence of seeing any sign as a superstructural representation of an economic base, Marxist theories pay the price of dismissing the materiality of image making.

An effective theory of visual interpretation has to concede the material reality of painting as pregnant with meaning. Images are active social discourse, not submissive to an external force, that would in fact deny their materiality. Images bathe "in the same circulation of signs which permeates or ventilates the rest of the social structure" (Bryson 1991: 66). To handle this fundamental contention, we must search for another theoretical alternative to perceptualism and economism. The image cannot be the ordinary depiction of what we presumably see, or a subordinate expression of positions in the social struggle. Images have a positivity of their own, they are not a negative profile of social relations. And the way that Bryson proposes to achieve this is to understand images as active projections in the discursive field of society, where they are fully significant elements, "not echoes or duplicates" (Bryson 1991: 70) of any thing. Images are modes of actions, strategies of use, forcefully dynamic in social life.

An important methodological repercussion of the projective conception of the image is its implicit denial of a hierarchy of signs. There is no legitimacy in purifying the discursive field of society, either through resorting to context or, following the steps of traditional art historians, by valuating specific art products as the paramount creations of the human spirit, at the expense of everything else. Society is an arena where signs collide, on equal stand, with one another. Meaning, or value, to use Moxey's appropriation of a central linguistic notion, "is not derived from its position relative to all the other signs that make up the system so much as from its position within all the other signs that make up culture" (Moxey 1992: 41). It is not an anything goes policy, but the belief that any attempt empowering us to enlighten the fading hieroglyph that we have inherited from the ever receding past is worthwhile. How could we previously discard theoretical constructs of the present as unable to deal with the past? How can we say that contemporary concerns do not fit into what was granted to the present? How can we separate past and present?

Griselda Pollock's "Feminism/Foucault-Surveillance/Sexuality" sets the tone for much of what will be read in *Visual Culture*. Pollock's essay is part of her sustained effort in criticizing social art history as forgetful of gender, in her view a crucial theme of any serious reflection on power relations. Traditional art historian's worries over the excellence of individuals deemed as geniuses is to be displaced by the analysis of the institutional gag that have silenced women, and more particularly, feminine artistic production. Pollock's reasoning springs from Linda Nochlin's (1988) widely influential attempt of rephrasing the desolate discussion on the absence or scarcity of women artists. What really matters is the cultural examination of institutional practices that have barred or disciplined women as social and also artistic actors. More than just producing a cultural analysis of specific ideological procedures, Pollock hopes to act upon contemporary culture, not only demonstrating the regretful masculine supremacy but also urging a radical reform in male tyranny. Feminist theory challenges all history as a conspiring agent of oppression.

Pollock claims that we should face first things first. Patriarchal and sexist practices antedate class discrimination as instruments of social submission. Class distinction is a historical phenomenon; it cannot be considered as the originating source of power relations. For many societies it would be unthinkable to separate infrastructure and superstructure, precisely the theoretical conception revealing the dominance of the economic base that explains modern power structures. Many social groups have opted for regarding kinship and its mating prescriptions as the weavers of the social fabric. The belief that all societies are based on the principles underlying industrialism, with its critical economic conflicts, is sheer ethnocentricity. Several practices in archaic societies stress that the distinction between the base and superstructure has no clear meaning. In kinship practices, as Claude Lévi-Strauss explained, women are considered valuable tokens of exchange. The exchange itself creates sociability and reserves a submissive role for women. Sociability, subordination and the constitution of feminine identity are altogether conjoined: "Man is positioned as the exchanger and women as a sign of the exchange as well as its object" (Pollock 1988: 31). Hence the representation of gender has to come to the foreground. Gender is "a transhistorical and unitary category" (Pollock 1988: 39) in any discussion aiming to discuss the origins of social subjugation.

After quoting contemporary authors as diverse as Michel Foucault, Jacques Lacan, Marxists, especially E.P. Thompson, and most obviously feminist militant thinkers, Pollock proceeds to investigate how representations ordered the body of women laborers working in the nineteenth-century mines. At the surface of images representing these bodies we figure a "conjunction of labor and sexuality" (Pollock 1994: 17). A set of extraordinary photographs depicting women, posing in both their working clothes and Sunday dresses, provides the clue for understanding the domestication of female sexuality, regulated by the social exclusion of the universe of the house, eternally feminine, from the outside world predominantly male, where labor thrives.

The separation of two social spheres functions as more than a neutral taxonomic grid. The bourgeois house advances an idealized model for social interaction and the bourgeois family is nothing short of a blissful haven, where disciplined and domesticated women ought to dwell happily. Reproductive sexuality rules the bourgeois home. But it becomes a moral guideline to be ascribed to all female social actors.

Such social values are clearly visible to our voyeur gaze. On page 27 of *Visual Culture* we see photographs of the same woman, Ellen Grounds, dressed in clothes that, at first, demarcate the frontiers of a female and a male universe, one domesticated and the other on the verge of breaking out of control. A picture shows Ellen Grounds meekly wearing a dress that follows the strictures of the bourgeois dressing code, and in another photograph, side by side, she proudly carries her laboring clothes, holding a shovel and what seems to be a mining screener. The laboring clothes are dirty in contrast with the bourgeois dress. It is a telling detail that while wearing her Sunday garments she is posed sitting near a fresh vase of flowers. Purity and chastity are transported, in metonymy, from the blooming flowers to Ellen Grounds herself, now represented as a tamed woman. The dirty labor clothes befit a potentially deviant social being, displaced from where it was naturally assigned. Besides representing this more than evident classificatory characterization, when photographed near Arthur Munby, the collector, owner and symbolic master of the pictures, himself "a minor civil servant and amateur investigative journalist" (Pollock 1994: 26), Ellen Grounds poses as a laborer but with clean clothes, as if touched by the magic wand of the disciplinary male at her side.

Women are visualized, controlled, disciplined, transformed into objects of knowledge and surveillance. In the process, photographic images are strategies of capillary power; they are active and normative grids. The social effectiveness of images derive not from what is suppressed, as a naïve conception of power entails, but through what is portrayed. Power may not be clearly visible all the time, but through visibility power comes to action.

We could connect Pollock's essay to several others in *Visual Culture*. Among them, John Tagg's "The discontinuous city" shares the same idea of power as a constitutive force of image making, in action over the social relations. The urban spectacle, nowhere so obvious as in Paris at the middle of the nineteenth century, is an overpowering agent, capable of distributing roles and organizing sociability. The city comes to existence through its organization. And its design, numbering, zoning, and rationalizing universal grid articulate the experience of the urban dweller. The city exhibits a visual configuration similar to what Tagg calls "the conventional conditions of western optical realism" (Tagg 1994: 90). The urban experience is akin to the regimes of representation that did beget perspective and photography.

Tagg recognizes that his study relies too heavily on the institutional effects of conventions over images, thus dismissing the issue of tangible resistance to social ordering. Every single social area bears the surveillance of a taxonomic power, and not only labor and sexuality, already pointed out by Pollock, but also paternal responsibility, psychological traits, internalized emotions. In short, everything that makes living identities possible. The basis is not the economic means of production; it is the dichotomy of male and female singularities in the urban setting.

The design of the city and its discrimination of public and private realms should be linked to the basic gender opposition. Women now parade their subordinate condition along urban avenues and alleys: "Women are the sign, but never the speaker" (Tagg 1994: 86). The articulation of different positions reinforces social discipline. The city is an instructional message, spelling implicit commands, and not any other kind of text.

Together, the macro order of the urban setting and the myriad of micro representations attain the goals of the panoptic power. Their conjunction forges a general "political strategy of representation" (Tagg 1994: 87), and so life thickens.

The city lives under the threat of disintegration. No other social sphere requires more reinforcement than an urban setting. Cities are invariably perceived as hives of evil. Their diversity requires steady control. As a document and a faithful record of reality, photography then assumes the function of a privileged mode of authority. Through photographs social reality is mapped out.

Multiplied by its limitless means of mechanical reproduction, photography could never be granted the cultural value of traditional art. But, as a result of its technical prospects, photography has an evidential value. Photographic technology is useful for the implementation of power strategies, "the power of evidence, record, and Truth" (Tagg 1988: 11). Photographs are from then on used for documents, and for surveying the details of urban life. "The photographs mark the beginning—but only the beginning—of a methodical documentation that has to differentiate itself in a field of urban representations: shunning the picturesque and the sensational, disdaining the moralism and humanism of philanthropic reformist photography, affecting a systematicness beyond and above that of commercial stereoscopic and postcard views, relinquishing the privilege of Art for the power of Truth" (Tagg 1988: 13). A photographic image validates observation, with the productive purpose of regulating, integrating, and governing social life. Photographs are smoothly attached to disciplinary cognitive modes and their practices, to medicine, to anatomy, to psychiatry; they are also used by the authorities responsible for public polices, or for police records and their technology. Photographs are the perfect witnesses, the flawless authenticators activating strategies of control.

The attributes of the practicing power perfectly fit the photographic expression: "impartial, objective, clean, compelling and modern" (Tagg 1994: 90). A unique discursive field is currently created with the purpose of conjugating the social and figurative orders. Only then can photography be seen as a neutral and unassuming power, ever more insidious for being so natural. Photographs mature into potent social operators.

Two other essays in *Visual Culture*, Lisa Tickner's "Man's Work?" and Mieke Bal's "Dead Flesh," try to confirm Pollock's indictment of an enduring masculine domination. For Tickner and Bal, image making is an accessory to a deplorable historical legacy. But Tickner and Bal show different argumentative tactics.

Tickner battles to mark gender traces in the works of British avant-garde artists between 1905 and 1915. The period is a moment of political turmoil, when labor unrest and feminist militancy emerge as undeniable forces in the social horizon. The old order agonizes, but as yet it was not buried. The times are ripe for a season of aberrations.

Once again, contemporary feminist interests lead to the revaluation of a definite historical point in art production. Modernism grows as the expression of masculinity and it is regarded by its cultural role in constituting female identity.

As an art style, Modernism thrived in the same milieu of urban societies. Change was a hopeful promise for all members of industrialized and modern urban gatherings. Women were to claim their political share in the new times. A visible sign of the pertinence of feminist demand was the strong reaction it caused and the efforts that were made to tame it. No other social sphere would be more fruitful for the emerging battle around feminist aspirations than culture. Culture is precisely the mold of social roles, therefore of femininity.

Tickner pursues a mellowed Saussurian definition of gender. If, in Saussurian terms, language is ordered by appositive values, the tag *woman* "becomes a relational term in a system of differences" (Tickner 1994: 45). The feminine self is seized by distinction with what is its other. And over the basic binary articulation a variety of social values is bonded to one another: functional against ornamental; pictorial opposed to decorative; engineer and leisure class; production and consumption; reality principle against pleasure principle; machine and body; active opposed to passive. The relationship of opposition inevitably conveys the threat of one term flooding the other.

Feminine art was then a possibility that created anxiety among male artists. Femininity was nothing less than feebleness, a synonym for mediocrity. Thus the hyperbolic representation of masculine features was to be the antidote for effeminacy. To portray the strains of that moment, Tickner charts mainly the biography of the rebellious figures of Augustus John and Wyndham Lewis.

Their bohemian lives are quite dissimilar. Augustus John will roam the English and French countryside as a gypsy patriarch, meanwhile Lewis aggressively advances over women of lower classes in the streets of Paris.

Lewis's phallic fixation finds artistic expression in aggressive artistic styles, violent geometries and the rambunctious prose of his grotesque novels. Augustus John remains an outdated pastoralist painter, in agreement with his wandering life. But around Lewis and John, there will be an emotional havoc and an artistic wasteland: illegitimate children, aborted talents, and domestic subservience.

Tickner denies that her goal is to supply biographies of each individual as ends in themselves. The lives of John and Lewis, as well as other British artists—Vanessa Bell, Jessie Etchells, Jessica Dismoor or Helen Saunders—should be seen as alternatives then socially available for men and women aspiring to be painters and sculptors. Nonetheless, I cannot help wondering what makes Lewis's boisterous rudeness and John's romanticism of gypsy caravans really representative of the times, and not mere idiosyncrasies? Of course, history is the conjunction of personal lives. But history is also and primarily a collective horizon. As such, biographies are little more than a record of events, so personal, no minuscule, so particular that to become a symptom of historical significance they require more than a chronicle of a life.

Unfortunately, Tickner does not dispense an answer for the objection. Lewis's shortsighted cult of masculinity is perfectly countered, at the same moment, by the ironic aestheticism of the Bloomsbury group. What makes Lewis's flag-waving maleness more representative than Bloomsbury's "homosexual component" (Tickner 1994: 53)? Bloomsbury's sexual options can be seen as a disavowal of Lewis's masks of masculinity. Or is it because the Bloomsbury group was a plain aggregation of individuals exclusively united by personality and class extraction? The same contention could apply to Lewis' Vorticism, or to any group of artists. I am not comfortable with the suggestion that Lewis's and John's biographies are historically more significant merely for the reason that they confirm Lisa Tickner's viewpoint.

Mieke Bal's "Dead Flesh, or the Smell of Painting" should be considered the obverse of Tickner's biographism. Bal would say that seeing a Rembrandt painting requires a more intricate operation than identifying it as the portrayal of actual events in a life. The recognition of the painter's common-law wife in a picture does not grant a lasting knowledge of it. Images are not the strict representations of concrete persons and surroundings.

Images are visual configurations manifesting classes of things. Images denote collections of objects and they cannot be easily specified as direct descriptions. On their own, images are universal representations. Similarly the word, "dog," alone represents a collective possibility. It will point to an existing animal only if conjugated to a syncategorematic term. Without a syncategorem, logic words such as "the," such as "a," such as "this," representations take flight, as uncertain as clouds. But images have no syncategoremical terms. Syncategorems are logical and textual devices. Does it imply that images cannot be read? If not, how can images convey meaning? In images, denotation is subjected to their connotative and therefore associative ties.

In an image, the density of connotation designates reality. According to Nelson Goodman, an image may appear to be the representation-of something, but certainly and foremost is representation-as. The representation-of something depends on an analogical cohesion with the represented object. Something else defines images. Goodman assumes that images cannot be described by their analogical correspondence. Let us take the case of twins, for example. Twins may be identical to one another, but we cannot say that one child is the image of the other sibling (Goodman 1972: 146). A picture of a person can be perceived as similar to whom it portrays, but the portrayed person is always dissimilar to the picture. To become more alike to a referent requires steps that would terminate the picture as a picture. The picture would become the represented person. Goodman suggests that a picture is consistently more similar to other pictures than to its perceived referents.[1]

Similarity in images is an aftereffect of the conventional conditions of their making, responsible for the capacity that an image has of being recognized. Images are not the uncompromising pictures of existing objects and events of the outside world. Therefore, the use of biographical data is a narrow option for interpreting images.

For Goodman, an image is an offspring of conventions, of habits, of the shared rules that created it. We recognize similarities because we trained for that purpose. Images have to be read, even those in perspective. Only guileless people could regard perspective as natural. The ability to read, and that is what we do when we see a painting in perspective or a photograph, is acquired (Goodman 1968: 14).

---

[1] Goodman's arguments are seductive, crafty, but circular. Iconicity and analogy are induced by neurological conditions guiding the perception of images. Twins would never be the depiction of one another. Twins, just like any event of the world, can be made into a representamen as long as they fulfill, through analogy, causality, or convention, the condition of standing for something else.

However critical of some details in Nelson Goodman's *Language of Art* (1968), such as his "positivistic privilege of sight as the most reliable sense organ" (Bal 1991: 258), Mieke Bal's quest is for a historical approach to collective representations. A picture of an agonizing woman indicates the conjunction between "death and femininity" (Bal 1994: 365). Lucrecia and Bathshebah depict the class of women. Images must be read in their distinctive way. Conventions and their collective nature are the clues to our reading. All in all, Bal's conception of image is as conventionalist as Nelson Goodman's.

Bal contends that Rembrandt's paintings are cultural texts. They are part of a discursive field tightly held together. Rembrandt's paintings illustrate and are explained by their insertion in a textual community, comprised of words and images read and extended to the seventeenth-century Dutch culture (Bal 1991: 420).

As autonomous and strictly conventional patterns, images lodge in a self-referred dominion. Purged of their attributes as designators, images escape from the strictures of truth and falsity. What separates utterances, verbal or visual, from facts is taken as groundless. "I say" and "I see" become equivalent. Images are analogous to speech acts, in which truth-values derive from the conditions of uttering them.

Biblical rapes stand for timeless sexual violence. They exculpate an unforgiven act. Rembrandt's painting, now at Washington, D.C., in the National Gallery, of Lucrecia pointing a dagger to herself, with open arms and with dejected gaze is seen as an ideological statement: "Rape is like self-murder (metaphor) because rape leads to self-murder (metonymy)" (Bal 1991: 70). The blame is laid on someone who is an innocent victim. The rapist is unjustly spared by the compositional decision of placing him outside of the image. Rembrandt's drawings of the execution of Else Christiaen are just the universal representation of women subjected to male sexual violence. Rembrandt's images are viewed as both masterful creations and arraigned as guilty for their participation in a dominant male culture, set on reducing females to nothingness. For Mieke Bal, visual representations and the ideologies of gender are closely intertwined.

Biblical narratives and the sketches of an actual execution refer to one another and can also be joined to Rembrandt's famous paintings of slaughtered oxen. An ox carcass spread wide open by a bar laid across its rib cage directs itself to crucifixion, rapes and sacrifices, not excluding images of opened bodies in Rembrandt's anatomy lessons. Representation is wrapped upon representation connecting signs to signs in a vortex, leading to infinite and unstoppable additions of contents, comparable to free associations, blending past and present in the hope that we will glimpse "what inaugurates modern representation" (Bal 1994: 380–381).

The hope is to explain the present from examining what is bestowed by the past. The historical trail delivers and disseminates representations that also bolster, perpetuate, and perfect the ruling codes. Pollock, Tagg, and Bal support a matching claim: Institutional codes, themselves a historical legacy, regulate our behavior. Images held us hostage.

The topic haunts Norman Bryson's (1994) paper, "Géricault and 'Masculinity'." Bryson argues that representations and culture are merging tides. The cultural conditions of masculinity and certain works of Géricault should never be inquired separately: "The two inquiries are one and the same" (Bryson 1994: 288). Representations build up the subjective possibilities of social life, and, for good or ill, masculinity is one of the most conspicuous cultural contents.

Bryson repudiates the criticism that this kind of analysis leads to a devaluation of paintings. An image would only be the example or the case inscribing a cultural principle, if we dismembered the discursive content of a picture from its iconographic configuration. And for that it is required to believe the most chronic tenet in our visual tradition: that images are invariably perceptual and so to judge them we would have to dispel anything outside of the mimetic criterion.

The outer world, and that means the whole of a culture, is never kept away from images. The gaze is not an innocent or harmless perception. When the image cleaves active and passive roles, and thus masculinity matures socially into the bearer of the look, while the female position is turned into an object, this is a statement. In no way do discourse and image preside over one another.

Even the discrimination of image and discourse according to their temporal gist is faulted. Images are as constrained to temporal contingencies as speech. How could we agree that images are timeless totalities and language a strictly progressive and approximative flow, if the state of totality in pictures "is never achieved, is always postponed, is always ahead" (Bryson 1988a: 185)? The interpretation of images cannot pretend that their discursive element has to be eradicated. The materiality of images embody cultural contents without being transformed into illustrations, into docile serfs of the word.

Now Bryson moves away from an already established portrayal of power relationships between the male gaze as active, and femininity as passive. Bryson's main concern in "Géricault and 'Masculinity'" is with what happens when the male gaze turns upon another male. It is a problem of creating identities. And identity results from a intricate interplay with alterity; as we can notice by not only admitting that the world is shaped into existence when we gaze it, but also realizing that the self is brought about through the gaze of others. In his contribution to *Visual Culture*, Ernest van Alphen states it clearly: "When I speak about the other, I remain caught into the process of defining and demarcating my self-image" (Alphen 1994: 260).

Self and other are not mere positions. They are functions of a constituting code, itself the donor of social meaning. Identification with assigned roles is more puzzling than what seemed to be. The inevitable exclusion of roles in relation to the individual commands "a continuous construction that has to go on until the subject's dying day" (Bryson 1994: 231). This arduous task, that Bryson perceives as an intolerable wrestle between representation and personal identities aspiring to be socialized, implies a dual motion: distinction from the other concurrent to affirmation of the self. The sexual attribution of an identity can be a shock comparable to the abrupt revelation of sexual differences perceived when the gazing child beholds the sex of the other gender. Each individual grows into a self that emerges from what is imposingly disparate from it.

Freudian theories provide the grounds for Bryson's rendition of the link between Géricault and masculinity. The starting point is "the polymorphousness of infantile sexuality" (Bryson 1994: 233). According to psychoanalytical contentions, the male child is caught in a paradoxical web of contradictory ties. The male child will helplessly strive to double the sexual identity of his father. He has to become what he cannot fully be. For the male child, the mother has the status of a forever interdicted object of desire. So, the self is under a strenuous split. An alienated other constitutes the child's self, not just from the idealized identity with his father, but accomplishing an afflicting contradiction between parts, between him and what he is not: The *Lust-Ich* (the pleasure-ego) will be domesticated into a *Real-Ich* (reality-ego). Therefore, what makes up any subjectivity is invariably doomed to failure. The feebleness of imaginary identification has to be mastered by the Symbolic Order, from where the masks and codes of masculinity will arise.

Identification comes from lack. A wuthering absence follows each one of the human subjects. Je est un autre. That discrepancy is most obviously realized when gazing a hyperbolic image of a muscular male body. The body turns into a phallus and there is no more vivid enactment of male ideals. But is that the only mask of masculinity? Géricault will supply another kind of discrepancy.

His male figures are under duress. Invulnerable masculinity is an idealized prototype far from individual experience. The soldiers are maimed and fragile. Invulnerability is a endowment from "other males who have it" (Bryson 1994: 244).

In each individual male body, we will find the incarnated destiny of the whole nation. The defeat of the French national army, painted with exactness by Géricault, finds expression in the lacerated and broken bodies of wounded soldiers. After perceiving images of mutilated soldiers ranked side by side with paintings that are a glorification of military hierarchy and pictures of mental inmates dressed up as soldiers, we arrive at the conclusion that straight voyeuristic gaze, separating genders, does not fully qualify as comprising male identity. The explanation would have to handle the complicated interactive identification of "the male subject, the male image, and the social hierarchy" (Bryson 1994: 258). Bryson discloses a vigorous description of how the codes of masculinity are fortified.

Géricault's paintings and drawings redeem the codes of masculinity in their ambiguity. Codes ring intermittently in the mind of the beholder, for they are anticipated by the unconscious sharing of their constitutive rules. And so "the visual impression can go on resonating within the mind after it has ceased to contemplate the actual image" (Bryson 1981: 3).

Codes undergird history; they echo even further than we may have thought. History is unified by the persistence of codes. We now move from the past to the present, receding back, in a modified way, to the past. Thus, Géricault's figures ripple through rebellious Rimbaud (1854–1891), born 30 years after the painter's death. The rage against the insisting Napoleonic projects is almost the same. In "Le Éclatant Victoire de Sarrebruck," Rimbaud represents the Emperor, Napoleon III, as "ferocius as Zeus, and as mild as papa" (féroce comme Zeus and doux comme papa); the soldier then put on his jacket and "turning toward the Leader, gets drunk on great names" (remet sa veste, et, tourné vers le Chef, s'étourdit de grands noms). Or else the image of the young soldier in "Le Dormeur du Val" sleeping in a peaceful valley, his mouth agape, and his hands on his breast, quiet. But he is dead: "There are two red holes in his right side" (Il a deux trous rouges au coté droit.)

There is another conjunction of Géricault and Rimbaud. The same bond between *dérèglement* and order, the derangement of the senses forcing its way through strict rhyming verses, is seen in Géricault's *The Raft of the Meduse*: a collapsed mass of bodies, floating over a billowing ocean, and raising as group to the apex of a rigid triangular composition.

In any account, identification is the blend of opposites. Imitation and empathy dominated by sameness do not suffice. In each individual subject, diversity festers in a plurality of *personae*, or if we wish, etymologically, masks. Identification assimilates ego to alterity. It is as Bryson portrayed and Rimbaud said, in a bitter letter to his teacher Izambard, on 13 May 1871: "It is wrong to say: I think. One ought to say: people think me" (c'est faux de dire: je pense. On devrait dire: on me pense). In their permanence, codes are at the heart of subjectivity.

The Drunken Boat

From the topsail of the present, the past looks like an ordered checkerboard, where future moves are settled beforehand. The unconditional use of the notion of code brings more than an illusionary atemporal lure; it forges a teleological conception of the temporal flow. History is seen as determined by the congruence of a lost or distant origin with the present. The lines of history are thus too neatly drawn.

But that does not disturb Ernst van Alphen (1994). As historical objectivity was deemed an impossibility, reading an image should be made into an activity laden with the interpreter's points of view. The interpretation of images is not the extraction of an untainted immanent meaning. Images were made to pluck out reactions, in fact collective responses, from visual messages. The past maybe lost, but the present is always here: *All is always now.* For Ernst van Alphen (1989: 131), "the readers are accomplices" of what is assigned to their apprehension. Any interpretation is necessarily ideological. Historical and social contexts of the works fade away with all the dreams of objectivity. Reading a historical image becomes a chosen political strategy. The present and the past are not radical others.

If Bryson referred to otherness as a constituting element in the construction of male identity, Keith Moxey's (1994b) "Hieronymus Bosch and the "World Upside Down": "The Case of the Garden of Earthly Delights," without doubt one of the luminous contributions to Visual Culture, presumably sees the past as a radically homogeneous alterity. And, in it, Alphen recognizes a latent political option.

Alphen argues that Moxey is swept by a contradiction, when he claims that the interpreter of an image is an inherent part of the interpretation, and at the same time avoids taking a clear political stance in his article. Moxey's priority would be historical and social context (Alphen 1994: 261), to be understood not only as a reasonable demand for objectivity, but also as an ideological position of the author, even more revealing because of an effect of his implicit conjectures.

Moxey would then be caught by the traditional historical options that he tried to avoid. The methodological option of relying upon the conjectured reception of an original audience of Bosch's paintings, in any case impossible to grasp, would be a flaw in Moxey's paper; as well as the symptom of kinship between Moxey's article and an insidious fashion of making art history.

Nonetheless, Alphen's critique betrays two visible problems. He complains that "Moxey refrains from declaring his own politics" (Alphen 1994: 261). But as Alphen himself stated in a previous article, a reading transcends the limits of a mere individual act of political choice: "In most aspects readings are not individual at all" (Alphen 1989: 121). Politics presumes consensus, whereas intellectual performances are judged by their critical reasoning and intellectual dissent. Sheer political allegiance is a barren landscape. More should be required.

Alphen also argues against Moxey's presumption of a uniform reception of Bosch's paintings by their viewers. According to Alphen, it would be a mistake to identify Bosch with "his own original audience" (Alphen 1994: 264). It is curious to observe how Alphen dodges the complexity of homogeneity, reducing the effect of images to the strict matching between the painter and his audience. But homogeneity is not an offspring of an unverifiable response of "those who first appreciated" (Alphen 1994: 264) the paintings. If there is homogeneity in the relationship between a painting and its audience, it is due to the tangibility of an underlying system of rules that allow the actual composition of a visual pattern. The system of rules can be retrieved; it is not hopelessly buried under the rubble of time. The existence of identifiable rules in an image allows and limits historical interpretations. It is precisely these rules what qualifies the reading of an image, regardless of a declared political position, that could easily be an arbitrary and reckless interpretation to be criticized with no mercy.

In contradiction to Alphen's allusion, Moxey's article manifests a definite stand against art history's traditional interpretations of Hieronymus Bosch's *Garden of the Earthly Delights*. The corpus of scholarly work devoted to Bosch qualified him as a ciphered and enigmatic maker, hovering above the social questions of his time. Thus, the key to his paintings was to be found in the iconological pinning-down of esoteric, allegorical, and alchemical sources inspiring his compositions. The task of deciphering Bosch then becomes not only an almost impossible task, but also a rarefied attempt.

Images are not expressions of ideas quietly waiting to be embodied in a pictorial composition. There is more to an image. Images are not restricted to faithfully depicting concepts that arrive from other cultural realms. Not only photographs but all images are involved in cultural action. They are socially operative.

The richness of Moxey's multilayered essay lies in his endeavor to deal with the intricacies of the social operation at work in Bosch's painting. *The Earthly Delight* acts publicly in the range of signs produced during its times, and represents a bid on Bosch's part to establish himself as a singular and individual creator. The power of the paintings indicates special qualities that would put Bosch above other painters, granted by his exhilaration of a divine token.

The two aims do not exclude one another. The socially accepted idea of fantasy helps the shaping of "genius," "a socially constructed category" (Moxey 1994b: 134). The overall pattern of Moxey's article sets him apart from previous interpreters of Bosch that reduce the painter's image creation to the stringent social function of creating inviolable visual enigmas to the lower strata of society.

The trouble with such conception is its implicit separation of form and content, making form an attribute of ruling themes. It presumes that visual compositions are the transparent rendering of previously existing concepts; in Bosch's case, the humanist doctrines of his patrons, members of the social elite. And it flatly disregards more complex theoretical options. The opacity of Bosch's paintings could well be not only a strategy of transforming himself into a cipher, but also a means of affirming his status as painter, similar to what Dürer and Leonardo, producing other kinds of works.

Bosch labored from sources that were common lore. His use of popular engravings and illuminated manuscripts[2] as recycled materials, neatly argued

---

[2] Sulzberger (1962) recognizes Bosch's pictorial compositions, weaving snippets of narrative into larger compositions, as similar to the design of illuminated manuscripts, especially the ones of the Master of Mary of Burgandy. The stylistic kinship also accounts for Bosch's travels in the Netherlands (Sulzberger 1962: 48) when he must have acquired the training for his famous panels. In another essay, Gibson (1972) recognizes Bosch as consistently linked to the Dutch tradition of art making, suggesting that the artist's early training may have been "in the workshop of an illustrator, perhaps at

by Moxey's paper, discloses the social purpose of an only apparent enigmatic art. The profusion of popular sources set in a dazzling arrangement—flaunting hares that go after hunters, henpecked husbands, a flute inside an anus, musical instruments serving for torture, pigs dressed as nuns kissing an uptight naked man, a die serving as a beret, and so many other oddities—incarnate the notion of a world upside down. Bosch's transformation of images poking fun at institutions had a dual purpose: From a public point of view, it led popular images into the cloisters of the higher strata of society, and from the artistic point of view, it expanded what was regarded as materials for high art. Then, the inversion of the world could mean more than a direct affirmation of the social order. Bosch earns his magical aura and is reinstated as a core artist of his century, which explains how he earned a niche in the collection of the noble, the rich, and the religiously orthodox patrons of his time, such as the unyielding bigot, Philip II.

The import of Moxey's article goes further than the scholarship on Bosch. It brings theoretical consequences and alternatives to a trend that is all too present in the studies of *Visual Culture*. Trying to unravel the conditions of image making, articles such as the ones of Mieke Bal, Griselda Pollock, John Tagg, Lisa Tickner, and Norman Bryson start from an obvious theoretical choice, granting a special niche to the concept of code.

Moxey's discussion of Bosch's *The Garden of Earthly Delights* favors a subtler analysis starting from the notion of code, which is a truism by now in semiotic theory, and moves well beyond it, in its care to deal with social action in a intricate manner. Codes are subsidiary to the action that they entail. Any determinism is nothing but an illusion of fixity created by the initial theoretical option for codes and their seduction of stability. Moxey moves not from codes to actions. He demonstrates how codes can be transformed by creativity, being therefore not rigid means of determination, but mere markers of possibilities.

Thomas Crow's "Observations on Style and History in French Painting of the Male Nude, 1785–1794," Whitney Davis's "The Renunciation of Reaction in Girodet's *Sleep of Endymion*," and Wofgang Kemp's "The Theater of Revolution: A New Interpretation of Jacques-Louis David's *Tennis Court Oath*" allude to each other. They display a detailed treatment of a common historical moment; and each article sheds light on the others. Nonetheless, I have to

---

Utrecht" (Gibson 1971: 130).

point out a vivid difference in their approach. Davis and Crow face French Classicist Style from the experiences and clashes of living social actors. But Kemp ponders about the action of representations referring to representations—signs growing into signs—in a semiotic process of endless branching out. Kemp is intent on demonstrating how this obsessive activity reserves a special role for images in history and social life.

In his effort to reply to the relationship between change and continuity in art forms, Thomas Crow discusses not only the possibility of interpreting images historically, but also argues what is the appropriate conception of historical links. A paradox now emerges. Is history a continuous sequence or the jolting utterance of discontinuities? Continuity seems to be tied to a formalistic conception of art making, dependent upon the historicist notion that a style by itself unfolds its possibilities, changing but remaining recognizable during the process of development. Actions are, thus, predetermined, and an unhistorical kernel hides inside the historical flow. There is no room for individual action. The alternative conception of historical ties would be the recognition of discontinuities that bars actions from one another, to a point that the prospect of history becomes problematic. Crow, then, wonders what choice has to be made. Is *The Sleep of Endymion* (1791), painted by Anne-Louis Girodet, a development of Jacques Louis David's classicism, or else a critical departure from it?

It is undisputable that David's civic world of public heroes, always drawn from antiquity, is absent from Girodet's painting. In *The Sleep of Endymion*, we encounter the image of a beautiful young man bathed by moonlight, tended and possessed in his slumber by the moongoddess Selene. The contradictions with paintings such as David's *Lictors Returning to Brutus the Bodies of his Sons* (1789) are evident. Girodet characterized a private scene underlined by eroticism. It is also true that Girodet's influential picture was the starting point of a series of paintings, which Whitney Davis points out as being "commonly understood by many commentators to exemplify a "decadent," post-revolutionary 'neoclassicism of reaction'" (Davis 1994: 168). But such interpretation is silent on the discrepancy between Girodet's picture and his actual commitment to revolutionary politics. How to conciliate the conflict of attitudes? A year later Girodet's would be painting again according to the canons of the French Classical style, as in *Hippocrates Refusing the Gifts of Artaxerxes* (1792).

A question must be answered: Seeing *The Sleep of Endymion* as the zero-degree of a reaction, are we not imposing a pattern that falsifies history? David's critical evaluation of Crow, another moment of editorial excellence in *Visual Culture*, admits that Crow's originality resides in his consideration of Girodet's painting as "a rhetorical statement within the context of an immediate contemporary "politics," artistic, professional and public" (Davis 1994: 169). Crow chooses to deduce his interpretation from events in Girodet's life, his relationship with David, a blend of empathy, admiration, and personal struggle, especially after the premature death of Jean-Germain Drouais, the master's favorite pupil. The temporary rejection of David's example is appraised as the expression of a competition, fostered by David himself.

The Sleep of Endymion insists on a different direction from Drouais's representation of a frail, ailing and dying athlete (1786), a picture of mutilated masculine prowess, whose visual qualities were minutely reversed by Girodet. Pain turns into erotic bliss. Crow believes that both images have to be "understood as moves in the same game begun by Drouais, with every encouragement from their common master" (Crow 1994: 153). Not only the pupils were acting upon each other's produced images, but David is permeated also by the process of mutual and implicit influence. Girodet's *Pietá* (1790) is the inspirational source for David's *Marat at His Last Breath* (1793). We can clearly see the visual affinities of Christ agonizing in the *Pietá* and Marat's death. The male nude in French painting then becomes infused with the interaction of all these pictorial constructions. The androgynous boy in David's *The Death of Bara* accommodates echoes of Girodet's Endymion. Styles do not generate themselves exclusively from the possibilities of their form. They are reached, step by step, without a previously instituted direction or goal.

Whitney Davis's critique of Crow's article should be appraised as a challenge of its microanalytic approach to topical politics, engaging David, Drouais, and Girodet. The contradiction between Girodet's revolutionary politics and *The Sleep of Endymion* does not bother Davis in the least. Whitney Davis is adamant: "The painting is just as complex, and perhaps as contradictory, as initially suspected" (Davis 1994: 192). In his option for a micro-historical inspection, Crow missed a larger facet of politics.

It is true that images exist in precise moments of history that allow their generation. But politics also implies more than the immediate conflict, strife or conjugation of forces on a strict local level. This horizontal understanding of political action excludes what Davis (1994: 177) calls "the vertical dimension" of politics, in which past, present and future interact.

Refusing the broader vertical dimension, Crow tries to level down the puzzling *Sleep of Endymion*. Crow's analysis reduces the meaning of the painting to its condition of production. For Davis, there is no reason for abandoning the notion that history comes from acts of replication, in fact from Girodet's reaction against David's overpowering influence; and how could Crow have missed that Girodet's *Endymion* is a deed in the make-up of masculine ideology?

The Sleep of Endymion inverts the generally ascribed masculine roles. Selene sexually posses Endymion, when he is sunken into unconsciousness. The painting reveals the performance of phallic acts without phallic desire, thus implying "a possibly homoerotic alternative" (Davis 1994: 183). Girodet's painting buries a certain brand of masculinity: phallic and exclusively public in its civil pledge. It renounces masculinity as strictly active, incompatible with "male beauty, sensuality, and homoeroticism" (Davis 1994: 190). The vertical dimension of interpreting images, that Davis requests, depends on forsaking politics as Crow conceived, namely a kind of action springing from rational or, at the other extreme, unconscious decisions. More important than anything, including the accomplishment of living social actors, is the admission that images are driving forces in history. If Crow moved from the interpretation of personal intentions to the making of representations, Davis calls for an analysis of images that start from their status of collective, and thus codified, representations.

In his work on the drama of the revolution and David's *Tennis Court Oath*, Wolfgang Kemp presents a stalwart argument against the idea that lived historical events are determinant in the constitution of images. The life of an image is of a different nature. Images take a life of their own. They are not compliant to events, not even to the ones that the image is requested to represent.

As a historical incident, the Tennis Court Oath happened on June 20 1789. The background of the incident goes back to the serious financial crisis that, during the summer of 1788, had enfeebled Louis XVI. At first, Louis XVI had called the deputies of the *Tiers État* to find a way out of the crisis, thus starting an uncontrollable reaction to his absolutism. The king perceived that his power was being undermined and suspended the scheduled meeting. Finally after a tense threats, six hundred French deputies decided to meet anyway in a tennis court at Versailles, resisting to the king's order to expel them from their usual meeting place. In the tennis court, the representatives swore to remain in permanent assembly until the drafting of a new constitution for France. It was the dawn of the revolutionary process, for "the authority of the king had to accommodate itself to the vows of the nation's representatives" (Bordes 1983: 15). A year later, Dubois-Crancé, a deputy of the parliament and an intimate friend of Jean-Louis David, claimed that the revolutionary landmark should be preserved. And also a painting should be commissioned to seize the symbolic importance of the court oath.

David was awarded the commission. Even if David started to work from newspaper reports and from actual eye witnesses (Bordes 1983: 40), his design setting the president of the parliament, Jean Silvain Bailly, frontally, facing the beholder, as though addressing it, is to be understood a meaningful representation rather than a mimetic staging of the event. The actual event is reordered during the process of designing the painting. Pictorial truth has prevalence over historical faithfulness.

If we compare the preliminary sketches of the scene with its final design—shown in a drawing, for the painting was never completed—it is evident that the vanishing lines of the final composition were gradually made to meet between the eyes of Bailly. The sketches were ongoing adaptations that consummated in a frontal motif. The option for a frontal composition had a purpose: Frontality is a standard of truth derived from the conjecture that an eyewitness has experienced the event. So, whatever is delineated stands as a testimony. David's *Tennis Oath* ought to be seen in this light.

Bailly faces the beholder of the picture, and the spectator's gaze coincides with Bailly. The play of eyes proclaims individualistic equality. Individualistic equality is the force unifying the painting. The six hundred historical actors raise their hands in oath to Bailly that, at the time, "acknowledges the viewer" (Kemp 1994: 208). The process blasted by the image is one of reciprocal circulation, moving from the representatives to the central figure of Bailly that transmits the power of the assembly to the beholder. The viewer then becomes a participant in the revolutionary moment. Bryson (1981: 143) qualifies Bailly's gesture as "the thunderbolt of potency." Images are anything but mere surrogates of what actually happened. Images are translations of events, builders of history, and also guidelines for what is to come. David's pictorial solutions resounds in the future. Kemp's article strips bare the indirect influence of David's *Tennis Court Oath* on the designs of revolutionary buildings.

After David's *Tennis Court Oath*, the image of a gazing eye appears everywhere. The eye takes the form of a circle, keeping a link with the original idea of equality—for a circle is an image of equidistance—but moving away from it. Although locked to social milestones, visual forms unfold according to an immanent logic. Handling other iconographic examples (vignettes, seals, groundplans of buildings, as well as other paintings) Kemp presents the course through which an image, as if it were a floating sign, is converted from its revolutionary expression of equality into becoming an emblem of surveillance. The French Revolution had then taken a different turn: Paranoia and terror taint revolutionary hope. Social conditions changed, and so did images.

Three more essays by Kaja Silverman, Constance Penley and Andrew Ross labor over strictly contemporary instances of image making. Penley's "Feminism, Psychoanalysis, and the Study of Popular Culture" and Ross's "The Ecology of Images" share a poignant immediacy. They are less scholarly papers than intellectual interventions over the topics of gender and ecology.

The starting point of both Ross and Penley is the inventory of images shuffled and offered by what could be called "popular culture." Popular culture is a fairly current but a hopelessly bad tag to describe mass media. The term *popular culture* is a misnomer, for the simple reason that its products have no folk roots. We are really talking about the production and the consumption of cultural artifacts on a massive and industrialized scale. The consumer is then reduced to the role of an numbed spectator of cultural donations. The consumer is an object of lure. We have to agree with the recommendation of the Frankfurt School that regards culture industry as a much better term for the phenomenon.

Culture industry is the offspring of a market society. It is so unlike anything else that the use of the label popular culture creates erroneous associations with traditional cultures, themselves preindustrial and outside of the demands of contemporary market society.

Preindustrial social networks are braided less through economic exchange than through moral duties common to social actors; as it can be guessed that, in folk societies, the isolation of a member of a group happens only if he was either expelled from the community or intentionally left to die because of age or illness (Thurnwald 1932: 281). On the other hand, market societies subvert everything that had been cherished by traditional societies. For that reason, Karl Polanyi (1968 and 1975) named the emergence of market societies, "the great transformation." To make it clearer—the economy of traditional and preindustrial societies is part of social relations, whereas, in a market society, social ties are embedded in the economy, so that economic relations not only exist in a self-sufficient manner, but also rule society as a whole.

Market societies are an inevitable consequence of industrialism. For, industrialism is more than a revolution in the productive sphere, resulting from the abandonment of animal and human traction for mechanical energy. The use of new sources of energy intensifies production, but requires the implementation of ever-growing markets to which industrialized products flow. The constant increase of industrial efficiency demands elastic markets in interminable growth, inclined to consume the productive surplus. Everything is thus transformed into a marketable good, including cultural products.

In market societies, tradition is weakened. Tradition is regarded as an obstacle. Industrial society elects change and technological mutation as their fundamental principle. The lived experience of social actors in societies directed by industrialism is unstable. Tradition is gnawed away by the unrelenting search for the new. In preindustrial communities, the task of social instruction lies on the extended group or the family. Now, after industrialism, this is almost impossible. Ceaseless technological innovation and a widespread compromise nourishing change erode any authority as a source of guidance. The social and the general values of the group are constantly being transmuted. In the age of ideological individualism, mass media accept the active role of tutoring and grounding social experience. Ross's approach to media images as productive in social life is fully justified. Images of war are more than simulacra. The social actor experiences images that are a substitution for reality. Images are a screen through which we can obtain experience. As shown in the last Gulf War, the Pentagon makes the military deployments, followed closely by the action of television images. An inventive partnership, comprised of the military command and CNN (Cable News Network), was consecrated: "In view of the job well done by the networks, the Pentagon decided not to release their own independent footage and propaganda in the United States" (Ross 1994: 324).

With ease, Ross distinguishes in those images the ideological contents justifying the war: the oily slickness of Arabs and petrol spills contaminating the waters of the Persian Gulf, the flames of hell erupting after bombs were thrown by airplanes, bringing justice to the enemies of democracy, and the triumphant predation of technology as a condition for freedom. After those images are put together, Ross demonstrates how technological invention is attached to old contents. Manichean polarities are renewed through the shroud of a deadly Nintendo artillery. The images of hell and heaven are divided by barbed semiotic frontiers delineating, side by side, destruction and enticing appeals to the consumption of goods trumpeted by television advertisements as a call to the promised land.

Ross contends that what we have through the media is not a glut but a scarcity of images, a wasteland of sameness plaguing visual culture. The social imaginary—or else, the inventory of visual solutions allocated to the members of the social group—endures severe restrictions.

In Constance Penley's charming article we can discern an alternative to the constant suggestion in *Visual Culture* that images are powerful devices in determining actions of viewers, as a result of contributing to their mental make-up. *Visual Culture* insists that images are indeed steadfast controllers and organizers of social behavior.

The psychoanalytic concept of fantasy presides over "Feminism, Psychoanalysis and the Study of Popular Culture." In fact, the original term for fantasy, *Phantasie*, that Freud borrowed from the German nurtures the intricate play of collective contents and personal transmutation of conventions. Fantasy builds a passage from an inventory of conventions to their active use by the subjects. So, Freud argues that the fantasies reveal the unconscious of the psychoanalyzed subject. In short, Fantasy is the stuff out of which subjectivity is made. A consequence can be inferred from the Freudian conclusion: Subjectivity is a psychic event and social accretion. Subjectivity is a compound of what is granted to us and that we make of it, after reshuffling conventions.

Fantasy is in itself a secondary elaboration, a tinkering with structuring contents common to us all, as what happens after a child perceives parental intercourse. The original scene is reconstructed by the subject, because it comes with the rumble of interdiction.

The great contribution of Constance Penley's article resides less on its application of psychoanalytic concepts than in the observation of an intriguing phenomenon: the slash fandom. Penley defines fandom as "a unique, hybrid genre of romance, pornography and utopian science fiction" (Penley 1994: 304). An aura of mystery surrounds slash fandom. Afraid of suffering consequences in their job or their private lives, the makers and the audience of slash fanzines avoid coming out in the open. The fanzines that concern Penley are the ones with stories, artwork, and poems built around a conjectured but explicitly homosexual liaison of Captain James T. Kirk and Mr. Spock, the well-known characters of the television serial *Star Trek.*[3]

---

[3] The slash marks publications depicting homosexual scenes. The slash fandom that Penly interprets is tagged as K/S for Kirk and Spock in love.

Fanzines portray a male homosexual tryst but paradoxically their audience and makers are comprised mainly of straight females. What sense can we make of it? Why should women cherish homosexual fantasies with male characters? The answer could not be mechanical. It springs from Penley's understanding that identity and gender are processes, the current presumption of feminist writing, similarly held by Griselda Pollock, Mieke Bal, Lisa Tichner, and Kaja Silverman in "Fassbinder and Lacan: A Reconsideration of Gaze, Look, and Image." Identity is not what is given, but what we make of what is given to us. An appropriation of male reactions, such as Kirk and Spock, serves a higher purpose. Fazines are not mere pornography. They retool the male psyche (Penley 1991: 158).

If the basic material is *Star Trek*, then the fantasy produced by women has to work with the Spock and Kirk, due not only to the fact that the other female characters in the television series are relegated to the background, always living submissive roles, but also because the origin of the sexual encounter of Spock and Kirk comes from an act of friendship, and not from raw desire. In one of the first stories of the slash fandom, Spock—being half Vulcan, half human—has a crisis of *pon farr*. *Pon farr* is a blood fever, a regular seven-year eruption of sexual desire that, unfulfilled, should kill Mr. Spock. Kirk feels that he has no choice but to save his dear friend, by having sex with him. Friendship then takes a different turn. The plot was appropriated and manipulated from an episode of Star Trek. It is a departure from the actual TV series, but it "could easily be made to be there" (Penley 1991: 137).

The conclusion to be reached is that Spock and Kirk experience a love that crosses gender barriers, expressing the desire of a relationship based on equality, thus transcending "the usual erotics of dominance and submission found in the typical romance formula, in which dominance and submission are invariably the respective roles of male and female" (Penley 1994: 317). It is clear that slash fanzines do not intend to change either Spock or Kirk into women, but rather keep them as males. Penley notes a general rejection to a story that gives a baby to Spock and Kirk. The whole point of the fantasy would be lost. Penley argues the interesting point that products of culture industry can be turned inside out to provide alternative contributions to the making of subjectivity. But I feel that Penley's strict reliance on psychoanalytic concepts, with their content-oriented views, leads her astray from figuring a radically semiotic interpretation of image making. Contrary to what Kaja Silverman stated in her influential book, *The Subject of Semiotics* (1983), I do not agree with the notion that psychoanalysis is central to semiotics, that the "human subject is to a large degree the subject of semiotics" (Silverman 1983: xvii). Psychoanalysis has an underlying theory of signs, uncompromisingly conventionalist, and responsible for a distorted and partial understanding of the semiotic process. Conventionalism draws a causal vicious circle. Codes are cultural for culture makes them; and culture is codified: A culture is the effect of codes. But if there are signs hanging above the doorsill of conventions, and how relevant they can be in the make-up of images, are questions morosely left out by conventionalist approaches.

Perhaps the most representative interpretation of images that the inextricable blend of psychoanalysis and conventionalism can aspire to is the kind of article that Kaja Silverman delivers in *Visual Culture*. Starting with a general theoretical concept, the distinction of *gaze* and *look* as derived from Lacanian thoughts on the making of subjectivity, coupled with the feminist assessment that masculinity is there in the act of gazing, Silverman surveys Fassbinder's movies.

Identity and gender are crossed and unveiled by the category of gaze. Gaze is not the neutral faculty that allows vision. The notion of gaze implies a collective look, stemming from the totality of a social ambience. The pervasiveness of gaze qualifies it as a product of a cultural framework. It acts upon the looker, making identity not a fluid drift, but stranded on social constructions. The look is an ordinary event; but gaze comes from an action inserting the subject in a cultural order. Silverman (1994: 274) describes gaze "as 'seing' itself being seen."

Gazing has a symbolic nature. And for that reason it is legitimate to postulate that the voyeur gaze incarnates the dominant power of masculinity, being thus patriarchal and phallic. The gaze is something other than the personal point of view, because it is constitutive of subjectivity. Gaze is not within the boundaries of desire. It rather belongs to what reorganizes desire. The look is inlaid into the gaze. Silverman set images and identity on the same level. "The subjects are 'photographed' through the frame of culturally intelligible images" (Silverman 1994: 292).

Kaja Siverman decks theoretical spins on gaze and subjectivity with shrewd analysis, sometimes frame by frame, of several Fassbinder's films: *Gods of the Plague*, *The American Soldier*, *The Marriage of Maria Braun*, among others. Film shots in their sequence are made into illustrations of psychoanalytic hypothesis. Even what psychoanalysis would have to say about identity does not provide a convincing interpretation of Fassbinder's bitter and disillusioned characters. It is the other way round: The minute description of actions of characters and the movements of the camera are explicative of the Lacanian theoretical enterprise that takes precedence over anything else. Through analogy, Silverman limits herself to recognizing the dominant categories in Lacan's psychoanalytical theory.

It is the same impression we have when reading Barthes's *Elements of Semiology* (1968). Barthes presents a linguistic concept and then lists examples that analogically illustrate it. However richer Silverman's analysis may be in relation to Barthes's rather mechanical inferences, both attempts are stale and suffer from having chosen the notion of code as their main theoretical option.

The history of images presented in the majority of papers compiled in *Visual Culture* circles around the pivotal discussion of the role played by codes, by shared conventions, in social life in general, and image making in particular. The interpretation of images is thus reduced to isolating the codes that yield their production. As in any message, visible or verbal, codes are systems of rules capable of discriminating the elements that will make up the message, as well as the combination of their terms, besides the determination of a correspondence between the sign and their denoted objects, notwithstanding the predictable response that will be triggered by the reception of the emitted signs. The option is altogether conventionalist, deterministic and content-oriented.

The Tender Trap

It is easy to fathom why, for historians and politically engaged interpreters of images, conventionalism has the happy chime of the undisputable. To consider images as resulting from conventions arbitrarily laid upon an unimposing reality seems quite befitting for historians that can then analyze the changes under the sway of time. And for the politically engaged interpreters of images, arbitrariness signals in the direction of liberation, an unseen land across the troubled sea of the present, not perceived as yet, but always a resounding promise.

Of all authors in *Visual Culture*, none is so explicit about the virtues of drastic and exclusive conventionalism as Alphen in his taking issue with Bryson's "Guéricault and 'Masculinity'." Alphen criticizes Bryson's conception of identification. Bryson's hazy view of identity would imply mere quest for power; it surmises a conflict between entities irreducible to one another.

Alphen claims that the process is far more complex than unqualified clash. It is an integration of partialities. The son that shies away from the sight of his father's shrivelled penis—as it occurs when Ham watches over Noah, naked and drunk—has in front of him not only the symbolic embodiment of a monolithic and absolute power, but also its frailty. The sexual member is coiled and underdeveloped; the son can then hope to emulate the partial power of masculinity. Power is not a severe alterity that would engulf the son into a gaping whirlpool threatening to drown him for ever. Frailty leaves the door open into identity and power is not fierce and unshakable. The nature of power is arbitrary. It can and will eventually change. Alphen leads the argument into a type of semiotics that can be viewed as an extreme brand of conventionalism.

The binding of historians and a conventionalist doctrine of signs is far more intricate than what Alphen suggests. It is not a matter of choice; it is a trend inlaid in the principles of writing art history. And to understand it, we have to examine the history of the history of art and the ensuing reaction to the legacy of Giorgio Vasari's (1511–1574) *Le vite dí più eccellenti architetti, pittori et scultori italiani* (1980).

Vasari's book underscores a conception of history in a linear and chronological series of biographies. Its sequence of life stories is more than just a narrative of events; time unfolds as a historical and artistic culmination. In Vasari's historiography, the rule of thumb is to essentialize biographic incidents. The history of art is reduced to an endogenous creation, cleaved from the social world. Social contextualization is but a minor issue. For the analysis of art, it is necessary just the normative judgment of the interpreter. And the interpreter is personified by Vasari, himself more of a critic than anything like a historian. But, as we saw before, strict biographic contextualization is an insufficient analytic criterion for the understanding of images. History of art seems to demand a culturalist interpretation, capable of placing the artwork in a social ambience, without which the narrative of a life dissolves itself into an inventory of anecdotes.

An implicit Kantianism overshadows the history of art that has followed after Vasari. There is a line connecting Vasari to Kant; both share a concept of history as an ongoing, sequential course. Vasari sees the apex of art history crowned by Michelangelo, whereas Kant perceives in the creative genius more than just the summit of artmaking. In any case, for Vasari and Kant, genius is the exemplary condition for artmaking.

As a direct consequence of Kantian thought, art history is converted into an objective and legitimate form of knowledge. Since Kant, there is a progressive retraction from the idea that creation is caged in the normative precept that the imitation of nature is the task of art. Art history uplifts when art frees itself from mimesis. Art historians have now to leave aside any concern with the fidelity of images to nature. Art has little to with natural beauty; art is "a beautiful representation of a thing" (Kant 1952: 172).

We now confront the thought that the interpretation of art has to do away with contentions unifying "the objective universality of pure reason and the subjective universality of the work of genius" (Didier-Huberman 1989: 47). There is a discontinuity between art, a product of human nature, and "ordinary nature" per se (Kamal 1986: 18). Art has to be recognized as art, conveying however the impression of being "a product of mere nature" (Kant 1952: 168); it should be a supreme but unobtrusive creation. Rules include nature. The tendency is to regard them as self-contained systems. It will take genius to alter the ordering of rules.

The subjective potency of genius generates stylistic mutations of artworks and justifies the existence of a historical approach to art. Freed from the obligation of judging artworks as assumed imitations of nature, art history understands creation as the fabric of an era. Even if the aesthetic schema inevitably uses the experience of the natural world, the creator "may transform the experience in accordance to the rules of representation practicized, say, by a particular school of painting" (Kamal 1986: 10). Indeed, rules are available through the workings of genius, whose subjective creativity gives away all forms of creation.

Genius forges "the ability to originate or give the rule to art" (Kamal 1986: 42). Rules and conventions, the providers of the schema of representation, are the productive substance of fine art. They are not rules for imitation, "but for following" (Kant 1952: 171). From this moment on, we can say that we are really talking of a historical approach to art, and its debt to Kantianism follows like a shade trailing along a shadow. The study of conventions shared by social actors will gradually come to be the cardinal issue of art making.

Another way of tracing the influence of Kantian thesis on art history could be detecting the effects of Cassirer's philosophy of *symbolic forms* over Panofsky, to whom, and by all means, contemporary historical approaches to art owe so much (Holly 1984: 158). So let us start with Kant, and then examine Cassirer and Panofsky.

According to Kant, knowledge does not come from an adaptation to what the external world grants to us. The categories underlining our understanding shape up empirical perception. The internal and the external senses of the subject—respectively, time and space, in fact, constructions of the mind—precede and organize experience. Space and time are forms of the sensible intuition. Kant labels them *a prioris*, and the *a prioris* are qualified as conditions for knowledge that is obviously not derived from experience, for geometry and arithmetic.

Neither space nor time could be described as concepts emerging from experience. We do not reach them through the reception of existing objects. We can imagine space and time without any existing object, but no object can ever be conceived without them. The *a priori* faculties of space and time create universalizing generalizations as well as their singular and empirical applicability to objects of the external world. Therefore, being *a priori*, space and time are founding representations without which the things of the world and the whole empirical dimension would be inaccessible.

Ernst Cassirer (1955a and 1955b) holds that Kant's reflection on the a prioris space and time, expressed in the section Transcendental Aesthetics of the *Critique of Pure Reason* (1973), has a larger scope. From Kant, we can extract a lesson that ought to be extended to the whole of a culture. The principles at work in Kant's description of space and time are recognizable in all cultural representations, in all symbolic forms.

Symbolic forms are synthetic unities. Representations in a given social surroundings are related to one another, forming the organic unity that we admit as culture. Culture fuses representamens and represented cultural notions. It fastens universality onto the fragmentation of the particular. Culture imposes an universal rule provoking all events in the sphere of human activities.

This philosophical conception of the nature of symbolic forms yields what Pierre Bourdieu considers "the most beautiful challenge ever made to positivism" (Panofsky 1970: 135): Erwin Panofsky's *Gothic Architecture and Scholasticism* (1957 and 1970). *Gothic Architecture and Scholasticism* stamps the similarities between gothic cathedrals and the structure of Aquinas's *Summa Theologica*. Panofsky's aimed to recompose the mental conditions that had produced apparently different offsprings: churches and a majestic philosophical *oeuvre*.

Culture and its array of symbolic forms are a prioris in the same sense that Kant portrays space and time, and appraises the categorical imperative of morality. The central notion of Kant's *Critique of Practical Reason* (1976), the categorical imperative, declares that we ought to act wishing our deeds to become universal laws. Human action must aspire to universality, transcending individual and personal interests. An action must be valid for all human beings and at all moments. This is the contract that makes humanity possible. It is what qualifies humanity as "always in progress toward the better, and will continued to be so henceforth" (Kant 1963: 148).

Kant's conception of the categorical imperative as an a priori amalgamates two tendencies up to then dominant in political theory, and tinges them with a finalist conception of history. Kant refuses to opt either for an idealized model of social life or for a hint of human action determined by situational interests. History is not the ruckus of selfish beings running wild. History insinuates the "totality of men united socially" (Kant 1963: 137). Kant stays somewhere between Plato and Machiavelli (Kein 1989: 326). In social morality, neither rarefied absolutism nor extreme relativism pleases Kant. The course of history demonstrates the urgency of conciliating the struggles of personal interests with a moral goal that is teleological and universalist.

Kantianism believes that human history walks toward a resolute goal, even it its laws are provisionally unknown to us (Kant 1959b: 29). The laws of history await their discovery To unveil them we should investigate the past as the donator of clues for what is about to come. Historical analysis receives from Kantianism its fundamental traces: The notion that the movement of history is sequential, linear, and the idea of a contract that, due to the formative power of conventions, regulates all historical happenings.

History balances contractual and finalist purposes. The central element that specifies history is the one that spells contractual relations, notwithstanding a more general and embracing contract of a cosmopolitan nature. History is our common duty. It is for us the responsibility of overcoming the conflict of particular situations, which can be successful if there is a contractual commitment to the whole humanity. The idea of a universal contract suggests the existence of a predetermined and hidden plan, stealthy present in political relations, moral order and all the modes of culture.

My purpose in laying down Kantian conceptions about history is to demonstrate that there is no contradiction between history as a finality and the contractual action of conventions. They are the two sides of the same coin, for a while circulating among historians. It is also true that today the finalist model of historiography has receded to the background, giving room for a demarcation of history as an anthropology of the past. History is a legitimate undertaking when it succeeds in placing the work of art inside the system that bred it. History of art then moves from a historicist finalism to the analysis of past conventions. The presumption is obvious: There are implicit rules generating culture and, therefore, artistic creations. These laws are the object of historians. The intent of art history is to unveil the rules, the cognitive codes, and the relation between objects created by the totality of culture. A system of rules is what determines the basic presence of an artwork (Holly 1984: 186). Rules are the prime reality of art making.

The maintenance of such a conventionalist approach is dependent upon the action of a given culture. Culture is an *a priori*, modelling existing individuals. The system of cultural institutions becomes similar to a unitary subject, omnipresent in historical phenomena.

The symbiotic nature of culture and codes is almost a platitude. Culture is a filter that we can not eliminate. Furthermore, codes are also vital for filtering and repositioning sensorial stimulus. To sustain this view, Roman Jakobson (1971: 339–340) quotes the observations of M. Aronson that, in a radio broadcast, tried to transmit natural noises of a train arriving at a station. The effect was disastrous. The informational value of natural noises is next to zero. There was no way of discriminating them clearly without conventions. Even to copy reality, it is necessary to use a mediating schema. The schema organizes our perceptual experiences and vindicates the necessity of considering the codes which are operative in a cultural milieu. In Aronson's experiment, the notion of code demands the acknowledgment of a fixed schema, regulating the fluctuating identification of perceived objects. It is the same postulation spoused by structural linguists, whom after Sausurre (1982) propounded that a prior system of rules is a condition for any utterance. In a language, the system of rules joins not a thing and a name, but a concept and a acoustic image, or, in other words, the natural representation of the word, depicted in the act of speaking (Saussure 1982: 98). Fixed as rules, conventions abate the arbitrariness of the linguistic sign. From the user's perspective, linguistic signs are far from arbitrary; the user deems it a necessary semiotic system, and that ensues because the system is *a priori*, created by collective consciousness acting upon individuals. Collective conventions precede and determine individual consciousness.

However, when these conceptions are employed to art history, the objects of analysis lose their individual characteristics and are transfigured into effects of a vast metaphysical creation (Holly 1984: 29), as is obvious in the concept of *Kunstwollen*, first conceived by Alois Riegl and then modified by Erwin Panofsky. *Kunstwollen* is a rarefied idealistic hypothesis; it grants intentions to an epoch. Nonetheless, common Kantian assumptions in both linguistic and art history have fostered the adoption of conventionalist semiotics in the interpretation of images. In what Margaret Iversen (1972) called the first phase of Reigl's work, he had tried to apply neogrammarian principles to the historiography of art. For Riegl, the art historian should examine artistic styles, with the purpose of isolating formative historic laws. It would be a venture similar to what linguistics used to do, in its effort of fashioning a comparative viewpoint in language studies, through their ordering in a historic series. Forms, either visual or linguistic, develop themselves, following a hidden plan unfolded along the course of history.

While Saussure ambiguously criticized neogrammarians, stating that they had left out important aspects of language in their studies, he simultaneously praised their contribution to the forsaking of the opinion that language is a self-sustained organism, in favor of understanding it as "the product of the collective mind of linguistic groups" (Aarsleff 1982: 311). Synchronic analysis and its emphasis on the prior system, without which there are no utterances, grow into the primary method, not only for linguists but also for art historians. So, both Riegl and Wölfflin call attention to the factor that artistic elements are also organized into systems. The acceptance of the system in a precise historical moment has to be explained by a kind of contractual agreement.

The system of art has the same contractual nature of the linguistic order. It is once again the double face of Kantianism: a teleological idea of history relocated as conventional contractualism. Seen from the conventionalist standpoint we recognize the identity between Saussurian linguistics and an active tendency in art history. This point was already made by Iversen (1972) in her assessment of Reigl's studies on the history of art styles, as well as Bryson's (1983: xii) consideration that art history has to consider as central the contributions of Saussurian linguistics.

There is no problem in recognizing that conventions have a positive a role in image making. The obstacle lies in conceding that the only process in images is the consummation of conventions. The most immediate effect of rigid conventionalism is the domestication of chance[4] and uncertainty, precisely the

---

[4] Hacking (1990) notes Kant's dislike for the word *determinismus*. *Predeterminismus* should be the correct expression for "our choices are predetermined by our motives, desires, and beliefs" (Hacking 1990: 152). An interpretation of images based on the *a priori* notion of code may not be deterministic in the strict sense of the word, but it is certainly predeterministic.

most persistent attributes of the historical process. History is then distorted and betrayed. The price to be paid for adopting a conventionalist theory of signs in historical writing is the inception of an furtive a historical narrative.

The Mystery of the Beginning, Again and Again

The denial of chance brought by the uncritical adoption of the concept of code is more than bewildering. Chance is an operative force in all manifestations of the universe, including history. The patterns that may be shaped as time progresses do not result from the action of predetermined principles. These patterns are a belated discovery. And the very recognition of an immense variety of patterns should serve as a strong argument for the existence of chance, toppling all design.

It is incorrect to assume that Saussurian theory of signs and its suggestion of an arbitrary trace in all representations could really account for historical change. Much more than Saussure's semiology, Peirce's semiotics and his cosmogonic philosophy[5] stress that there is a lasting state of indetermination in the gifts of nature, arising after the spontaneity of origins. So, "an element of pure chance survives and will remain until the world becomes an absolutely perfect, rational, and symmetrical system, in which mind is at last crystallized in the infinitely distant future" (Peirce 1992: 297).

The process is described as the outcome of the action of the mind fitting the manifold of sensuous impressions into a unifying and continuous grid that sometimes will spell necessity. But what we always have is "approximate regularities" (Peirce 1992: 306). The succeeding regularity can only be in itself precarious. The rest—under the guise of diversity, irregularity, multiplicity and all modes of transformation—is the product of chance. This metaphysical reasoning transpires from nature to history; they are magnified and sampled across time.

The word that describes the action of the mind is probability. Only occasionally, when dealing with self-contained axiomatic systems of propositions, the mind responds with necessary conclusions. As the mind formulates three kinds of inference—induction, deduction and hypothesis—all the processes are shaped by probability: "The inductive and hypothetic forms of

---

[5] For an appraisal of Peirce's cosmogony, an often neglected and misunderstood part of his philosophy, see Turley (1977).

inference are essentially probable inferences, not necessary; while deduction may be either necessary or probable" (Peirce 1992: 329). Necessity is more of an exception than a rule. At its best, probability directs all processes.

Any thought stemming from Peirce's consideration of chance has to be discriminated from theories dependent upon conventionalist axioms. With Peirce, we will uncover a different postulate about history, a sense of knowledge as a fallible enterprise, as well as the idea that signs are not ruled by antedating patterns. Signs are renewed functions through the action of representations moved over by endless chance and change. Besides all this, we will confront a departure from the conceived relation between matter and mind, implicit in conventionalist theories.

Signifier and signified, respectively the material and the conceptual aspect of a sign bonded by a conventional rule, presuppose a barring of matter and mind, so common in the linguistic tradition loomed up from the seventeenth century. The essence of the sign, its utmost reality, should be sought in what lies beyond matter. Skipping through the controversy involving the primordial relevance of either the innateness of the mind or the arbitrariness of the sign as the central problem in linguistic theory, we have to admit that Saussurian and Chomskian linguistics share similar general precepts. As we can see in Chomsky's allusion that grammatical transformations are always the product of rules relating a more abstract structure, qualified as deep structure, to the actual material sentence. A dualistic nature haunts Chomsky's theory of language: *Surface structure* is the material body of the sentence, and *deep structure* its mind, or, if we wish, its soul. Besides this, there are other streams in linguistic history: They are the ideas influenced by Locke that also state the importance of rules in language—themselves not innate—but "made by man and conventions" (Aarsleff 1982: 27). Lockean tradition reaching Saussure thrives on declaring that a sign deals with ideas, rather than things. The arbitrary relation between signifier and signified departs from what Aarlesff (1982) calls the Adamic doctrines of language. Such doctrines are prone to naturalize the link between signifier and signified. However, in many ways the Cartesian and Lockean traditions overlap and merge. Aarsleff (1982) has masterfully painted this picture.

From a Peircean perspective, the exclusion of mind and matter—the founding belief of conventionalist theories—simply cannot apply. Two quotations should be enough to settle this point: "Matter is effete mind" (Peirce 1992: 293) and "all matter is really mind" (Peirce 1992: 361). The conclusion to be drawn is that matter and mind are continuous. They are not exclusive, but discerned from one another in terms of degree. The mind acts and is capable of creating, through the establishment of continuities, the conditions for escaping and transfiguring whatever aspires to be its rule. On the other hand, solely matter is subjected to stiff rules that guide it.

The coalescence of matter and mind brings chance to the foreground, placing it as the central agency in natural and historical processes. Order, its patterns—and by extension, any form of coding—are always precariously stable: They are on the verge of dissolving themselves. Unless the whole process is completed, unless history has ended, any design is provisional.

Not even the great historical constructs could ever be free from this kind of dissipation. What was held in favor will be uprooted sooner or later. That is to be learnt from Michael Ann Holly's article, "Wölfflin and the Imagining of the Baroque," in *Visual Culture*.

The effectiveness of Wölfflin's categories hinge not only on his extraordinary power of unifying themes and objects, but also on his exacting effort in producing the identity of the baroque from its opposition to another mode of seeing and representing the world, handed over to us by the Renaissance culture.

Holly claims that, after Wölfflin's *Principles of Art History*, we are left with strictures for perceiving artworks that pertain to the Renaissance and afterwards. Since Wölfflin, these historical periods stop being the scattering of objects, events, ideas, and personalities. They are made into sets "structured upon contrasting optical modalities: linear versus painterly perception, planar versus recessional spatial articulation, clear versus relatively unclear compositional strategies" (Holly 1994: 346). We are now compelled to see, comparatively, Leonardo's and Tintoretto's Last Supper; one painting elucidates and interprets the other.

For Holly, Wölfflin's fashion of organizing polarities creates a method of vision, clearly voiced in the veneer of his style. Writing art history requires a complex and shifting rendition, encircling at the same time its object and the very act of narrating history. To understand it in its full stature we must account for both extremes of the process, what Holly calls, quoting Wölfflin, the double root of style.

Historical discourse is recast under the surprising influence of the artwork it handles and what was up to then regarded as passive. The excellence and relative persistence of Wölfllin's interpretation arises from the precise matching of its object with the analytic discourse it propounds. Holly (1994: 356) concludes brilliantly that "the works of art of the period compositionally prefigured their own historiographic response."

The final inference is that Wölfllin's method cannot be consigned to another historical moment; history does not repeat itself. Holly's assessment overhauls Wölfflin's analysis, insinuating that the historic process brings with it change, metamorphosis, and transience. It is the dark fabric of the historical flow. Holly's critique is forceful because Wölfllin' historiography, intent on crystallizing the codes at work in a particular period, is not mirrored methodologically in her subtle evaluation.

From Peircean semiotics, history can learn to avoid the enticement of deterministic conceptions brought forward by strictly conventionalist doctrines. Consciously or not, theoretical concerns about signs are a core issue for historians. Historical interpretation is always inferential. No one has direct access to historical reality (Ginzburg 1991: 84). In itself, the past is as unattainable as the thing-in-itself. Historical analysis are evermore mediated by signs.

Historical interpretations thus require a complete theory of signs, whose basic grounds—informed by the flux of time—are certainly possibility and chance, but without discarding the normative role of facts and also considering the constraints that conventions impose upon signs circulating at a precise moment. Taking a detour from the essays in *Visual Culture*, in the next section we will see possibility, fact and convention acting in a concrete historic analysis.

Those Memories, This Rembrandt, That Spinoza

The demand for such a comprehensive theory of signs, embracing concurrently hypothesis, normative facts and conventions, can be glimpsed if we consider the successes and failures of a particular historic interpretation. Let us tackle a forgotten theme of historical analysis: the presumed association between Rembrandt and Spinoza. Recent scholarship has neglected this alliance, not because it is an unattractive theme. Far from it: What could be more interesting than the personal interaction of two major figures of the seventeenth century, which would grant us an insight on the common points and mutual influence of philosophy and the visual arts? In Stuart Hampshire's monograph on Spinoza, we come to a reverberation of this possibility, when he describes the city of Amsterdam, that sheltered Spinoza, as "full of Jewish faces of the type that Rembrandt painted" (Hampshire 1978: 228). It is a remote suggestion of the meeting between Rembrandt and Spinoza.

If we just had a historic document of their encounter—a marginal note in a personal diary, a reference in a letter, or a representation of Spinoza in a Rembrandt painting—the claim would move from mere possibility to the status of a historical fact.

Even at this early moment in our investigation, there is a strong tendency to fasten Rembrandt to Spinoza. Of course, it is an action of the mind craving continuity. But the support for this junction has the restricted logic status of sheer possibility. Suspicion of the ties between Rembrandt and Spinoza creeps up because we know that we need more than a mere possible connection. Guesswork can be endless, an infinite creation that multiplies itself to indistinctness. Connections are contrived, but knowledge requires a normative principle, capable of sorting out what was produced. We are left in the midst of a whirlwind. The infinite addition opened up by limitless accumulative connection has to stop. So we are in search of facts that would legitimize or falsify the continuous connection.[6]

There is no doubt that Rembrandt and Spinoza could have met. A very early piece on the theme (Coppin 1916) asserts that in 1636 both men were going through personal setbacks. Spinoza was expelled from the Amsterdam's Jewish community. Rembrandt had been declared bankrupt; he saw his belonging taken away from his house.

Against the grain, Rembrandt had used the Jewish faces of Amsterdam's *Joden-Breedestratt*, the Old Jewish Quarter, as models for his drawings and paintings. Rembrandt lived near the house where Spinoza was born. They must have been around each other. Rembrandt was not an absolute outsider to the Jewish community. He knew cabalistic mystics; he was acquainted with the important leaders of the Amsterdam Jewish community, such as Menassé-ben-Israël, and he had also painted the portrait of the Jewish physician Ephraim Bonus, among others. But, even so we cannot be sure of the depth of Rembrandt's association with the Jewish community: It may be that it was merely familiarity with the more prominent members of the group, or with the models that sat for his pictures. Schwarz (1991: 284) mentions three

[6] Bab (1934) is an example of coupling Rembrandt to Spinoza with an ideological purpose. During the raise of Nazi hostilities to Jews, it was a clear political position to connect an eminent Jewish philosopher to a great European artist.

documented contacts between Rembrandt and the Jews and all of them litigious. In 1637, Samuel D'Orta accused Rembrandt of an unfair dealing of a print. Later on, in 1654, there is a recorded dispute about work in a house with Daniel Pinto, and, in February of the same year, Diego D'Andrada refused to accept a painting commissioned to Rembrandt on the grounds of lack of resemblance between the portrait of a girl and the sitter.

Nonetheless, some links between Spinoza and Rembrandt can be forged. Spinoza himself was an assiduous visitor of Amsterdam's Menonite's circles. Rembrandt had Menonite patrons and a Menonite disciple: Samuel van Hoogstraten (Coppin 1916: 171–172). It is also possible that through his contacts with political officials, with Mr. de Zuylichten, Rembrandt was introduced to Cartesian philosophy, the springboard of Spinoza's thought. In fact, Rembrandt's extant letters, collected by H. Gerson (1961), were addressed to Constantijn Huygens, himself a proponent of the new scientific spirit in the Netherlands, as well as directly responsible for important artistic patronage on behalf of the House of Orange. The contact with Huygens was not occasional: "Rembrandt kept contact with members of the distinguished Huygens family from the beginning to the end of his career" (Slive 1953: 43). But the factual problem remains, for no one can determine whether Huygens had any other common theme of discussion with Rembrandt apart from the kind of business interaction that is expected between a patron and an artist. We came back to the initial point. How can we rate the possibility that Rembrandt was familiar with philosophy?

It is unlikely. Rembrandt lived in a cultural environment where artists had very little interest in intellectual or philosophical disputes. Montias's (1982, 1987, 1988, 1989 and 1990) socio-economic analysis of the artistic craft in the Netherlands demonstrates that not even plain literacy was a necessary request for the exercise of the artistic profession. It is reasonable to presume that, for artists and craftsmen, what mattered was that artmaking became a very lucrative craft. Art was a flourishing commercial enterprise bringing, in the middle of the sixteenth century, daily wages that were fifty per cent greater than those of an ordinary workman; and later on, "the ratio was more like three or four to one" (Montias 1990: 365). In 1630, Rembrandt's charges for painting a portrait were high, ranging from "50 guilders for a single head to 500 guilders for a full-height, life-size work" (Schwarz 1991: 143). And, for Rembrandt, there was no shortage of the more expensive commissions. Compared to the honorable, respected, but poorly paid profession of preachers, we can have an idea of what Rembrandt's paintings were worth. For 500 guilders, precisely the price of a large Rembrandt portrait, a preacher would be receiving the best possible annual wages that would allow him and his family to live in near abundance (Zumthor 1989: 380). During the year of 1675, the annual rent of a sumptuous house in Amsterdam would be 700 guilders (Zumthor 1989: 274).

Putting this together with the observation that the social atmosphere that dominated the Netherlands was one ruled by tolerant values, especially if we compare it to other places in Europe, we have the picture of a society where social distinction was not exclusively a result of having an educated background laden with intellectual concerns. The tolerance prevailing in the Dutch world was in direct connection with the general success of its main economic activity: commerce. Dutch commerce required a social tinge that toned down social hierarchy: "Free enterprise was for everyone" (Méchoulan 1992: 75). However simplified this assessment of the Netherlands may be in relation to the actual political and social conflicts of the time, it is a valid general assumption. Everyone had the right to engage in economic transactions, everyone paid taxes, except the privileged nobility that kept its exceptional treatment without social legitimacy. The nobility existed in virtual social exile, being a source of outrage. This is certainly a contradiction in Dutch society, and the same trend could be seen in the coexistence of an internationalized economy, itself the utmost expression of modernity, with the antique system of guilds.

It is, therefore, probable that such traces of Amsterdam's political and social milieu may have encouraged Rembrandt to go from depicting Biblical scenes to search for inspiration in the faces of the Jewish community. He perceived a clear and common identity between Jews and Christians, as being equals. As it had no immediate bond with personalized relationships, Rembrandt's painting of Jews were not in search of individuals, but rather making a open-minded and universalist statement about Jewishness, frequently persecuted and seen, from the dominant Christian perspective, as the enemy within, the executors and deniers of the Messiah. Around 1635, Rembrandt makes a clear statement around a Jewish theme, when painting Balthasar's Feast. In the background of the painting, near God's hand and shining in a circle of light, there is a message written in Hebrew.

Montias's accounts of the economics of artmaking in Dutch seventeenth-century art insinuate that definite changes in art styles were consonant with a search for an artistic production capable of both creating and expanding a potentially lucrative market. Aesthetic alternatives went hand in hand with economic choice. Simpler styles would be effective in lowering the price of the paintings, for "the prime factor in determining a given art work's cost" (Montias 1988: 25), namely, the cost of labor, would have come down. All this matched to a reduction of expenses in materials generated what Montias calls "product innovations." This kind of art would sell better in a market whose trend was democratic expansion. The changes were pervasive: "Many abandoned history painting for other subjects, including portraits, landscapes, and still lives" (Montias 1987: 459). Rembrandt's production was usually dictated by the demands of the market. It is the contraction of the market that, around 1645, makes him stop painting landscapes (Schwarz 1991: 245). Elitist patrons, like Huygens, would still be important for the public commission of paintings. But they were not indispensable.[7] As a painter, Rembrandt had strong ties to the patronage of the political power of the cities where he lived. Schwarz (1991) painstakingly reweaves Rembrandt's ties to forgotten patrons and sitters that commissioned his works. Through notorious leaders and influential members of Leyden, The Hague, and Amsterdam, Rembrandt received important contracts that projected him into favor with wealthy businessmen and affluent people.

The *Anatomy Lecture of Doctor Nicolaes Tulp* was more than a depiction of scene, or a group portrait of a dissection of a corpse; Dr. Tulp, whose baptismal name was Claes Pietersz, was a local political figure: "town member of Amsterdam town council from 1622 on, alderman for numerous terms starting in 1622, and four times burgomaster, beginning in 1654" (Schwarz 1991: 144). Schwarz (1991: 142) thus insists that this group portrait is a political picture. The actual anatomy lecture coincided with the opening of a university in Amsterdam: It happened in January 31, 1632, "the last day of the political year in Amsterdam, the day before the election of new burgomasters and aldermen" (Schwarz 1991: 145). It is noteworthy that Rembrandt at the same time painted individual portraits of important people in the city. The market now

---

[7] Schwarz (1991: 73) argues that by 1633 Huygens's early enthusiasm for Rembrandt "had cooled to a freezing point." In a poem about the resemblance between Jacques de Gheyn and his picture, Huygens was offensive: "the hand is that of Rembrandt, the features are de Gheyn's/Admire it, reader, though it's not de Gheyn at all" (Schwarz 1991: 97). Yet, earlier on, Slive (1953: 19) advised against a literal interpretation of Huygens's verse: "they can be interpreted as a rhetorical compliment of the sitter, instead of adverse criticism of the painter."

market now included the emerging and wealthy bourgeoisie, thus diminishing the ascendancy of the intellectual elite over artisans and artists. Glassmakers, embroiderers, stone masons could be, as a group, both literate and illiterate; whereas painters, bookmakers and printers would be generally literate. The guild of Lucas, on the other hand, would be all literate. Artmaking did not demand a refined educated background, or even special intellectual concerns, much less the intricacies of philosophy. But the exercise of public office demanded a classical and humanistic education (Zumthor 1989: 136). The elaborate literary background of a painting sprung mainly from the educated commissioner of the work.

At one point, it was thought that Rembrandt's *Man with a Magnifying Glass* (1668) depicted Spinoza. But this is a vain hope. The intense picture of a meditating glass-grinder could be one of Spinoza, or equally, as it was argued, Titus, Rembrandt's son and his constant model. Once again, the facts run counter to wishes opened up by possibility: In 1668, Titus and Spinoza were younger than the sitter with the magnifying glass, Titus was then 27 and Spinoza 36 years old. And Spinoza had been expelled as heretic, 12 years earlier, from the Jewish community of Amsterdam (Muller 1968: 253). We come to the agonizing center of a maze.

If Rembrandt did not really meet Spinoza, this does not preclude the recognition of a deeper affinity between them. The reliance on biographic and factual data could be of help in establishing this identity, but in no way is it the only means. Shifting to a higher level of analysis, we would find the kind of historical conventionalism, and its semiotics of codes, unraveled in several essays of *Visual Culture*.

However different their intellectual choices may seem, it is the same set of assumptions that ruled what Valentiner (1957) had done when dealing with Rembrandt and Spinoza. Valentiner stressed mainly that, regardless of having actually met or not, Spinoza and Rembrandt were historical contemporaries. They were the products of the same epoch (Valentiner 1957: 79). A philosophical oeuvre and a pictorial production would then necessarily have the formative presence of a common force. This insight allowed Valentiner to postulate the existence of a unique drive exerting force over creators that had never been in direct contact with one another. Furthermore, Valentiner supposed that the epoch would contrive parallelism in philosophy and the visual arts: Spinoza is to Descartes what Franz Hals is to Rembrandt. This pairing an utter disappointment and a misleading clue. It is a simplistic opposition locking, side by side, two traces that are supposed to be the symptoms of rationalist and intuitive streaks in seventeenth-century Dutch culture.

The weakness of Valentiner's association is obvious if we refer it to the different conclusion that George Simmel (1950) proposes when discussing Rembrandt and Spinoza. Spinoza is an adversary to Rembrandt. Spinoza and Rembrandt are incompatible (Simmel 1950: 57). The mechanistic philosophy and the deterministic outline that inspired Spinoza cannot be recognized in Rembrandt.

As a whole, and beyond the commercial nature of the painter's enterprise, Rembrandt's obsession with self-portraits could be interpreted as more than just the minute representation of physical changes; in them, a whole life plucks off from the conjunction of instants. The representation of a self is constructed. In his production of self-portraits, Rembrandt makes himself, changing the tradition of painting portraits to his own direction, and thus enhancing "his personal identity" (Chapman 1990: 47). It is not a search for mysterious interior depths, but a straight forward act of self-depiction. Examining Rembrandt's self-portraits, Chapman (1990) perceives in them the creation of a socially acceptable image for Rembrandt's contemporaries: a development from historical paintings into a new brand of individualism. Rembrandt's vision of a totality is the embodiment of a unity made from irreducible moments.

Simmel sees no other way but to discern Rembrandt from Spinoza. In Spinoza, the understanding of individual things is constrained by the eternity clasped by the essence of the mind. We do not contemplate eternity, and "nonetheless we feel and we know that we are eternal" (1963: *Ethics* 5, Prop. XXIII). And eternity cannot be defined from time or even explained by duration. Duration is a mirage lasting as long as our bodies last. Eternity is essentiality rather than the indefinite continuation of what is perishable.

Rembrandt takes the converse stand; totality is revealed by "the constant presence of the instants" (Simmel 1950: 17). Each one of Rembrandt's paintings celebrates the idea that what matters is the addition of instants. A pose is a moment. But it is only through the capture of fleeting instants that the flow of life is discovered. Totality does not frame the instant. Looking at Rembrandt's paintings we understand totality as an afterthought.

Thus, comparing Valentiner to Simmel, we see how their interpretation of the parallels of Rembrandt and Spinoza are inconsonant. Simmel's appraisal is superior do Valentiner's in his effort to face the internal complexity of each one of his objects. Simmel's choice is for treating the diversity of each cognitive construction. It is possible to compare Spinoza and Rembrandt as long as we do not erase their distinctions. An interpretation of the ties between philosophical arguments and artistic creations should go not from the materialization of a cultural structure into concrete life, but the other way round, from life to general representations.

Rembrandt's pictorial compositions are strange to the geometrical method of Spinoza. Rembrandt's paintings express a living person, a vital plenitude, "an unsurmountable individuality," as Banfi (1970: 300) says, reflecting upon Simmel's treatment of Rembrandt. The unruffled and uncompromising determinism of Spinoza has no place in Rembrandt. Rembrandt exhibits insoluble tensions, polarized by the dilemmas of personal life and its trying choices. The Calvinist idea of vocation integrates the unity of humanity. Each human being has a destiny to fulfill; we have a call. The anguish of living comes from our efforts in transforming what is predestined into a vocation. Life is a grave, austere, and serious liturgy. With Calvin and Rembrandt, "it is the same path going toward the light, through countless troubles and suffering" (Wencelius 1937: 229). This is happening to all humans, for we share a common grace.[8]

Rembrandt is reconciled with inevitable defeats, and Spinoza dwells in timeless joy. For Spinoza, the quality of our happiness comes from our love of eternity. Mind is united with nature that is godly; "infinite alone feeds the mind with pleasure and it is free from all pain; so it is much to be desired and with all our might" (1963: *On the Correction of the Understanding* I, 8). An individual is not just there in itself; it continues in other thinking minds and ideas; it belongs to a totality. Understanding is, therefore, the illumination of eternity.

Rembrandt's pictorial depiction of transience—singular gestures, frozen for a moment, and at the brink of an abyss—is not in keeping with Spinoza's idea

---

[8] Guéroult (1968a: 385–386) criticizes any brisk approximation of Spinoza's theism to other notions of God, either Cartesian, Calvinist, or Jansenist. Spinoza's theism is not wholly coincident with Jewish or Christian conceptions of God. In fact, only two of Spinoza's definitions of God could conform to other theisms: the notion that we are in God, without being God, and the contention that our existence comes from and persists through the very existence of God. Guéroult (1968a: 386) observes that four other elements that Spinoza handles to define God are beyond traditional theological conceptions: the idea that we are modes of God's substance;that we have an identity with God's manner of being; that our bodies are attributes of God; that we are one with God, for the act that makes us exist and the one that brings God to cause are the same.

that the love of transience is weak and urges us to search for stronger and stronger objects of love that only eternity can appease: "The mind does not shift its attention away from finite things to God; rather in the light of the idea of God it comes to a new perception of finite things in themselves" (Lloyd 1987: 214).

Other discrepancies between Rembrandt and Spinoza can be pointed out. Morrison (1989: 363) has even claimed that a philosophical reflection about art and beauty has to shy away from Spinozism. Spinoza's philosophy determines that our imagination creates beauty, but this is inevitably a minor mode of judgment. Beauty is not a real property of things; it is simple reaction, an affection created over the perceiving mind. Beauty has no objectivity; the impression of beauty varies immensely in all of the reactions that it produces. Beauty can only be measured through usefulness. "In itself, or in relation to God, nothing is beautiful or ugly" (Morrison 1989: 360). The lack of an objective nature in artmaking is, for Morrison, Spinoza's motivation for disregarding art completely, to the extreme of denying it a place in his system.[9]

Spinoza's arguments about art's lack of objectivity are then appended to his moral rationalism. If the imagination that created beauty is passive in relation to the eternal part of the mind, that is to say, the intellect (1963: *Ethics* 5, Prop. XL, Corollary), then the passive trace of the imagination makes it inferior to reason. Such submissive faculty, the imagination, is a source of error, that has to be bonded to the ultimate demands of reason. Imagination is incapable of granting what our mind so eagerly craves: eternity.

To all this, it must be added that Spinoza's critique of representation drives him away from any identity with Rembrandt's pictorial production. Spinoza's

---

[9] Selsam (1935) claims that, in Spinoza, aesthetics is not an exterior element of his philosophy. Aesthetic experience is at the very core of Spinoza's *Ethics*. "There is a most intimate and inescapable bond between Spinoza's moral doctrine and the type of method by which it is expounded" (Selsam 1935: 260). The knowledge of truth, required by morality, is the source of beauty. The deductive method, displayed in Spinoza's book, guarantees the perception of aesthetic beauty, which in turn is the condition for morality. Nonetheless, Selsam's contention is wrong on two counts, in its disregard for the negative judgement that Spinoza makes of beauty, subsuming it under the inferior faculty of imagination, as well as forgetting that Spinoza's geometric method of composing his *Ethics* is less an aesthetic expression than a cognitive postulation, "centered around the idea of a complete deduction of properties from a special understanding of the essence of things" (De Dijn 1986; 68).

founding idea that God is Cause of Itself (*causa sui*), not involving the concept of anything else, denies a solid cognitive rank to representation.

Defined as a being of infinite attributes, God will be reached not through its representation, but through what immediately partakes of its nature. The knowledge of God, conceived by Itself and for whom nothing is hidden, is absolute affirmation, and it will come by reason, not by the senses. Reason transcends correspondence, parallelism or even dependency of the finite mode to the infinite one. Present things are more vivid than their representations. Cause (*natura naturans*) is to be preferred to any affection (*natura naturata*) in the same way that an active nature is superior to a passive one.

Being is measured by plenitude. "The more reality or being a thing has, the more attributes will have" (1963: *Ethics* 1, Prop. IX). Of all beings, the one that aggregates more attributes is the one to be valued the most. And this perceptions leads to a requirement devaluating representation. Any dualism is imperfection. And representations are at least dual, a product of the interaction of representamens and their objects. A real unity would integrate the plenitude of the sensible world; but the full unity is God, that can and will do away with representation. It is not in appearance but in reason that plenitude exists.

An immanent force is at work in existence. The endeavor of preserving oneself is the very essence of a thing, any thing, and the basis for virtue (1963: *Ethics* 4, Prop. XII, Proof). Spinoza's philosophy makes no room for dualism; it is concerned with determining the conditions of an intellectual dynamism, actualizing eternal potency. The absolute infinite substance is indivisible and dispenses with explanation. Spinoza's detour from Descartes becomes the passage going from dualistic imperfection to an aspired unity, *Deus sive Natura,*[10] or else, "all things are in God" (1963: *Ethics* 1, Appendix). The principle of substance plenitude asserts that "extension is an attribute of the absolutely infinite being" (Donogan 1989: 117). What could be called separately mind and matter is different attribution of the same infinite substance. So, Spinoza profess that extension is an integral attribute of God. As God's attribute, matter will abide rest and motion. In God, "the thinking thing" (1963: *Ethics* 1, Prop. 1), the rule is inclusion that surmounts all modes of disjunctive representation.

---

[10] The laws of Nature express God's essence (Donagan 1989: 57). Nature is a not possibility chosen among many others; it is the only determined solution. The world is out there as it should be, resting upon its persistent nature, offering itself to be grasped by understanding.

Representation is neither inevitable nor an end in itself. From an eternal perspective, from what we aim to be, there is no contingency. Contingency and possibility, the grounds of representation, are irrelevant from the point of view of a totality. Human understanding is fallible because the human mind is caught in a web of representations. But true knowledge moves beyond representation, and it is granted by understanding.

For Spinoza's philosophy, understanding and imagination are distinct in their nature and capabilities. Understanding is an endeavor guided by reason, whereas imagination is an affair of the senses. Intellectual understanding responds to how things are in themselves—infinite, indivisible, unique, and necessary—whereas imagination accounts for divisibility, finitude, division in parts, and possibility.

Closer to the profusion of words, imagination is a source of mistake, error, and inaccuracy. In their inclusiveness and generality, words cannot exclude contradiction: They are doomed to harbor diverse representations. Dealing with the strictures of ideas, understanding is unitarian and necessary; its task is to do away with contradiction. In an idea there is no mediation. "An idea does not consist in the image of anything, nor in words" (1963: *Ethics* 2, Prop. XLIX, Note). An idea clings immanently to its thing: "The order and connection of ideas is the same as the order and connection of things" (1963: *Ethics* 2, Prop. VII). To comprehend this proposition, the use of a mirror as a metaphor can be misleading. So, when Matheron (1969: 73) says that, according to Spinoza, the interaction with the outside world offers to us our reflection, the idea is that, in fact, there is no duality, nor transfigured representation. Nothing that sticks to the representation of appearances shall be worthy of plenitude. If Rembrandt's paintings are representations of appearances, then Spinoza and Rembrandt cannot be reconciled.

How could anyone ever reduce the dissimilarity of Rembrandt and Spinoza to a unvarying unity? The only way would be through the conjecture that human actions are beyond the intentions of the actors, as they follow the same flow of time. History is thus transfigured into a supraindividual force. Identity of works are then perceived in detriment of their difference.[11]

---

[11] Gebhardt's (1926) analysis of the links between Rembrandt and Spinoza is an example of this tendency. He calls for the recognition of a unity in distinct works. Stronger than any superficial discrepancy is the action of time as "the force that expresses itself in a form" (Gebhardt 1926: 164). For Gebhardt, the extreme positions of Rembrandt and Spinoza condense the possibilities of a historical moment crystallized in a dominant

We are back to a consistent dilemma in historical analysis. What to do: to force uniformities or else to relish in ruptures? The circularity and the fluidity of the replies to the question may be a sign of its irrelevance.

Looking closely at Michel Foucault's theory of history, we can see that there is no easy choice to be made. Apparently, Foucault's nihilist drums call for rupture. History is discontinuous. The archaeologists, a new brand of historians, have to be rid "of a whole mass of notions, each of which, in its own way, diversifies the theme of continuity" (Foucault 1976: 21). Discontinuities are effects of the arbitrary grid imposed culturally to specific historic expansions. But within each *episteme*, within each enunciative field, there is a deep unity, whose main trace is regularity. Then Foucault makes a clear option: The task of the archaeologist of knowledge is to deal with "enunciative homogeneity" (Foucault 1976: 145). Enunciative homogeneity indicates the identity of cultural productions and does not come around from authorship or even the material unity of an oeuvre. Epistemes are the product of fundamental cognitive codes, operating from an unconscious strata, generating ruptures with the past, but setting the directions for discursive dispersion: Epistemes are "generative grammars of cognitive language" (Merquior 1987: 37). Within itself, each episteme is not arbitrary; they are ruled by necessity. An episteme obeys "the laws of a certain code of knowledge" (Foucault 1973: ix). So, Major-Poetzl (1983: 165) is right in her criticism that Foucault's *The Order of Things* "imposed a uniformity of thought on periods as long as a century and a half."

The exclusiveness of each one of Foucault's archaelogical descriptions yields the misconception that the cognitive trends pertaining to the past are buried for ever in the subsequent historical period: "It is all or nothing at all in the period of each episteme" (Aarsleff 1982: 23). It is therefore no wonder that most critical commentators of Foucault's archaeology complain not so much of what is included in the descriptions, but of what is left out, as either forgotten or inconsequential. Foucault's summary of what he calls the classical episteme is another surprising impoverishment. Among his exclusions from the core of representative figures of the seventeenth century, we will find Rembrandt and Spinoza.[12] Foucault reductively elects, as representative of the Classical

---

style, the Baroque. But it is difficult to see how Spinoza's philosophy and its symmetric, cold, rational method of exposition fits into the classification of Baroque.

12 In an amazingly inept reading of Spinoza, Foucault (1973: 70) says that Spinoza,

period, *La Logique* (Arnauld and Nicole 1970) and *The Grammar* (Arnauld and Lancelot 1992) of Port Royal.

Port-Royal's *La Logique* and *The Grammar* are viewed as relevant for seventeenth-century history not because of the actual editorial fortune of the books when published in 1662. Foucault would certainly rule out these data as too narrowly empirical. But it is a fact that Port-Royal's *Logique* was influential after its issuing. According to Blanché (1985: 182), fifty French editions of *La Logique* came out in two centuries, notwithstanding several English versions, and twelve Latin translations aimed at Germanic countries.

Arnauld and Nicole's book owed its success to the revolutionary nature of its conception. Contrary to traditional manuals of logic that were abstruse in their formal technicalities, *La Logique* never lost track of its practical objective. It emphasized that reasoning depended on acts of judgment. And the judgments were considered part of actual life. Logic is defined as an art that teaches us how to think better, through our learning of how to distinguish truth from falsity: "It is through judgments that one must conduct one's life, as well as rule one's actions, and become happy or unhappy" (Arnauld and Nicole 1970: 109).

La Logique is thus normative. Its normative values came directly from the general conception that, as a discipline, logic should be involved in clarifying and perfecting judgment. This allowed Foucault to see *La Logique* as a rupture with Renaissance thought, for Renaissance thought had restricted itself to encourage the production of new representations. During the Renaissance the universe was seen in a process of constant transformation. But sooner or later the endless production of representations came to an impasse, demanding the creation of criteria that would serve as means for judgment. This was the task of the Classical Age.

---

along with Descartes and Malebranche, sees imagination as "both the locus of error and the power of attaining truth, even mathematical truth." But any attentive interpretation of Spinoza rules out imagination as the source of mathematical knowledge. Spinoza emphatically argues that the mind should be curbed of confused notions, thus placing mathematics at the side of the intellect, far away from imagination. Another example of Spinoza's discredit of the imagination is his radical criticism of religious revelation. Prophecies should not be taken as authoritative, because they are the products of feeble, imperfect, and inconstant imagination. For Spinoza, "prophetic knowledge is inferior to natural knowledge" (Popkin 1977: 231).

How should we eliminate erroneous intellectual productions? How would Port-Royal fulfill its project of placing judgment at the core of intellectual productions? To answer such questions, Arnauld and Nicole argue that language represents thought. For that reason, Marin (1975: 41) sees in Port-Royal's texts an absolute parallelism between logic and grammar. Language and thought are excluded from one another, and this separation engenders a normative criterion. "The function of language is to name, that is, to raise up a representation or point it out" (Foucault 1973: 104). The task of the logician is to consider ideas in their relation to words and words as related to ideas (Arnauld and Nicole 1970: 60). In *The Grammar*, the authors are adamant: Words were invented with the sole purpose of revealing our thoughts (Arnauld and Lancelot 1992: 27). The judgmental consideration of words linked to things is the manner through which identity, differentiation, measurement, and order are known. Identity, differentiation, measurement, and order are normative means. So, we can gather that the exteriority of signs, expressing ideas, in relation to things is the effective condition for normative judgments.

When a grammarian classifies words into substantives and adjectives, the classification follows a distinct philosophical image of the universe. The distinction of words into substantives and adjectives reflects the differences between things and their manners of being: "The substances subsist in themselves, meanwhile the accidents only exist through substances" (Arnauld and Lancelot 1992: 30). The logical and grammatical rule of any proposition is one of agreement, or, if we wish, concord. The hierarchy of substances and accidents is directly mirrored by the grammatical form fitting adjectives to substantives. In a sentence, the subject attracts the attributes; the subject determines the attributes (Arnauld and Lancelot 1992: 76). The use of the notion of substance, as the dominant mode of being, responds to an essential property of language in Classical thought.

Thus, language is not expression but discourse (Foucault 1973: 92). The elementary unit of language is the proposition. Without substance underlying both nature and the propositions declaring the properties of the world, how could we have representations? Substance creates the conditions for representation in the Classical Age; after being defined as differentiated, representations and represented things are in direct correspondence with mediating ideas. Freed from the chore of representing objects, conjunctions (such as and, no, therefore, if, among others) signify the workings of the mind (Arnauld and Lancelot 1992: 134). A negative conjunction indicates a judgment. An interrogation signals the wish to have a reply. But language and thought are inevitably dual. A proposition expresses an idea that designates reality. The authors of Port-Royal move from language to language, handling samples of French, Latin, Greek, and Italian because they believe that underneath the surface of a sentence each utterance hides a logical proposition. The connection of the dual elements, of language and thought, is obtained through the Cartesian principle of *adequaetio*.

Adequaetio is a muffled reverberation of a Cartesian view active, through Arnauld,[13] in both *The Grammar* and *La Logique* of Port-Royal. Nothing is further from Spinoza's unity of God and our understanding. For Spinoza, in all of its forms, dualism is a sign of imperfection and incompleteness. The differences separating Spinoza from Descartes are striking; no recourse to a subterranean historical layer, as put forward by Foucault, is justified.

If we consider how Descartes and Spinoza deal with the fundamental theme of the unity in diversity, we become aware of their incompatibility: Descartes places it at the level of human beings, and Spinoza at the level of God (Guéroult 1968a: 229). Their discrepancy cannot be bridged. Spinoza's dismissal of dualism is uncompromising; a determined existence with a finite cause necessarily has to be ascertained by another cause, and so on to infinity. Either the regression comes to a halt—and then we have a finite existence determined by an infinite cause—or else we must put up with an idea absurd enough to shock the wits out of any rigorous thinker.

With this in mind, Spinoza maintains that the infinite substance, God, harbors infinite attributes. In Spinoza, Descartes's dual distinction of *cogitatio* and *extensio*, is unified into a single substance. Duality is a fallacy; the dual terms are the expression of an infinite substance. Spinoza moves beyond Descartes. He rejects what Descartes said in *The Principles of Philosophy*: That we, as finite beings, could never comprehend infinite perfection (Descartes

---

[13] It has been pointed out that Descartes is not a homogeneous influence over Port-Royal. Lewis (1950) and Nadler (1992) contest the idea that Cartesianism is the source of Port-Royal's work. Strictly speaking, only Arnauld could be considered a Cartesian follower. Lakoff (1969) demonstrated that the most important influence over Lancelot's and Arnauld's theory of language was not Descartes, but rather Franciscus Sanctius; and Aarsleff (1992: 105) established that "practically all universal grammarians" have a debt with Sanctius. Clerico (1977) reviews Sanctius oscillating critical fortune.

1968: 227). Spinoza insists that the understanding of infinity is a condition for understanding existence. Cartesian split of *cogitatio* and *extensio* makes infinity incomprehensible. For Descartes, our errors stem from a lack of perfection; Spinoza asserts that error resides in the privation of knowledge, itself the cause of any erroneous statement (Guéroult 1968b: 314).

Spinoza's rejection of dualism led him to exclude painting, a progeny of representative imagination, as secondary to the major task of contemplating eternity. Does a dualistic conceptual framework, like Port-Royal, stand a better chance of explaining visual arts? At first, it seems that painting has no place in Port-Royal's reflections. No clear reference is made in *La Logique*, whose starting point is really the relation between word and ideas. Then, how do we fit paintings in the intellectual production of the Classical episteme? Ostensibly there is no way to do it, at least not if we uphold Foucault's contentions about Port-Royal's *Grammar* and *La Logique* as being "the most perfect expressions" (Marin 1970: 28) of the Classical Age.

For the authors of Port-Royal, there is no serious consideration of the visual arts. But what can we infer about painting from their postulation of a transparency ruling language and thought? The first point would be that paintings or visuality are segregated from Port-Royal's model. The only way to consider painting within this framework would be to see it under the general guise of representation. Representation is common to both language and visuality. Words are not visual things, but there are visual things that can function as signs, through similarity or analogy. Now we find an argument that can be relevant for an assessment of painting.

Either in language, or in the case of painting, or of the linguistic sign, or even the pictorial sign, any sign is a double; and this double is a substitution (Marin 1970: 2). When we have visual signs functioning as surrogates, the substitution aspires to immediacy through direct analogy, rejecting whatever does not fulfill the condition of perfect similitude.

Absolute similitude is the desired paradigm. How could we ever deny that an image in a mirror is a natural sign of the person mirrored? In front of my image in a mirror, the reaction is immediate: "That is me" (Marin 1991: 282). An image thus stops being a representation. After the recognition, the duality is gone. But that is not the kind of unity that Spinoza would cherish: It is a debased unity, grounded in illusion, for the represented object cannot be separated from what represents it. It is "an instant of identification in which representation becomes a real presence" (Marin 1991: 289).

As natural signs, paintings follow the specular principle: "Without preface or ado, we say of a portrait of Caesar that the portrait is Caesar, and of a map of Italy that the map is Italy" (Arnauld and Nicole 1970: 205). If visual illusion is the principal responsibility of pictorial representation, how can it be part of the judgmental assignment of reasoning, whose goal is to discriminate falsity from truth?

For Port-Royal, painting would always be at the fringe of representations. Painting is subsumed under the perfection of mirrors, themselves the pictorial signs that without mediation represent the natural world. Port-Royal's doctrines do not treat painting as a legitimate form of representation. The conclusion should be that Port-Royal despises, and condemns pictorial representations. So, do we have to exclude painting from analysis of the episteme of the Classical Age?

As the author of a substantial and subtle interpretation of the bonds between Port-Royal and Pascalian philosophy, Louis Marin would agree with the idea that Port-Royal's theoretical conceptions dismiss paintings as legitimate modes of judgment. But Marin also tried to downplay this estimation. Did the authors of Port-Royal really believe in such rigid exclusion? If so, how should we interpret Phillipe de Champaigne's (1602–1674) close biographical connections with the Jansenists of Port-Royal?

In a departure from canonical interpretations of Champaigne that used to state how little influence Port-Royal had exerted over the painter, Marin set out to inquire whether that is true. If Champaigne's paintings did follow Port-Royal's dogma, would we have to qualify them as the paradigm for image making during the Classical Age?

A strict probe of Champaigne's paintings is not enough to unravel the riddle. Hence Marin (1970: 12) refers to a fragment of Champaigne's lecture on the use of shadows in religious paintings, calling it "a true theology of shadow." In a religious painting, shadows serve to express divine creations, when we identify the forms of actual delineated objects. Paintings make visible what had up to then been invisible. Existence literally comes to light. But images should be subsidiary to the texts that they imply. In themselves, painted images are stringent appeals to the eye: How could an image reach the soul? The answer is: through the viewer's interpretation of the depicted scene that was directly taken from the Scriptures. The divine word is then revealed. But it is not hidden or ciphered anymore; the divine word was discovered in the play of light and shadow forming the sacred text (Marin 1970: 15). Painting is a fiat, it is eternity lit in an instant. In this idea, Marin (1970: 18) recognizes the influence of Pascal.

For Marin, Champaigne's paintings, as any portrait ought to do in its task of substituting the sitter, oscillate between the rendering of extreme individuality and the expression of a higher impersonal value hovering above us, incarnated from the Christian conception of grace. The blending of personal call and impersonal forces is not impossible. Silence, retreat, and prayer are the personal conditions that define the soul as the locus of grace. Consequently, Marin decides for the amalgam of Port-Royal's religious doctrines and Champaigne's paintings.

But Marin's exercise is both canny and problematic. Champaigne's works cannot claim to be a supreme achievement of seventeenth-century painting. They are no match for Rembrandt. Not only in their formal achievement, but also in the ideas that they convey, Champaigne and Rembrandt are incomparable. Champaigne's paintings present grace as being cold and hierarchical. Champaigne has nothing to do with the Calvinist notion of grace that Rembrandt puts forward. Rembrandt is dramatic, Protestant, and individualistic.

The only common point to be seen in Champaigne and Rembrandt is their use of gestures in pictorial compositions. For Rembrandt, gestures are what define each painted figure. Gestures are just what Rembrandt has to offer, after his choice of isolating "his subjects within their own world of contemplation" (Rosenberg 1948, vol 1: 64). They may be gestures of expertise dissecting a corpse. They may be suspended gestures of members of a gild, sitting for the very group portrait that we are seeing, or else, an arrogant posture in a self-portrait, a letter being passed from one person to another, the sharpening of a quill, the writing at a desk, a joyous celebration of personal triumph, raising a glass, with his wife on the lap, or even the countless minute postures of Rembrandt's sitters, threatening expression, but holding it, not allowing anything to come out.

Here we have little to go on. How can we explain the relevance or importance of these gestures in Rembrandt's paintings and drawings? It is inevitable thinking of Rembrant's correspondence with Huygens, however scant and elusive its suggestions, for with the exception of a dubious and much disputed mention to his own works, Rembrandt's letters are mainly the record of an economic transaction concerning the commission of a series of Passion paintings for the *stadholder*.

Huygens's commission was the culmination of his early favorable appraisal of Rembrandt. Around 1630, Huygens described the excellence of Rembrandt's paintings with impassioned exactitude. Rembrandt's paintings were more than mere imitation of a visual scene. Huygens said that they presented a translation into visual forms of what Rembrandt saw with his mind's eye. A supreme example of this pictorial achievement was a painting of 1629, showing a repentant Judas returning the 30 pieces of silver to the chief priests and elders. Huygens's commentary focused on Rembrandt's enactment of Judas's gestures: "That single gesture of the desperate Judas—that single gesture, I say, of a raging, whining Judas, grovelling for the mercy he no longer hopes for or dares to show the smallest sign of expecting, his frightful visage, hair torn out of his head, his rent garment, his arms twisted, his hands clenched bloodlessly tight, fallen to his knees in a heedless outburst—that body, wholly contorted in pathetic despair, I place against all the tasteful art of all time past, and recommend to the attention of all ignoramus—I have disputed them elsewhere—who hold that our age is incapable of doing or saying anything better than was already said or the ancients have achieved." These are Huygens's literal words, translated by Schwarz (1991: 74).

In a letter to Huygens, dated January, 1639, Rembrandt follows the hint and qualifies two of his recently finished pictures, *The Resurrection* and *The Entombment of Christ*, as the expression of "the greatest and most natural movement" (Gerson 1961: 38). This is the only registered hint of Rembrandt to his own paintings. The rest in his letters is just haggling about the price of the paintings.

Concerning Rembrandt's words, historians simply cannot reach an agreement. What does the expression *die meeste end die naetureelste beweechgelickheijt* effectively mean? Is it "the greatest and most natural movement" or "the most innate emotion"? Is the movement depicted in itself, for its own compositional sake, or is it the representation of movement according to the psychological traces of the characters in the painting?

Rosenberg (1948, vol. 1: 16) endorses the translation as "the greatest and most natural movement," taking sides against H. E. van Gelder's interpretation of the sentence as inward emotion. Rosenberg argues that this would be more in keeping with the paintings themselves that are renditions of movement, and furthermore, it would be in accord with what Rosenberg (1948, vol 1: 226) calls "the aesthetics of the period." On the other hand, Fuchs (1969: 34) asserts that there is no reason to exclude the meaning of movement from its purpose of presenting the psychological overtones of the scene. For Fuchs, the expression means inner commotion, emotions visibly recognized from the outward movement of the bodies. In fact, this is the experience the viewer has when contemplating the picture. Fuchs professes that *beweechgelickheijt* can stand for movement and emotion, whose kinship is perceived when we pair up the words motion and emotion. White (1984: 68) considers both meanings as relevant, since movement would also be an appropriate description of the main visual quality of the *Resurrection*, whereas emotion would be pertinent to qualify the expressions and actions of the figures surrounding the dead Christ.

Is the impossibility of coming to terms with this cryptic expressions merely a historical or even a philological problem? It may be that historians are mislead in forgetting the context in which the expression was used. Rembrandt was then addressing Huygens from whom he may have heard this expression. Rembrandt seemed to quote an expression that Huygens would recognize as his own, with the sole purpose of pleasing his influential patron. In the same letter that Rembrandt uses the enigmatic expression, he also offers a gift to Huygens, as a token of appreciation. The gift is "one piece 10 feet long and eight feet high for my lord's own house" (Gerson 1961: 38). Comparing the dimensions of the gift with Rembrandt's production at the time, the conclusion must be that the painting is *The Blinding of Samson*. Due to its violent theme, and grandiloquent composition, the offering of this precise painting as a gift could only be a reinforcement of Huygens's previous estimation of Rembrandt. Slive (1953: 23) adds that Rembrandt also knew of Huygens's admiration for Rubens's painting of a Medusa, another gruesome, violent, and emotional painting, nonetheless prized as an aesthetic achievement. Rembrandt was well aware of what a commendatory Huygens would bring to him in future contracts.[14] Rembrandt was playing a game, confirming what he knew it was Huygens's interpretation of his work, and in the background of all this, we can hear Huygens's description of Rembrandt's painting of Judas, the penitent.

Die meeste end die natureeleste beweechgelickheijt may not be Rembrandt's expression. And it is not an exclusive creation of Huygens, either. The expression is related to contemporary ideas that Huygens deemed

---

[14] Slive is right on the mark when he argues that Huygens's later disregard of Rembrandt s most likely due to the painter's abandonment of extreme emotional gestures, "the great inward emotion," for the rendering of restrained gestures. Huygens was "not prepared to follow Rembrandt's departure from the style of High Baroque" (Slive 1953: 26).

intellectually valuable. The clue to understand it is Francis Bacon's major influence over Huygens.[15]

Bacon's conception of Nature is surprisingly close to the tendencies of seventeenth-century Dutch painting. Bacon sees Nature as wholly self-sufficient. Hence, the return to Nature—in its full immediacy, similar to what Dutch painters were doing, craving for a direct glimpse of external reality—becomes the best cognitive option. On the other hand, moving away from Nature brings the risk of being lost in a tangle of representations.

It sounds like a paradox. To know is to link up similar observations. But representations are what leads away from Nature. What to do? In fact, the only thing to do is to admit that this is the core of Baconian philosophy. There is an unbreachable split of two bodies of philosophy in Baconian thought (Rees 1984: 298).

We can easily see in Bacon a defense of analogy as condition of knowledge, due to analogy's power of generating representations. Analogy conjures up mental representations of objects, but analogy is not enough. This is a symptom of Bacon's "ambivalence toward imagination" (Park, Datson and Galison 1984: 288). So Bacon calls for a method capable of reforming understanding. The reform of knowledge comes through induction. The new inductive method would serve as a prescriptive norm. It is not a mere revamping of the old Aristotelian induction through simple enumeration. The new inductive method depends on negative empirical instances that are intended to function as a means of testing the generated representations.

But Bacon is not consistently inductive. He recognizes that there is room for a variety of solutions. Somewhere, he also argues for a diametrically opposed conception of nature, revealed by another method of examining natural events, closer to "a systematic, deductive model of interpreting the phenomena of nature" (Rees 1984: 298). So Bacon ended up "fashioning a system that combined intrinsically different modes of thought, modes represented in Paracelsianism and the Scientific Revolution, and created a unique if unstable

---

[15] Colie (1956: 72–91) dedicates a whole chapter of her study of the English influence over Huygens to Bacon. Huygens cherished Bacon as an intellectual hero. This influence was not subdued, not even after Bacon's negative impression over Huygens as proud, vain, and pompous. Alpers (1993) tries to determine the Baconian influence over Dutch art, through Huygens. Thanks to Bacon's influence, Dutch art opts for minute description of the sensible world, abandoning the Italian tradition of narrative painting.

synthesis designed to rehabilitate the geocentric world picture" (Rees 1975). Bacon is a reactionary, as well as a thinker concerned with the reform of knowledge. The abandonment of tradition is a requirement for scientific progress. Bacon's project of reforming knowledge basically descends from his unwavering critique of representations.

In themselves, representations are always under suspicion. Cognitive problems occur when representations drives us away from the only source of true knowledge: Nature. And this is precisely the problem with words, with ordinary language. Bacon considers language an idol; and this is due to his recognition that words and things are not isomorphic with each other. Rhetorical dexterity does not contrive the grounds for judgment, words are what muddle judgment. Rhetoric has one fruitful purpose: persuasion (Rossi 1984: 290), and it should be reduced to the role of disseminating scientific ideas (Park 1984: 290). Rhetoric cannot generate the advancement of empirical science.

The question of empirical truth requires another path, that we can perceive considering the natural relation of words to the natural world: "Words have no existence other than as signs pointing to their referents in the world. An ideal language, therefore, is one that clearly and transparently represents the thing it signifies" (Elsky 1984: 452). But this is not to say that there can be a directly analogical correspondence between verbal sign and reality. The direct, natural and most transparent sign is the Adamic gesture of pointing. Pointing names things without the use of words.

Gestures are residues from the Edenic moment of perfect congruence of signs and things Gestures are a universal language. In fact, there are two notations of things: one, analogical, composed of gestures and hieroglyph; and another, conventional, whose best example is the word. Analogical notation is, by definition, superior to any convention mediating representations and nature. Gestures are the direct revelation of an essence. Gestures are prior to conventions; they are like hieroglyph, or else, natural ciphers, in their claim to universality. And Bacon had alluded to the convenience of such "system of real characters in the *De Augmentis Scientiarum* of 1605" (Knowlson 1975: 45). Similar to hieroglyphs, gestures establish a direct correspondence of things and notions, dispensing with any need for mediation (Rossi 1965: 150). Error comes from being distant from things. The therapy to our mistakes consists in returning to directness and analogy, as sources of natural notations. The Baconian task of reforming knowledge can tear the veil hiding Nature from us. We will then become once again like Adam in Paradise. We will see things as they are, after having recovered the "Adamic knowledge of the nature of things" (Cooper 1992: 98). Huygens's emphasis on the excellence of Rembrandt's depiction of gestures was the highest compliment that a Baconian could make to any form of representation.

When considered side by side, the nuances of representations created by the seventeenth century are amazingly distinct. Spinoza, Rembrandt, and Port-Royal show no unity. Their sense may well be precisely this dispersion. At close range, it is impossible to recognize the action of a common historical undercurrent, uniformed as a set of conventions.

Conventionalism precludes a fundamental perception of sign production; meaning is not obtained by an abstract model ruling the users of signs as if they were marionettes. The unruly crew of history glides without a rudder. Transient history is more of a lost boat moving through with no guides to carry it.

Meaning comes from the material occurrences of signs, from acts of handling and transforming them, from the contact driven by the deliverance of signs. Conventionalist interpretations are simplistic and reductive. Conventionalism sticks to a dimension prior to semiotic action. And living history is thus left out of the analysis.

You Wonder How It All Came About

David Summers's "Form and Gender" is the last chapter of *Visual Culture* and a harrowing scrutiny of a central assumption in art history. In this time of widespread disaffection, "Form and Gender" renders the best service that feminist critique of image making could ever get. Rounding up epistemologically sound arguments, and without resort to the easy and unconvincing idea of a pervasive male conspiracy against women, Summers answers why femininity is structurally disregarded by the concerns of traditional art history. In short, Summers (1994b: 405) sees the skull beneath the skin, and points his finger to the "strongly gendered idea of form."

Form is the mutant concept that grounds art history. Art historians are unfailing formalists: They always start from the undisputed definition that works of art are "essentially forms or 'compositions' of forms" (1994b: 384). So, Summers's attack on the neutrality of form has the sharp peal of doom. Is it feasible to approach art-making historically, now that its central operative concept has been indicted as an incurable distortion?

In a previous paper, Summers (1989) placed form, the descriptive tool of art history, at the core of nineteenth-century metaphysics. Form has nearer roots in Kantian aesthetics and its ensuing emphasis on the non-mimetic nature of artistic representation. Form comes from the human spirit that delivers itself from the constraints of nature.

Without the shackles of natural necessity, forms develop autonomously. They acquire a life of their own, being independent and free agents of artistic processes. To use form as a means of description implies isolating it from content, or merging it with content to the point of mutual determination. It is not difficult to see why form comes to the conceptual foreground of historical analysis, transformed into a privileged language for describing art works. Painting, sculpture, architecture are classified as visual arts, not only because they can be described as visual forms: The concept of form is the proper way to describe them (Summers 1981: 301). Forms are essential to artistic making, and serve, in their change, as the justification of historical approaches to art.

Formalist description is a structural mapping out of actual works. Its language is the language of shapes. Art history does not start from a description of what is depicted, but from how form is achieved: "The painted surface becomes a plane, and in general we abstract from three dimensions to two, from centers of gravity to verticals, from horizons to horizontals, simplifying as we go" (Summers 1989: 377). Through the glint of shapes lies what is visually experienced. Around this dichotomy of form and content, interpretative positions are taken: either considering meaning as directly expressed in the formal configuration of visuality, or else as the concept enshrined in forms. Forms always prevail.

The evolution of forms is history; but not the living sequence of actual lives. It is something more than that; forms express totalities, such as nations, races, epochs. Now there is the presumption that a unifying principle is at work involving continuity and more than local cultural identity. The language of forms suggests the existence of an even higher totality. With the idea of form, history of art becomes "a kind of universal cultural history" (Summers 1989: 375). It is the achievement of a timeless and ahistorical human spirit, generating ever-changing and nonetheless continuous organic unities.

Is this conceptual framework neutral? Of course, it is not. Summers observes how biased are the effects of using form as a descriptive vocabulary, itself isolated of a higher priority, akin to Aristotle's claim that semen is the efficient cause of life itself. In that interpretation, matter is a passive substratum, both an imperfection and a lacking. "Matter is a feminine principle of perfect potentiality, and form is a masculine principle of perfect activity" (Summers 1994: 397). The social consequences of the uncritical adoption of these notions are more than evident. Gender hierarchy is instituted upon biological inferiority, naturalized and seen as unquestionable. Upon this basic structural distinction, other notions are piled up. Form is rational, logical and intellectual; matter is irrational, illogical and pertaining to the senses. The distinction of form and matter and its subsequent assessment that form is the superior and dominant principle finds its way in a series of hierarchical levels.

Form shapes matter, as "bronze (matter) may be poured into any shape, and the shape (form) is determined by the imagination of the craftsman" (Summers 1989: 397). When form is abstracted from mater, the superior capacity of the intellect is championed. It all fits with the generalized idea that "the female is an incomplete or mutilated male" (Summers 1994b: 394). Indeed, the idea of organic unity postulated hierarchy. Earlier on, in *The Judgment of Sense*, Summers (1987) had demonstrated that the Renaissance aesthetic tradition considered art making a result of a central conception; mental work is incomparable to manual labor. So, after the Renaissance, art making is thought of as a supreme creation; the artist is the modeler of forms out of raw and inferior matter; artistic creation is the action of a superior demiurge, whose genius is capable of doubling nature, through the rendering of the naturalist language of vision. The classification imposed by the notion of form is recognizable in a whole range of highs and lows: active and passive; father and mother; limited and unlimited; odd and even; light and dark; order and chaos; determinate and indeterminate; good and bad. And in all those pairs, the categories are "hierarchical, rather than symmetrical, the first being superior, just as form and matter are both necessary principles but form is higher" (Summers 1994b: 398). In its essentialism (what describes it but essence?) form is by nature exclusive and segregating.

With acuity, Summers indicates that the understanding of form does change. During its long and influential course, form is turned into something more vital than shape; "the higher form was intelligible and was identified with essence or soul or end or idea and came to 'form' or inform the lower" (Summers 1987: 196). The pair form and matter eventually becomes the dichotomy subject/object. In the transformation, hierarchy persists. The object has to adapt to the ruling of the subject, not only as grammar compelled, but also in epistemological terms: Ideas presumably innate to the human mind are then seen as the source and warranty of certainty. To understand the import of this assumption, we should refer to the Cartesian formula: The thinking process, the *cogitatio*, is the source of the basic certainty of our existence; *cogito, ergo sum* (I think, therefore I am).

A new conception of vision can be perceived during this subtle mutation; and it challenges the traditional primacy of sight, for sight had been given a special place in the order of senses, since the Middle Ages and until the Renaissance. Sight was the "most mind-like of the senses" (Summers 1994b: 402); it was the sense that would reveal the intelligibility of experience. We can see how this was true in Augustine's discussion on time: The past is redefined as memory, the future as expectation, and the present as sight. Memory is inner visualization. Thus sight is the dominant sense. Even "the first appeal of speech was to the inner eye of the beholder" (Summers 1987: 39).

Cartesian optics rejected the dominance of sight. From then on, vision depended on the mind that interprets what was gathered through contemplation. The stimulated mind constructs its object: "Visual information is a code or a language the mind succeeds in understanding in its own terms" (Wilson 1993: 162). Form is made into a construction of the mind.

But it is in Kantian transcendental aesthetics that the formative nature of the mind finds its full expression; the phenomenal world is redescribed as a construction of a priori faculties. Form and matter are not the same as in Aristotelian metaphysics, but they remain forcefully active.

The gender bias still lingers. Summers asserts that in the next historical moment, in what became known as the Romantic legacy, the singularity of creative genius is depicted as a virile power, a masculine spiritual force. The inversion is startling. Once feminine, imagination matures into a driving generating force; but the armature of concepts—eternally present in art history, and composed of form and matter—is left untouched.

Only superficially, the most recent trend in art history, the "linguistic turn" presuming that art being language-like could be interpreted by linguistic categories, did effectively break away with the millennial tradition of framing experience in terms of form. This "linguistic imperialism" is in perfect accordance with the previous mutations of form as a descriptive principle of the visual arts. Language is arbitrary, or rather unmotivated, in relation to nature; and, in the Romantic legacy, conceptualized by Kant, art is also non-mimetic. The linguistic and the artistic experience are constructions following or departing from rules rather than a direct expression of natural reality.

In the case of linguistic experience, onomatopoeic signs are no argument against the arbitrariness of linguistic conventions. Onomatopoeic words are just marginal elements in language. The comparison of what could otherwise be seen as straight imitations of natural sounds, such as Sausurre's (1983: 69) reference to the barking of dogs in French language, *ouaoua*, when matched to its German counterpart, *wauwau*—bares evident sound differences. A linguistic sign is never directly motivated by its referent. Imitation of nature has no place in language-structures (*langue*). There is no necessary, natural, or imitative link between the linguistic sign and its significance. If that is the case, we are left with a fundamental definition of linguistic experience, whose transposition to the sphere of art will bring deep consequences. Language is pure order connecting sound and thought. The linguistic elements are part of a system giving "rise to a form, not a substance" (Saussure 1983: 111). Saussure's conception of language as form implies that, as a set of conventions, language is bounded to a community. The nature of language is considered social, not individual.

Summers (1982) had argued that conventions were central but hushed concepts in art history. Similar to the linguistic notion, in art history "convention is identified with the group, with 'them,' who are the natural enemies of the 'I'" (Summers 1982: 105). The mind, that was seen in Kantian terms as the dominion of the individual, forceful, and masculine genius, is transformed into a suprapersonal and collective force. For Saussure, semiology, the study of signs in the midst of social life, forms "part of social psychology, and hence of general psychology" (Saussure 1983: 15). Signifier and signified, acoustic image and concept, or else respectively matter and form, are "psychological, and are connected in the brain by an associative link; this is a point of major importance" Saussure (1983: 66) warns us. Yet, in language and art, the arbitrariness of conventions is in no way reduced to the free choice of the speaker and the creator. The individual is powerless to change and alter what is socially granted to him. This truism in linguistics may not be as rigid to art as it is to the speaker, nonetheless the manner in which the Romantic legacy defined genius is now displaced to social life.

Reading Summers's indictment of the constantly renewed form and matter polarity makes it difficult to agree with Ernst van Alphen's (1994: 271) claim that "Saussure's penetrating radicality concerning the arbitrariness of the signifier-signified relation" can be an alternative to the traditional impasses in the interpretation of images. Clothed as novelty, Saussurian conventionalism, like other modes of conventionalist solution, is a truly an old-fashioned approach.[16] The same criticism can be raised against any conventionalist

---

[16] Saussure has roots in nineteenth-century thought. Aarsleff (1982: 356–371) revealed the depth of Saussure's debt to Hyppolite Taine (1828–1893). Several of Saussure's notions defining language—the idea of linguistic value, signs as the joining of sound and

interpretation: feminist or otherwise. Concerning the first sentence in the editors's introduction to *Visual Culture*, "the academy is visibly changing" (Bryson, Holly, and Moxey 1994: xv), it must be remarked that it has not changed enough, not yet.

However reluctant Summers may be to believe that the simple excision of the concept of form can be of any good to art history, he knows that an alternative must be found. Some of Summers's latest publications (1986, 1991 and 1994a) are extracts from a manuscript in progress in which he shows concern not only with what he calls conceptual images, but also with finding a new analytic vocabulary for image interpretation. Conceptual images are a variety of artifacts produced at the margin of illusionist art; they are abundant in several cultures and can be seen in objects of use, ritualistic or not. To understand conceptual images, form is blatantly ineffective. Summers gropes for concepts that can lead him away from dominant naturalism in Western art. He contrasts substitutive images and planar ones. Substitutive images direct the gaze to the outside, whereas planar images are the construction of real spatial interaction within the configuration of the image itself. Planar images are indifferent to the depiction of the virtual space. In them, the outside space is self-contained within the picture.

An image can be free from strict reference to the appearance of the natural world that it could represent. The extensive use of split and bilateral symmetry, cutting across cultures so distant in time or space, is a crucial problem to be considered in the evaluation of images. It serves as a strong argument against the idea that conventions shared by a specific culture determine image making. The intermittent occurrence of symmetrical solutions means that images should not be reduced to either aesthetics or expression. Summers (1986: 34) contends that such visual patterning is "the result of the significance of operations within the conditions of the possibility of making images altogether."

The configurations of conceptual images shies away from naturalistic representations. Conceptual images disregard foreshortening or the modelling of visual appearance. They materialize a visual concept. Conceptual pictures

---

concept, collective structures forced upon the individual—are directly taken from Taine's work. Taine is also a decisive influence over Foucault. Taine's contention that each age has a dominant spirit is strikingly similar to Foucault's episteme. And "this mold was first of all formed by language, by what Taine in fact also called 'le discourse'" (Aarslef 1982: 23).

are mental constructions embodied in the immediate, preconventional properties fashioning images. Summers suggests that the mental nature of conceptual images originates in memory, rather than the direct perception of the natural world. The qualification and consequences of image as doing, as a product of actual handling, as "facture," "obviously related (like "artifact" itself) to the word 'fact'" (Summers 1994a: 592), are liberating. In this conceptualization, we do not find the constraints of illusionist tradition.

It is still early to pronounce a definite comment on Summers's accomplishments. He is perfectly aware that attempts such as the influential redefinition of T. J. Clark of "the history of art not as the history of forms, but as a complex history of codes" (Summers 1989: 389) are far from comforting. The reliance on code is no hedge against the stealthy resurrection of form.

Visual Culture collects the last breath of conventionalist interpretations of image. In this extraordinary book, Summer's "Form and Gender" signals the landmark of a new starting point, and for it another theory of signs is requested, capable of accounting for conventions, but not at the expense of everything. It is possible to compare Summers's quasi-morphological approach to signs, transforming themselves according to internal formal unfoldings, across time and cultures, with Moxey's idea of an active creative agency, undoing conventions, thus turning the world upside down.

The pairing of different conceptual solutions to the interpretation of images can be the condition for enriching the interaction of semiotics and art history. It is thus urgent to have a theory of signs capable of accounting for both the preconventional dimension of sign production and the transfiguration of conventions altogether. The dialogue of art history and semiotics will then begin.

CHAPTER 5

Heidegger Says Being, and Representation Is Dead

DURING his lifetime task of unveiling in awe the gaping abyss of metaphysics, Martin Heidegger (1889–1976) said little about fine arts. Scattered clues are here and there: comments on Greek temples, on Vincent van Gogh's painting of peasant shoes, a lecture on art and space (Heidegger 1976: 98–106), and also a clumsy effort in relating what he considered to be the wasteland of Abstract Art to man's spiritual slavery in a planetary atomic age (Heidegger 1957: 41); or passing remarks considering modern art as either destructive or obscure (Heidegger 1981: 64). But is that enough to consider Heidegger's reflections influential or even explanatory of a semiotics of image and the visual arts?[1]

This chapter will be worlds away from recent and apparently endless disputes about politics[2] in Heidegger's biography, such as the real meaning of

---

[1] David Kolb's review of the divided legacy of Heideggerian influence in America does not present a single reference on the impact of Heidegger over the philosophical treatment of the visual arts (Kolb 1991:140–51).

[2] This debate can easily produce astonishing absurdities, as we may see in Lyotard's argument about Heidegger and "the Jews." Lyotard tries clumsily to understand Heidegger's silence on the extermination of "the Jews," extending the definition of "Jews" to include a supposedly enlarged community of Others, a fictitious residue in the spirit of the Occident. "The Jews" are therefore everywhere; they are so dispersed that they can be indistinguishable and certainly forgotten. What is forgetting but a form of extermination? Talking of the general community of Others, Lyotard also talks of no one. Auschwitz is silenced in this far-fetched generality, and Heidegger rests in peace. Nevertheless, Lyotard rightly points out that Manichean judgments can be a serious obstacle to assess the German thinker. We should not trust the mistaken syllogism: "if Heidegger, then Nazi; if not Nazi, then [not] Heidegger. This alternative does not allow for thinking, rather it freezes everything in a position" (Lyotard 1990:51). But, on the other hand, wild generalization is just the easy way out for the surprise of admitting that a major thinker is involved in, and fascinated by, a great evil. It is sheer deception, what Lyotard (1990:59) does when he advises not to "mix Heidegger's thought with his

his 1934 resignation as the University of Freiburg's Rector. In here there will be no definite explanation for his joining the National Socialist Party. Was this a by-product of Heidegger's backwardness and political naïveté or was it a necessary unfolding of his philosophical premises? Was he an ordinary Nazi or was he trapped and ensnared by the intellectual dilemmas of his time and country? Did Heidegger's political options and convictions taint his thought? Was he an ideologue of Nazism or an irrelevant voice for his Nazi leaders? Maybe those are important issues to contemporary history of ideas, but for anyone closely interested in Heidegger's contribution to the understanding of the visual arts, if we take them as a point of departure, they may lead nowhere. Heidegger's theoretical standpoints must at first be considered as he stated them.

With Heidegger, traditional notions of interpreting a work of art are at stake. Interpreting is considered a violent act of possession, a misleading appropriation. Interpretation then becomes the easiest way to lead us astray from the essence of the work of art, for it belongs to the material nature of the art work to resist analysis. When we try to capture a work of art through interpretation, we lose it. It is an essential point of Heidegger's assumptions that if we wish to understand the nature of the work of art, we must primarily refer to its manifestation as a phenomenon. As a thing among the things of the world, the work of art manifest itself. For Heidegger, the condition to understand artistic creation is to establish the intraworldy principles of the art work. Heidegger considers this to be in fact the right way to approach artistic creations, as long as we ascribe them to the primal question of Being.

It is a constant demand of Heideggerian thought that we inquire into the nature of Being that articulates intraworldly principles. Ontological knowledge takes precedence over any other inquiry. For Heidegger, there is no issue more fundamental than inquiring into the manifold meaning of Being. It is the dominant task of philosophy to seek for the way of Being, but correctly approaching *things-in-being* from the point of view of Being. This distinction is clear in German: *Sein* (Being) and *das seiende* (beings); or in French, *l'Être* (Being) and *les étants* (beings).

"politics" and the sociohistorical context in which it played." And why not? Why should we screen away this important element in any investigation? Was not this precisely what Heidegger did to the metaphysical tradition?

What do we talk about when we talk about Being? For sure, something more than metaphysics. Early on, Heidegger stated that metaphysics is no more than a stage in the inquiry into Being. Metaphysics is a deviation responsible for the forgetting of the question of Being. So, if the effects of metaphysical heritage are accountable for hiding the true sense of Being, Heidegger sets himself on undoing their dogmas. The question of Being is essentially the question of Its history.

Heidegger's Way

Dorothea Frede (1993) argued that however conventional and undistinguished Heidegger's early monographs may seem to be, they must be considered important steps in his development. Heidegger's critique of empirical psychologism in *Die Lehre vom Urteil im Psychologismus; ein kritisch-positiver Beitrag zur Logik* led him to Husserlian phenomenology. It was a definite detour from Aristotelian conceptions of substance and their naturalist ontology. Heidegger's 1915 habilitation dissertation, "The Doctrine of Categories and Signification in Duns Scotus," only deepened his criticism of Aristotelian treatment of Being. He asked himself: Are the categories of Being read from Nature, or are they read into? If all "objects" depend on their meaning that is bestowed on them by the subject, and if they are always part of a wider network of referential totality, then it must be the philosopher's task to work out in what sense there is a structure of meaning that stands in relations or conditions what one might call the structure of reality (Frede 1993: 48). That was the first condition for Heidegger's later insight into the importance of language for the question of Being. Language, interpreted meaning and referred object did not mirror each other. Heidegger could then perceive that the antique metaphysical tenets of Aristotle's correspondence theory, or even Cartesian conceptions of truth as the adequation of things to thought (*adequatio rei et intellectus*), had to be abandoned. Our previous comprehension can easily take over our categorical objects and therefore drive us away from the true question of Being.

If there is no key for the structure of reality on strictly abstract terms, the solution inevitably arrives from the investigation of actual existence, in fact from the living human experience that created those categories. Phenomenology, as conceived by Husserl, was once again a possible shelter on Heidegger's path: "The Husserlian idea of an a priori pure grammar reigns in Heidegger's dissertation" (Pöggeler 1967: 31). With the difference that

Heidegger added historicity to living human experience. Living human experience is ultimately historical.

At first, everything seems to be in the right place. Phenomenological analysis of life conditions could well be the tool for criticizing metaphysics. Phenomenology returns to living experience, and this implies a suspicion of metaphysical tenets. To describe a phenomenon means to store away ontological debris. We should then have a clear recognition of Being in its immediacy: Being as it is there.

History was once more the great divide. Heidegger could not readily accept Husserl's option for Cartesianism. Heidegger felt that he should keep away from Descartes. Cartesianism was just another landmark in the road of metaphysics, a hindrance to any ontological investigations. As a philosophy emerging from the *cogito*, Cartesianism centered itself on the subject. Cartesian philosophy is a moment in what Heidegger presumes to be the long-standing history of forgetting Being.

Any knowledge deriving from a philosophy of the subject stops at the ontic level of a scientific project. Heidegger esteems Descartes as a philosopher of the Age of Representation. For Descartes, the world is figured as in a picture (*Bild*). The subject faces the object, and contemplates the world standing in front of a window. The world is an image (Heidegger 1962b: 136). This representational model transforms Being into a presence under the subject's gaze. Made into an image, the world's traces are persistence, immutability, and permanence. Those are attributes of entities. Only entities, never Being, should be manipulated at the subject's will.

Different conceptions of Being entail different ways of approaching natural phenomena. In a Cartesian conception, the world is duly understood in mathematical terms, for mathematics, with its project of permanency, is a presence under the subject's sight. Living entities are measured by numbers and spatial magnitudes. Numerical framework and axiomatic deductions unify experience. The Cartesian definition of truth as adequation would lead to the dead end of mathematical exactness. The result is a projection of mathematical properties over things; with it emerges the belief that the world is essentially mathematical. Scientific laws just discover the constancy of what could be ordinarily perceived as in a flux. So, the present rules over other time dimensions. Defined as evidence by Descartes, and considered necessary for any scientific project, ontic certainty, a mathematical derivation, obstructs the ontological revelation of Being. Also entrapped in metaphysical contentions, traditional theology conceives eternity under the form of the present.

Looking from the point of view of his critique of science and technology, or even considering his earlier judgement of Cartesian world ontology as defective (Heidegger 1962a: 128), we could not describe Heidegger's thought as a kind of anthropology, or even as an existential philosophy. Like everything else in any moment of the Heideggerian project, the phenomenological analysis of everyday life is conditioned to the unique priority of Being. The subject, a conjunction of ego and substance in the form of the absolute foundation, is not the goal of Heidegger's reflections. Contrary to Descartes, Heidegger does not rely on a hierarchy of distinct substances: *ego cogito* and *res corporea*. The subject is not detached from the world. It is precisely in the midst of his relation with the world that the subject emerges as a questioning being.

According to Heidegger, of all entities that can be analyzed, we are the ontological priority, the royal road for the understanding of Being. And this is so because the very act of asking about our own existence puts ourselves in question. No other entity in the world can do it. For the *Dasein*, in other words the Being that we are thrown in the world out there, and for the Dasein only there is the possibility of inquiring into Being. But we should learn how to think about the difficult question of Being in the right way.

If we want to understand existence in terms of Being, we have to confront a radical examination of existence itself. According to Heidegger, what metaphysics defines as existence is not fully existence, but a restricted form of "presence-at-hand." If it were the complete spectrum of existence, it could not be solely based on the philosophical premises of scientific thought and, therefore, its metaphysics. Metaphysics of scientific thought presumes a mutual and radical exclusion of the subject in relation to its object. For that reason, metaphysics does not cover the complete horizon of existence. It is obvious that Heidegger has to refuse to put the world in "brackets," as Husserlian phenomenology suggested. The solution lies elsewhere. Permanency, fixity and stability are instances of the present, exerting an unacceptable restriction on Being. Dasein's authenticity brings with it the extreme request of facing instability and finitude. Even in the early works that lead to *Being and Time*, the Dasein is not defined as living in time: It is time itself (Kisiel 1989: 15).

Time draws the horizon of Being. To ask about the nature of time is a form of investigating Being. Time and Being cannot be separated from each other; they are opened to one another. What is time? Unfortunately that is the wrong question. The aim of overcoming metaphysics demands another questioning attitude. It is a serious mistake to reduce time to any form of presence or substance. If time were something, our answer would immediately break time down to the dimension of an entity, ruled by metaphysical constraints of presence, certainty, and evidence. We cannot really say that time is. This form of the verb to be creates the distorted impression that the present is the reigning dimension of time. Linguistic utterances hinder the investigation of time and Being. There is a high price to pay for any imprecise formulation of the nexus between time and Being. When ordinary language talks carelessly about the question of time and Being, there is always the imminent danger of transforming them into fixed objects, into things. Neither time nor Being are entities or even substances. Here, language use must be careful. There is Being and there is time; but it is a serious mistake to say that time is, or that Being is. Time is not, time happens. In the same sense, Being is not: it cannot be defined in terms of presence and entities. Being is destined to happen; it is sent. So, time and Being are given. Their experience is one of revelation, as a truly bestowed gift. They reach us because they are in themselves a reaching (Heidegger 1978: 12).

Time cannot be understood as a sequence of measurable instants. Only the time of clocks and watches is composed of fixed moments in succession. The time of chronometers materializes the principle of time and Being as present. But time is more than a succession of *nows*: "we are still prisoners of the Aristotelian representation of time: succession, dimension for a quantitative or qualitative calculation of duration" (Derrida 1989: 92).

Time as a presence should be represented in a different manner. Temporal presence is simply different from the now and its wished-for precision. Presence implies a unified dimension. And this unified dimension will certainly include the absences that are past and future. Instead of exclusion, it should be mutual giving, conjunction of belongings, gathering of nearness.

Temporality must be other than spatial conceptualization. Time-space with its three-dimensions is apparently under the dominance of the present. Nevertheless, considerations over the strict nature of temporality can be surprising: "the unity of time's three-dimensions consists in the interplay of each toward each. This interplay proves to be the true extending, playing in the heart of time, the fourth dimension, so to speak, not only so to speak, but in the nature of the matter. True time is four-dimensional" (Heidegger 1978: 15). The giving opens up the fourth dimension. The presence of time should not be substantialized as the mere juxtaposition of unitary moments.

Those reflections on *Time and Being*, presented in a 1962 lecture at Freiburg, are a belated response to the fact that Heidegger left his *opus magnum Being and Time* incomplete. In *Being and Time*, he had declared that the understanding of authentic temporality comes from Dasein's possibilities. And by authentic temporality, Heidegger meant Dasein's projection of his fundamental mode of Being-toward-death. For Heidegger, the most important of human possibilities is death. Heidegger's famous contention that the Dasein dies alone deserves comment. Death as a lonely affair, as Edwards (1979) argued, is a senseless exaggeration on the part of Heidegger. More often than not, human beings die among other human beings; in fact, to die alone is the exception and not the rule; it is more frequent to die surrounded by the hubbub of daily life. The fact that the overwhelming majority of deaths do occur in public is no reason to consider them unauthentic; it would be just outrageous to disqualify them, either when it is an accident, an agony in hospital, a death in a battle-field or even a suicide. Suicide can be more than a strictly private affair: It can be a destructive message left for the living. In that case it would be a death for the other. If that is not what Heidegger meant when he declared the quintessential solitude of death, then what he seemed to imply is that death is a unique event. But any other event of human existence cannot be repeated. Singularity is not the exclusive definition of death.

What if Heidegger wished to convey that the consciousness of death is a distinctive human possibility? Once again, objections may be raised. We would then be hastily presuming what is sheer anthropocentrism and also unverifiable: That animals are not aware of the possibility of their death. Edwards (1979: 60) concedes this to Heideggeer, but how could animals be really ignorant of their finitude, if they try, when they can, to fly away from death in a natural environment where predation is so frequent. Heideggerians could reply, quoting their master, that death is an essentially human affair; animals perish: They have no idea of death (Heidegger 1971: 178). That would still be an insufficient argument: the fact remains that some thread of awareness is always there, lighting up the animal in flight from its predator. Perhaps it is very difficult to grasp the existential consequences that the awareness of death brings forth to animals, but we should not dismiss this awareness as non-existent. Or else Heidegger meant that death's uniqueness makes it impossible to represent, which is not true for there are all over cultures, verbal and visual imagery representing it. Or perhaps Heidegger intends us to realize that death in itself cannot be fully represented, but that is also true of any experience: Representations never completely capture what they mean to represent. Death may well be beyond any representation because it is a thorough annihilation.

When the Dasein is conscious of death, he forecasts his frailty, and understands his finitude and precariousness. At this moment, the Dasein experiences total temporality. Temporality is then a unity of diversities, something more than just the adding of past, present and future. The temporal unity projects each moment—either past, present, or future—beyond itself. Temporal unity allows the projection of each moment outside itself. In that sense, existential analytic hoped to reach Being through the interpretation of Dasein's structural possibilities. Thus, Being and Time would bring about a crossing of ontic and ontological possibilities. But Heidegger never showed the last section of the book, "Time and Being," that would complete the full circle of Being and Time. And by 1947, Heidegger published his letter on humanism to Jean Beaufret, admitting that, as a project, Being and Time would never be realized. The language of Being and Time was still loaded with insidious metaphysics. So, it was necessary to make a complete reversal, to do the turning (*Die Kehre*). As usual, Heidegger commanded the interpretation of his works. He provided the clue for a presumed unity of Heideggerian thought. The strictly existential analytic of *Being and Time* was left behind, and now the stress was on language.

Language is where ontological revelation takes place. A tense relationship prevails in language: With language, as with thought, there is always the possibility of illusion and error. Language creates Being, and at the same time language also makes it possible to lose Being (Waelhens 1971: 278). The representative character of speech is enough to put it under suspicion. Under the strictures of grammatical expression, Being waits to be revealed, coming Itself to language. Being is eternally under way to language (Heidegger 1977a: 239). It could be said that the unity of Heidegger's thought relies on the ontological question to be answered, but are we talking of unity, or of a dead end? How could the singularity that is the trace of the Dasein, in the form of its being there, be compatible with the utmost generality of Being that is even more extreme than any lower form of generality given by concepts or even by the representations in ordinary language? In existential analytic, generality was publicness, the they into which Dasein is thrown. Heideggerian existential analytic was concerned with singular positions of discourse (*Rede*), or with idle talk (*Gerede*). Now, the turning (*Die Kehre*) would be dealing with language (*Sprach*).

Heidegger's Crossroads

It is difficult to agree with Heidegger's contention that this turning (*Kehre*) does not arise from self-centered concerns. He argues that the turning is of primordial importance. Heidegger's system of thought unfolded itself naturally. His texts illuminate one another. "The Age of World Picture" (Heidegger 1977b: 115–154) showed that metaphysical principles are at work in the technological realm; and that technicity is not a neutral affair; it is a risk for the possibility of being human. Instability, frailty, and risk are also intrinsic parts of Dasein's destiny. There is always the peril for the Dasein to become a thing among things. Man can become an inert passive thing to be manipulated. Then, for lack of care, Being would be lost. Heidegger says with alarm that mankind ought to consider this threat seriously.[3] The ontological question remained a central part of Heidegger's concerns. But is the presumed unity of his concerns so inexorable, or is this unity a mere effect of Heidegger's direct influence over the overwhelming majority of his commentators? In reference to this question, Pierre Bourdieu (1991: 91) takes a precise stand, describing Heidegger's ontology as a political strategy, as the creation of a self-regulating system which adjusts itself to periods of deepened crisis; that is why Heidegger survived the Nazi regime, and its demise.

Heidegger took great trouble over the years to rectify himself. With Heidegger, the one who thought of Being as forgotten, too many things are always left behind: such as his intermittent references to German destiny as both an ontological prophecy and a political position. For Heidegger, a special brand of people, not incidentally creators in German, are assigned to guard the house of Being. Being talks directly to the elected, in German, through Germany. Germans are the chosen people. The leading role of Germany is undeniable: The world becomes historical throughout the nations in contact with the chosen

---

[3] Technology and its implicit metaphysics cannot be blamed for the evils of society. Evil derives from the social organization, from human interaction, not from any rational procedure, however much social relations and human reason may be welded. That is not to say that technology is neutral, but to see it as it is: an instrument of action, not the culprit, the cause of violence against anything, much less Being. Heidgger takes a clear stand against technicity, qualifying it as falsification, a veil. Scientific methods of measurement obscure the experience of Being. Science does not question itself: It appears under the guise of pure evidence and sheer technological empowerment.

ones. "The homeland of this historical dwelling is nearness to Being" (Heidegger 1977a: 218). It is surprising that, for so long, so many commentators have ignored all those clues, so evident all the time. Levinas (1989: 485) states clearly that he knew of Heidegger's sympathy for Nazi ideology from 1933. In his last interview, published just after his death, when he was 86 years old, Heidegger mentioned his political choices in the 1930s as an intellectual mission to reform the German University, also insisting that the Germans had the special task of saving Western civilization from the doom of technicity. Whereas Moehling (1981) faithfully echoed Heidegger's claim that he accepted the Rectorship as a rescue mission of German University, Ferry and Renaut (1990: 28) ridiculed this justification. As a counterpart of all this, Heidegger presumed a profound kinship between German language and the Greek language of philosophy, to the point of saying that even when the French start to think they speak German (Heidegger 1981: 64). Otherwise thinking would not be thinking. How can all this be forgotten? The choice of purifying Heidegger's text is more than just mere lip-service, it is heart-rendering obedience.[4] Never was jingoism so explicitly hidden.

And then, when Heidegger talks about rootlessness as a wicked trace of modernity, it is possible to see this as an innocent praise for the purity of the quiet and the solitude of idealized peasant life, shepherding Being, as well as an antisemitic figuration of the Wandering Jew (Bourdieu 1991: 57). Thus, if urban life is uprooted, it is associated with Jewishness, contrary to rural life, which is chosen to keep authentic values, so similar to Dasein's authentic potentiality-for-Being-as-a-whole, described in *Being and Time* (Heidegger 1962a: 349–380). Only in the tracks of German woods we are bound to find the clearance of Being.

Heidegger's thoughts are not as autonomous as he would like us to think, his contentions are constantly positions to be understood in relation to his contemporaries. Bourdieu (1991) mentions that Heidegger's book on Kantian metaphysics is more than a historical assessment of Kant. It is essentially a critique of Cassirer's Neo-Kantianism. Nevertheless, Heidegger heartily detested contextualization of his thinking. He considered such attempts as a conspiracy to bastardize his ontological efforts: useless sociologism. As a conjurer, Heidegger leads us to believe that his destination never really

---

[4] It is amazing to read Derrida finding an exquisite sense of humor—a wild, grave, and yet dangerous comicality (Derrida 1989: 68)—in Heidegger's dour remarks.

changed; the ontological goal persisted in his slow approximation to the truth of Being, and at the same time there was a radical rupture, an offshoot of the main road.

In *Being and Time*, Heidegger starts from ourselves as Daseins to access the meaning of Being. In the turning, Being manifest itself in language. In this new byway, Heidegger recognizes language as the undeniable event (Heidegger 1971: 193), where speaking transcends chattering. Language is defined as a call, where the diversity of thought and world is reunited. Language is more than naming. Saying is all-embracing; it is even more encompassing than naming. Naming is an instance of saying. Being is said and not necessarily named. If language were just naming, it would be weakened to remain as correspondence. Correspondence springs from the splitting of subject and object; it has vivid Cartesian overtones. Heidegger aims at something purer. Pure language surpasses designation. Bestowing, grounding, and opening are the essential features of language; those features are, at least for Heidegger, the opposite of correspondence.

The world is not there, before language, waiting to be designated. Language opens up the world, and so, in the opening of this world, things are called to light. The call of language "entrusts world to things, and simultaneously keeps the things in their splendor of world. The world grants to things their presence. Things bear world. World grants things" (Heidegger 1971: 201–202). One totality calls another: Language brings the world that bears things. Now language speaks and man should listen.

Language speaks through an internal dimension, beyond the adequation of subject and object, prevalent in the representational thinking of Cartesian correspondence theory. Through the interior dimension of language man becomes Being, thus responding to the ontologic demand of belonging to Being. Heidegger declares that this belonging is given to thought through the concept of *Ereignis*. Heidegger also asserts that he used the term in early unpublished manuscripts.

The concept of Ereignis should be approached with care. Linguistic difficulty in translating the word is just part of the problem.[5] Ereignis is a

[5] In the English translation of Heidegger's lecture "Zeit und Sein," Ereignis becomes the event of Appropriation (Heidegger 1972:19). The French translation sticks to the original word in German and just mentions in a note that the current sense of Ereignis is the event, what it arrives; Ereignen is "to let come to itself," in the sense of making it come to itself (Heidegger 1976:51). On the other hand, the Portuguese translation tries to

fuzzy concept; its fuzziness comes from the nature of Ereignis itself. As happened with Being and time, it is a vain task to try to define Ereignis with a direct answer. Heidegger's indirect answer outlines Ereignis as what determines the common belonging of Being and time. Ereignis must be conceived as the clearing where time and Being come to light in the manner of an event.

How could Heidegger conciliate his project of overcoming metaphysics with the unavoidable fact that he had to expresses himself in a language loaded with metaphysical assumptions? He felt he had to avoid precise definitions, at the price of pedantry or vagueness. If Heidegger had approached time and Being cautiously, defining them as happenings, with Ereignis, a condition for either time or Being, it could not be different. Ereignis occurs, appropriating. Ereignis could never be a kind of Being, but Being is a kind of Ereignis. Ereignis express a peculiar form of presence: anchorage and repose. Dominated by exclusive concerns with substantialized entities, metaphysical thought would never reach those conclusions. Therefore, Heidegger deemed himself liberated from the metaphysics in language. He could then announce his triumphant victory over the dominance of ontic permanence.

What does Heidegger talk about when he talks about language? What kind of language is he referring to? Ordinary language or something else? For Heidegger, the splendorous advent of Being cannot be housed by the chatter of ordinary language. Ordinary language with its logical and grammatical structures is closely related to metaphysics. Ordinary language structures experience according to the reductive mode of subject and object, adequate and interior to each other. Metaphysical conceptions present in ordinary language have tamed the revealing possibility of language. We do not see Being, we are condemned to the perception of entities. The metaphysical framework of ordinary language reduces every designation to an exclusive model based on ontic principles and the temporal dimension of the present. Whatever this brand of language ruled by metaphysics talks about, it will be in the image of entities, joining what ought to be kept separately. If we talked of nothingness, nothingness would immediately become something, as only entities could be.

---

respect the polymorphous sense of Ereignis; it is rendered as "acontecimento-apropriação," literally appropriation-event. Pöggeler (1975:172) mentions that with Ereignis, there is a whole new question: "The meaning of Being is thought of as the event of appropriation."

Entities and nothingness would be indistinguishable, and the discourse on nothingness then fails. That is the same conclusion that Heidegger reached when analyzing Being and time. Therefore, language must certainly be something else than ordinary language, drawing another perspective untainted by metaphysics. In this immaculate language, one could clearly see occurrences that ordinary language could not really talk about. To hear language is like locking over an edge when one is barred from even declaring that there is something over there. Through ordinary language, we perceive just echoes, rippling from the logical insufficiency of common talk about Being, time, and nothingness.

There is a linkage between what comes to light and transcendency. Anguish, as a non-determined existent, opens up nothingness. Anguish is not only beyond words: Anguish deletes the possibility of expression. Anguish is a fear in itself, a fear independent of any expression, a fear without a necessary counterpart coming from outside of the anguished mind, a mood without an object. In the state of anguish, pure Dasein (pure Being-there) is still at work, suspended, wordless. Anguish is its own self-expression.

Because correspondence is the unquestionable premise of unquestioning metaphysics, Heidegger feels all along that thinking is pure expression, akin to the lyrical poetry of Hölderling and Georg Trakl,[6] with no outside instances that could either refute it or verify it. Thinking becomes autonomous, and it is possible to infer its appropriateness from a self-referential criterion. That is why Heidegger was always so careful with providing himself the clues that would amend all the variations in his thought over the years. It is not only arrogance or stubbornness that leads Heidegger to recompose the apparent loose threads in his writings. For him, thinking was essentially a language creation. If that was originally so with the world, why not with thinking? Heideggerian thinking is ruled by internal cannons established during the utterance of statements.

---

[6] Thinking, art, and poetry should share the same ground. After his lecture "What is Metaphysics" Heidegger turned more and more to poetry, even if he himself suggested that, ever since his student days, he was under the spell of Hölderling's lyrical verses. Both Richardson (1963) and Bernasconi (1985) emphasize that Heidegger's "The Origin of the Work of Art" must be read in relation to his essays on poetry. Nevertheless, we may wonder if this primacy of poetry is an unsurmountable demand of Heidegger's thought, or if it just expresses a lack of interest in visual art on the part of his commentators.

Rorty (1991: 44) has a good point in saying that thought, in Heidegger, begins with a willing suspension of verification. There is no objective way in which one could distinguish useless subtleties such as "the presentness of factuality so characteristic of metaphysics from the presencing (*Answesen*) of Being." In fact, if Being cannot be figured out as a thing of the world, then how could it have been forgotten? If Being were a pure event, how would it differ from any other entity? We are on the verge of an unredeemable contradiction. But Heideggerians request us to be persuaded and seduced just by Heidegger's elocution. For a considerable number of followers, Heidegger's oracular words beget blind devotion. It must be enough for all interpreters that Heidegger himself considers a mistake to look for any confirmation of Being.

Ereignis, Anguish, self-questioning are symptoms of extremes that are not dependent upon external references or correspondence. Those symptoms correspond to each other and refer to themselves only. A thought is at its origin, and therefore essentially, a language performance, irreducible to the limits of ordinary language. Language, and no more than language, should prevail, lighting up the world in a state of perpetual self-reference.

Heidegger is completely against representationalism. His presuppositions are such that he is at ease in performing statements that are in direct confrontation with the traditional correspondence standard of being either truth or false. Heidegger's utterances are more of a biblical fiat, as in the case of God saying "let there be light" and the light comes about, with no interval in between God's saying and the existence of light. A pompous statement is just enough. The link between representation and experience is done away. There should be no break between representation and experience. Existence emerges from the act of performing self-referential utterances.

Heidegger's etymological analysis of what he presumes to be the guiding-words of thinking, such as λογοζ, φυζιζ, παρουσια, αλεϑεια, are an intrinsic part of his critique of representationalism. Words are not directed toward external references. It is a metaphysical illusion to think that predicates are out there, waiting to be seized. Therefore, language analysis can just hope to follow the traces leading to the glades where words originated. However exact, etymological analyses are of no proof-value. They are a linguistic abstraction, to which current language usage is both blind and indifferent. Etymological analysis can only provide the sacred ambiance of thinking, through the weaving of articulated linguistic remittances Heideggerians, such as Gadamer

(1975: 510), are satisfied with this, and may even think that this vindicates Heidegger's recourse to etymologies. There is no possible proof, no objective verification, nothing more than presumed "advance achievements of conceptual analysis" (Gadamer 1975: 92–93).

What is objectivity but a manner of articulation, a form of binding? So, meaning is tied to what is judged as well as the act of judging itself (Heidegger 1962a: 195). To predicate a quality about a thing of the world is nothing like referring to a representational meaning. Predication lies within the entity itself. Assertion does not put forward external predicates of intraworldly beings. What is made accurate is not the external predicate. Accuracy in terms of language is not a relationship of correspondence, it comes from intrinsic bindings visible in the world. Heidegger then postulates that an assertion is a conception. When one says "the hammer is heavy," it also meant that "heaviness belongs to the hammer," or that "the hammer has the property of heaviness." Linguistic statements are developed means of conceiving and judging (Heidegger 1962a: 199).

Heideggerian Games

With this in mind, we can approach Heidegger's lectures delivered around 1935 and 1936, and collected as "The Origin of the Work of Art" in *Holzweg* (1950). However much we may consider them a landmark in Heidegger's famous reversal (*Kehre*), the style of those lectures is typically Heideggerian and their starting point is a question about the very existence of art. Gadamer (1985: 51) was there in Frankfurt at the three-hour lecture; and mentions that Dolf Sternberger, reporting the event for the *Frankfurter Zeitung*, called it "The Deserted Landscape." But Gadamer thinks that the negative reaction could only be ascribed to the deformed view of a journalist. Philosophers should think otherwise; so, for Jacques Derrida (1978: 24), "The Origin of the Work of Art" is one of the last great discourses on art.

By origin what Heidegger has in mind is really "the source whence something springs; that which renders it possible for a thing to rise up (*entspringen lassen*) as what it is and how it is" (Richardson 1963: 403). Heidegger refuses to see the work of art in either Romantic or psychological terms. The work of art is more than just the display of genius, or even the subjective expression of psychological drives determining creation. As forms of subjective individualism, Romanticism and psychologism are genuine offsprings of metaphysics. If it is not the artist who makes the work of art, is it the other way round, the art work making the artist? There is now a suspicion that we are going round in circles; the artist and the work of art may well be existences of the same kind. Then the origin, as the source of essence and nature, lies elsewhere.

The center of everything is art itself, the original event that creates both works and their artists. Also, if it is the case that art exists, being not just a word or an empty abstraction, then art ought to be a real presence engaged there in the work of art. In this way, Heidegger takes a definite stand, defining art in the strict terms of the work itself. So, art is to be revealed primarily through the work and its properties as a thing-in-the-world.

Things are singular occurrences in the world, and around them properties are gathered. That forces us to take art in its final materiality. Works of art have the attributes that things have. It is as material events, as self-sufficient presences (Heidegger 1971: 29), that they present themselves to our contemplation. Art works must not be understood as modes of representation. They do not represent. They are. And one consequence of this is that Heidegger's essay on the origin of the work of art is not only about the original source of art; it is also about the end of art (Bernasconi 1985: 36). Heidegger (1971: 76) acknowledged that "the beginning already contains the end latent within itself."

The art work does not portray anything. It exists and its existence is defined as a gathering. Heidegger's reflections could not ever be called a philosophy of art, except in the vaguest way. Representation and interpretation, as central categories of philosophy, are absent in it. This is spread all over in Heidegger's works. Even language cannot be represented. Hence Heidegger condemns translations from Greek originals into Roman-Latin. The nature of the ideas disappears when transposed into another language. Their essence is distorted; authenticity is lost. There is no way in which we could translate or even interpret without distorting their self-contained occurrence. Translation is always a deformed interpretation.

The work of art reposes in its materiality. The art work is a thing in the world, resting upon and springing from the earth. The Greek temple fits in the surrounding landscape, and simultaneously creates a unity transcending its strict existence. When a beholder faces the temple, he recognizes the multiple forms of life, birth and death, calamity and grace, victory and fall, endurance and dwindle, shaping human destiny (Heidegger 1977a: 168). Most likely, Dreyfus had this passage in mind when he wrote that the art work cannot exist alone.

Through its worldly aspect, the work of art solicits culture to make its working explicit and encompassing (Dreyfus 1993: 300).

Does the temple represent cultural values? Is it a representational construction? Heidegger would certainly answer no. It is part of the nature of the work of art to bring forth the totality of existence, in the same way that language reveals existing things. In Heidegger's lecture on art and space, sculpture plays the same role as the Greek temple; it is there, and its existence aggregates the surrounding space. In this space, places erupt and sacredness comes forth or then hides out (Heidegger 1976: 102). Now things existing in space can belong to each other, living in this discovered clearance.

As an original element of this process, earth is more than just physical nature; it comes forth and shelters. But earth does not repose quietly in its *quidditas*. Earth strives perpetually against the world. The world shows reluctant earth. The source of the art work is simultaneously creation and preservation (Stultberg 1973: 263); the world creates and earth preserves. Thus, we can recognize universality in this struggle between world and earth; but, at the same time, the world disclosed in the work of art brings with it a concrete, historical, and particular intelligibility (Walhaens 1971: 289).

Earth and world are different from each other, and therefore inseparable: "The world grants itself on earth, and earth juts through world" (Heidegger 1977a: 172). In the same way that everydayness was an event of the world to be structurally analyzed in *Being and Time*, now, at the turning, materiality, a counterpart of everydayness, shows itself as the immediate appearance of art works. Nevertheless the art work has another role other than existing there, resting upon earth. Through the work of art emerges what Heidegger presumes to be the evidence of an original happening. The art work blazes, as a thunderbolt reveals the articulations hiding in the dark, where the totality of existence is appeased. Then, we can see the totality of earth, that otherwise would be self-concealing. Earth resists the manipulation of the world set up by the art work.

Heidegger's arguments overcome the initial definition of the work of art as a thing in this world, a thing among things. Now Heidegger examines how the work of art is simultaneously made into a thing, so distinct from any non-fabricated natural happening.

The work of art is made. But is it something to be used? Functions rule things of use. What is the function in an art work? When we talk about function, we are immediately thinking of tools. Things of use are different from things of the world in general because they are more than just material occurrence. Does this mean that in things of use, form is a major concern? Heidegger considers form a concept overloaded with metaphysical implications. Form should be superseded as a concept. It belongs to the same Aristotelian tradition tarnishing time that Heidegger wished to be refuted in *Being and Time*. Form belongs to a theory that emphasizes substance as the immanent cause to which things in their intimacy were given. If we abandon form and stick to thinking usefulness, we will see that usefulness is a formative act and a choice of material, this in itself an act. Matter and form are grounded in usefulness (Heidegger 1971: 28). Usefulness, as a worldly act, informs earthly materials. When tools are made, materials that arose from earth become artifacts. This is the classification of *Vorhandeinheit* and *Zuhandeiheit* that Brandom (1983) considers central categories of being in Heidegger's fundamental ontology. In the face of a produced tool, there is no reason to speak of isolated form and matter.

In a world swayed by tools, necessary for human survival, what role does a work of art play? To answer this, Heidegger turns mimesis inside out. The proper way to deal with it is not to go from the thing to the art work, but to go from the work of art to the thing. Strictly speaking, in Heidegger's contentions, some form of ambivalent mimesis is still there, even if reformed, and even if he took great care to dismiss it as an outdated conception (Heidegger 1971: 36).

The work of art does not entirely mirror the represented thing. Heidegger wishes to produce a theory of truth, possibly a different type of theory of truth, free from standards of correspondence. Heidegger wrongly believes that all analogical representations are coarse correspondences. In fact the analogical faculty, from which all imitation springs, is more than servile copy: It is responsible for creative processes that reconstruct the world. Nevertheless, Heidegger insists that any kind of correspondence is an unredeemable mistake. How is it possible to think of reality after Berkeley's *esse-percepi* that identified the physical and the psychical worlds (Heidegger 1973: 64)? Is reality unreachable, is it an illusion or can we posit it?

Heidegger denies a transparent and mirror-like relationship between representations and the outside events. He cannot accept the Husserlian notion of a pure ego a matching understanding with cognitive objects.

Truth must be somewhat different from mimesis. Truth transcends the representational framework of Cartesian correspondence theory. A work of art is supposed to be an act of revelation, an ontological event, beyond the authority of things and their effect of correspondence. Heidegger asserts that it is feasible to perceive reality from the contemplation of art works such as Vincent van Gogh's painting of peasant shoes. The work of art does what any expression ought to do. It does not imitate external events; it appropriates reality; it shapes a self-contained occurrence. When language names a thing of the world, it does more than just designate through correspondence. The expression takes hold of what is designated, and so Heidegger (1977a: 154) asks: "Is the structure of a simple propositional statement (the combination of subject and predicate) the mirror image of the structure of the thing (the union of substance with accident) or could it be that even the structure of the thing as thus envisaged is a projection of the framework of the sentence?" In the same way, van Gogh's painting is laid upon reality, disclosing a particular mode of being without the metaphysics of subject and predicate, substance and accident, form and matter.

Expression betokens existence. Is that an illusion? Or can we substantialize existence from performed expressions? A statement that predicates something suggests existence, but it does mean that what it describes must always apply to something actually existing. Heidegger believes that it can be a description without a fact, like so many fictional constructions; in this case there is no possible criterion that could drive us out of this self-contained, self-referent expression. We either take it or not.

When Heidegger talked of Being, he suggested the possibility of saying "Being" as an indication of existence, when in fact is an extrapolation of its function as a linguistic and logical operator; "being" is just an operator that allows the performance of an expression and does not warrant an object as existing. We are now following Edwards's (1992) critique of Heidegger's premises. Existence is a logical presupposition in any utterance, but it cannot have the same status as facts. Existing objects are physical, but existence in itself is irreducible to physicality and actuality. Actuality would be a kind of existence, in fact an indexical existence. As a condition for facts, existence belongs to another level, distinct from actuality. It is difficult not to agree with Edwards's contention that Heidegger makes the cardinal mistake of forcing physicality into existence. From a different point of view, but equally relevant, Kahn (1973: 416) concludes, after careful analysis of the verb "be" in Ancient Greek, that there is a striking disparity between the conception of Being in Greek philosophers and *Sein* in Heidegger. Greek philosophers and the early Heidegger are talking of different things. Any existential starting point is incompatible with Being as such, the non-personal form constantly present in the primordial Greek thinkers. The confusion is absolute: for Heidegger, "is" as predicative becomes indistinguishable from "is" as identity, and also from the "is" of existence (Edwards 1992: 459).

Heidegger's vague formulations leads him to substantialize existence without things, derived from the autonomy of expression without referents, that nevertheless forges the impression of existence itself. It is Heidegger's demand that we must be in a Godot-like situation, waiting without something to wait for, a search without an object and yet a good search. Heidegger tries to console us, saying that this is the authentic task of thinking. It is this or to be trapped by the shackles of representational thought.

To overcome representationalism we must admit more than just the autonomy of expression, as something that cannot be subsumed in any mode of referentiality. It is another framework defining reality, an imposition on external things and events, exclusively determined by internal rules of expression, autonomous and forceful enough to substitute with its presence any referred object. In that case, expression will be an event as real as any other fact. A work of art exists with the same status as other independent objects of the world, either tools or natural things. That seems to be a radical departure from mimesis.

Tools, natural things and works of art are independent from references. They exist on their own. Are they mimetic? Do they comply with analogical conditions that direct our gaze to look at external references and pictures in a similar way? Is that enough to overcome mimesis completely? Certainly not; the same analogical process is at work whether looking at pictures as an adequate pictorial expression presented in front of our eyes; or whether looking at things from what pictures showed us.

A significant part of Heidegger's conference "The Thing" seems to stem from Johannes Vermeer's *Maid Servant Pouring Milk*, a painting done around 1660, shown at the Amsterdam Rijksmuseum. One may wonder if Heidegger, who admitted to Schapiro (1968: 205) seeing van Gogh's peasant shoes in Amsterdam, did in fact see Vermeer's painting. Nevertheless the definition of a jug as thing finds its expression in Vermeer's maid looking attentively to milk outpouring from the jug and flowing into another clay vessel. The jug is really a vessel, whose function is to hold anything (Heidegger 1971: 168). And the attentive maid regards the jug a vessel; she is carefully holding the jug with both hands. Through Vermeer's painting the jug-character of the jug is not concealed anymore. The only difference is that Heidegger talks of wine and water, never mentioning milk. This iconographic source has gone unnoticed up to now.[7]

Mimesis is more than copy; the notion of revealed truth becoming and happening in an art work is quite distinct from the mimetic grasping of essential properties of natural objects. The work of art is considered mimetic because it is self-subsisting as any mode of existence; or, in Heideggerian jargon, it is the totality of the earth and the creation of the world.

Heidegger's notion of mimesis claims to be essentially different from traditional notions of mimesis. It does not rely on correspondence with what is sensorially perceived or even rationally inferred from the outside world. And without an idea of correspondence, mimesis stops being a philosophical category offering a representational norm. Heidegger glorifies self-reference: an immersion in itself regardless of any ideal norm for representing beings.

Therefore, Gadamer concludes that the play, as an effect of self-referred rules, becomes the key for understanding the being of art works. Now it is clear that Heideggerian thought is radically conventionalist. Playing a game extracts its *raison d'être* from itself. Playing is self-representation (Gadamer 1975: 97). Playing and art are self-absorbing events. When we are involved with them, we are unable to distinguish anything but their presentation closed within themselves. Playing and art work have structural similarities; they occur in an autonomous space, where self-absorption is both an effect of the autonomy of rules and a condition for its act of make-believe, setting up a world full of meaning in its own. Rosenstein (1976) and Fink (1966) express similar points of view about Heideggerian aesthetics. But Bossart (1968: 60) finds it necessary to establish a distinction between art and game: Playing a game is a socialized event; art erects a world of its own.

In a work of art, an essence is at work in the same way that self-referred rules create occurrences in playing. An art work is another proposition about the universe, substituting previous systems of representation. A new framework takes the place of another. Reference and correspondence with anything outside of the work are plainly secondary; they are sheer aftereffects. A work of art is more than just representation. If it were strictly representation, we could then

---

[7] Therefore, van Gogh's shoes are not the only use of illustration by Heidegger. If Derrida (1978:334) finds the use of van Gogh's painting ridiculous and lamentable, incompatible with Heidegger's seriousness and rigor, what would he make of this fragment in "The Thing"?

reduce its judgement to a criterion of right or wrong correspondence. When Heidegger talks about truth coming forth in a work of art, he surely means that the art work "opens up a whole world and sheds light on a unified whole of existing reality" (Jaeger 1958: 61).

For Heidegger, what an art work reveals serves as evidence that it is a source of knowledge, having little to do with ideas of mimesis as normative procedure. Mimesis as an aesthetic norm is nothing but a historical product on the brink of either extinction or disregard. Heideggerianism presumes that another kind of mimesis is at work in the becoming of an art work. And it is not a normative mimesis, but the production of Being coming to itself, entailing the very condition for representation, through the unity of man, actual existing things in the world, and Being. All of this is due to a discourse more primordial than any form of representationalism. Heideggerians firmly believe that it is the coming of Being (Brogan 1984: 355).

A Heidegger Not Heideggerian Enough

However much Heidegger tried to avoid the lure of representationalism, he was besieged by it. We may see his ideas in a straightforward representative relation to his time. Against his direct wish, Heidegger's contentions are also historical products. They do not arise in a timeless void. So to keep a full perspective of Heidegger's reflections on the work of art, we must remember that he shifted from previous concerns with existential analysis. Therefore, it is significative that Heidegger's piece on the origin of the work of art was drafted in 1935, approximately at the time when Hitler delivered his Nuremberg speech on art and architecture, demanding that art ought guide the formation of the new German Spirit. Heidegger was then thinking of German, and by extension Western, history in terms of Greek tragedies. And this coincided with Hitler's presumptions of providing the German people with new myths (Zimmerman 1990: 94). But Zimmerman is careful to make it clear that the convergence of Hitler and Heidegger is never complete. Both saw Greek architecture as the sign of a golden artistic age. Hitler requested that the political artist should help forge the "New Man" dreamt by National Socialism, whereas Heidegger clearly declared that no artistic construction could ever be totally free of the inevitable human frailty and finitude (Zimmerman 1990: 100). Heidegger kept a consistently critical attitude toward modernity. His apocalyptic views are incompatible with ideas of engineering a new breed of men, resulting from technological progress. Heidegger never looks toward the future. Hope was lost in an Edenic past. He is searching for lost authenticity in an age gone astray.

In another way a faithful defender, a good Heideggerian guardian, Derrida (1989) says that all of this ensued because Heidegger could never transcend some limits. It was as though Heidegger was taken aback by the very radical novelty of his own thinking. Some issues that should have been thoroughly examined to the point of clearing them were simply left unthought. What should have been a necessary critical deconstruction is left undone. Heidegger's attraction for Germanism is due in fact to his impossibility of overcoming the question of the Spirit (*Geist*). Otherwise unwanted residues crept up in his works, and he believed that metaphysical tenets such as soul, subject, spiritual values, essence, national destiny would in the end spiritualize National Socialism. Here we have subtleties: Derrida never states forthright, without tact, that Heidegger adopted Nazi doctrines as a result of his clinging to the old metaphysics of humanism; Heidegger reached for Nazi empathy as a result of a connivance with the spirit of his age (Ferry and Renaut 1990: 49). In the end, Derrida's extremely theoreticist explanation blames it all on a theoretical mishap. Heidegger got stuck in conceptions that, properly faced, should have been superseded. And this is not just the question of the Spirit of an elected nation, namely Germany. Heidegger's emphasis on the category of truth brought with it a heavy price to pay. Paradoxically, Heidegger's reflections on the work of art remained representational (Derrida 1978: 420), in spite of his partial critique of representationalism.

If Heidegger wanted to describe van Gogh's painting as an adequate means of revelation, duplicated in actual objects existing in the world out there, then he had some problems to tackle. His early criticism of representationalist conceptions slackened, driving him to an untenable contradiction. Following Heidegger's initial premises on representation, van Gogh's painting should be a unique event, and could not be considered representational because there is nothing in the world of existence to be fully substituted by it; and therefore, the proper way to deal with this picture is not take it as a direct reference to a singular pair of shoes, but rather as a clue for the understanding of the equipmental being of peasant shoes. In that case, there would be no direct reference to facts. But to reach the universal ground of this precise equipment, its universal essence, Heidegger sticks to a descriptive method very similar to phenomenological analysis. Bartky observes that in "The Origin of the Work of Art" Heidegger criticizes metaphysical conceptual schemes; and at the same time, trusts that a description of the art work will capture the essence of what is depicted, in an almost Husserlian manner. The painting spells the secrets of the world it reveals. The essence of the art work "can just be 'seen' by the receptive viewer" (Bartky 1981: 272).

Besides this methodological criticism, another serious reproach can be raised against Heidegger. Those are not really peasant shoes. If that is so, then Heidegger failed completely. It would then be no use to say that Heidegger's description is not an ordinary one, but it seized a more encompassing generality, the equipmental Being of peasant's shoes (Kockelmans 1985: 131), as the sign of Being's emergence. Nonetheless, there is no excuse. How could he be right about the universal essence of this thing, the peasant shoes, if Heidegger is wrong in identifying it as a thing of this world? Much to the irritation of a whole horizon of Heideggerians, this is what Meyer Schapiro (1968: 203–209; and 1982: 349–360) firmly maintained.

What is Schapiro's argument? In the first place, the theme of van Gogh's painting is not easily identifiable. Heidegger (1977a: 163) admits that the painted shoes are an image difficult to decipher: "there is nothing surrounding this pair of peasant shoes in or to which they might belong—only an undefined space. There are not even clods of soil from the field or the field-path sticking to them, which would at least hint at their use."

Then, how to proceed? An iconology should be deciphered in relation to other forms that could offer a more precise indication. It is part of any iconological presumption that we can relate images analogically to other images or to other sources. Thus, the key to an image may well be an element that is not an image, such as a literary, scientific, or philosophical text. The meaning of an image can be found in correspondence to other forms of expression regardless of any artistic or cultural evaluation. Analogy is not directed toward an external referent. Schapiro offers as a clue to van Gogh's painting Knut Hamsun's description of a pair of shoes in *Hunger*, a novel written around the time that van Gogh painted those shoes.

Other evidence shows the possibility that van Gogh painted his own shoes as a personal object and not an extolling depiction of rural life. The shoes belong to Van Gogh, and at that moment he was dwelling in urban areas (Schapiro 1968: 205). In 1886–7, van Gogh was living in Paris, away from Holland, not painting in dark colors subjects derived from Dutch peasant life. One of the paintings that Heidegger might have used as an illustration of his philosophical ideas was dated 1887. So, most likely the painting referred to urban and not peasant life. Van Gogh's image of peasant wooden shoes is formally different with a smoother painted surface. In a later picture of "a peasant's leather slippers, he has turned them with their backs to the viewer" (Schapiro 1968: 207). The shoes that Heidegger mentioned are there in front of us, facing the viewer, following a common pattern of pictorial truth, derived from the experience of an eyewitness, in front of things, like the painter facing both his canvas and his subjects.

In the same way, several of Hamsun's novels, such as *En vandrer spiller med sordin* (1906) and *Den sidste glœde* (1909), translated as *With Muted Strings* and *Look Back in Happiness*, the hero is a wanderer, with clear autobiographical characteristics. Van Gogh's shoes are also autobiographical, basically a veiled self-portrait, and rhetorically, a synecdoche. And more, Schapiro considers Knut Hamsun's description of shoes, the ghost of the wanderer's other I, as more adequate to explain van Gogh's painting, because van Gogh had also lived, during this period, the life of a drifter, roaming from place to place.

Even though Derrida criticized Heidegger's fall into a representationalist trap, he focused most of his assault on Schapiro. For Derrida, Schapiro jumped to an abrupt conclusion. Derrida argues: The fact that van Gogh lived around 1887 in Paris, far away from peasants, is not sufficient evidence to conclude that those shoes are personal objects. Van Gogh could very well have lived in Paris then, and still painted peasant shoes. What does really matter: the date of the painting or the painted picture? Schapiro reproached Heidegger's guess and at the same time raised his bid even more, coming to the wild conclusion that van Gogh painted his own shoes (Derrida 1987: 312). Derrida prefers to raise doubts. There is no way in which anyone, Heidegger or Schapiro, could be certain that this is a pair of shoes. Are they a pair? They are not a pair. Van Gogh painted two left feet of different pairs of shoes. Then, following Schapiro's biographytis, does that mean that they, a personal object, are a symbol of van Gogh's bisexual tendencies (Derrida 1978: 317)?

Derrida's ingenious remark avoids the question. It is ironic. Otherwise, it would confirm Schapiro's dispute that the shoes are van Gogh's self-representation. Derrida cunningly ignores the fact that Schapiro's argument relies also on other sources. It is as though Derrida skipped the end of Schapiro's text, where Gauguin, who shared quarters with van Gogh, is quoted as declaring that he heard the Dutch painter talk about a pair of shoes in their studio. They were van Gogh's shoes, and also a subject of a magnificent painting, a still life (Schapiro 1968: 208). With them, he walked to preach in Belgium, where he had taken care of a victim of a fire upon whom the doctors have given up. As if by miracle, the victim recovered, and van Gogh kept the shoes as an important memento of his life. Another version for the shoes, still personal objects, is told in Rotonchamp's Paul Gauguin 1848–1903; the shoes are the ones with which van Gogh walked from Holland to Belgium. In a 1981 post-scriptum to his essay, Schapiro (1982: 359) also notices that during a visit of Fanz Gauzi to his studio, van Gogh comments on one of his just finished shoe paintings, depicting a pair bought in a flea market. Whatever the case, the objects belong to van Gogh: They are not peasant shoes.

It is part of Derrida's argumentative strategy not to answer any question directly. Derrida takes a detour around the issue, while creating the impression that he has dealt effectively with the problem. A good example is the way he assesses Hamsun's description of the drifter's shoes as a personal object analogous to van Gogh's still life. Derrida then wonders if Schapiro knew that Heidegger mentions Hamsun in *Introduction to Metaphysics*, just before commenting on van Gogh's paintings (Derrida 1978: 432). But that is not the point. Derrida's commentaries are a choreography depicting the void. Schapiro did not presume any intellectual antagonism between Hamsun and Heidegger. What Schapiro did was to search in Hamsun for a clue to decipher the nature of van Gogh's painting. A better objection would be to question whether van Gogh ever read Hamsun. No way. That would be biographism, a criterion of verification unworthy of a deconstruction approach. Refusing to face the problem up front, Derrida brings to the foreground an irrelevant issue.

Derrida's arguments stem from a footnote of the editorial board of *Macula*, the journal where the French translation of Schapiro's article was published. *Macula* (1978, vol. 3/4: 6–10) points out that the American version of Hamsun's novel describes the wanderer's shoes as "they affected me, like a ghost of my other I—breathing portion of my very self." Macula translates this in the main text as "une partie respirant de moi-même," and simultaneously, in the footnote number seven as "une partie vivant de mon propre moi." In Derrida's comments, "the breating part of my very self" is exclusively rendered as "une partie vivant de mon propre soi," which is in fact "a living part of my own self." The translation is not altogether precise and it is curious that a presumed master of textual analysis, like Derrida, does not reproduce this ambivalence, sticking in the end to a biased rendering. "Breathing" could well refer to walking, the very action of van Gogh crossing countries, from Holland to Belgium, stated by Schapiro. Literally "breathing part" may be more appropriate than "living part," however near they may seem; but with this nuance, Derrida's claims for the undecidability of whether Hamsun's text refers to a presumed ghostly double of van Gogh or to Vincent himself are simply weakened. The choice of translating "breathing part" as "living part" leads our attention to the subject Vincent van Gogh and not to his act of walking. Derrida would rather resort to irony than face the issue. Irony is a false way of tackling the question. Then, Derrida diverts us to wonder if van Gogh's painted shoes are a mysterious gift from previous life, and therefore imputing an otherwise unthought of mysticism to Schapiro, or are they objects personalizing the painter? Now the issue is not whether Heidegger made a mistake in assuming hastily that those are peasant shoes. Heidegger is miraculously preserved. The issue does not allude to Heidegger anymore. All in all, Derrida produces a passionate defense of Heidegger (Crowther 1989: 273).

It is revealing that the vast majority of Heidegger's commentators avoided checking the appropriateness of his claims. Here there is more at stake than just a matter of minor detail concerning the false attribution of shoes, either urban or rural. If the kind of argument that Heidegger propounds despises external evidence as metaphysics, then what are we left with? Certainly the authoritarian expression of a master, *magister dixit*, that cannot be falsified, and in which we must trust. Through the master illumination comes.

Heideggerianism is a neo-scholasticism, or rather an up-dated patristic philosophy. Kocklemans (1984: 176), for instance, dismisses Schapiro's criticism. Kocklemans may even admit that Heidegger's contention is not without its problems. But that is all; he does not say what those problems are. Now Derrida comes handily and Kocklemans (1985: 126) tells us that "Derrida has effectively dealt with Shapiro's criticism insofar as it is without sufficient grounds," and not another word. In a later work, Kocklemans (1985: 126) returns to the issue, saying that Schapiro still thinks within the boundaries of aesthetics and the history of art, old-fashioned products of metaphysics from which Heidegger generously tried to set us free. Very few Heideggerians voice the possibility of Heidegger having taken a flight of fancy.

For Derrida, the dispute between Heidegger and Schapiro is futile. Then, why take a stand in favor of one or another? According to Heidegger, van Gogh's painting depicts shoes that worked in a field, whereas Schapiro sees them as city shoes, directly related to van Gogh himself. What bothers Derrida is that both Heidegger's and Schapiro's analyses are in fact related to referentialism and spring from "a desire for attribution" (1978: 297). Therefore, they are not talking about representational truth, Derrida consoles us: it is a matter of personal appropriation. No facts, or data could be applied to the painting so that truth could be determined about van Gogh's still life. All it amounts to is a personal choice of Heidegger and Schapiro. Heidegger identified himself with peasant life, and Schapiro with city dwelling, a personal homage to his friend Kurt Goldstein, a Jew like Schapiro. We cannot but agree with Carrier (1988: 220) when he says that "Shapiro had reason enough to criticize that detail in an essay in *Festchrift* for a refugee from the Nazis."

Derrida is unfortunately unable to see this. So the opposition between the authenticity of rural life and the lack of authenticity of urban dwellers lurks in his discussion of the problem. He asserts that truth is a foreign category to the debate. Derrida regrets that Heidegger could not get rid of it. Heidegger was not referring directly to one specific painting by van Gogh. Heidegger could not be interested in truth and therefore representation. His reflection was dealing with the truth of truth, which is a concern prior to representation, an indispensable condition for knowing what referring to means (Derrida 1978: 368). It is a pity that Heidegger did not perceive this.

Even if Derrida does not say it clearly, we can guess what his solution for avoiding representationalism is. Two of his four parts in *La Vérité dans la peinture* are samples of an extremely subjective mode of composition. It is again, an even more radical act of *magister dixit* disregarding any verification. After all, what matters is not truth, but, at the very best, sense. We are at the threshold of hallucinatory subjectivity. But, is it not a Heideggerian presumption that all forms of subjectivity come from metaphysics? So, if that is the case, does Derrida overcome metaphysical tenets?

Derrida puts himself consciously at the center of his own conceptual drift. He just refuses to write interpretative essays on art, whether about a contemporary painter such as Valerio Adami, or Gérard Titus-Carmel's exhibition at the Center Georges Pompidou.[8] It is very significant that Derrida records his puns and metaphors on those artists in a diary form. Why should we comment on those pieces? The texts are rather interventions where Derrida's very performance should be enough to produce our naïve and pious recognition that his act of saying causes immediately what he said. All along there was no need for illustration of any sort. Images and writing have similar autonomy. The central metaphor of the visual arts is a painter looking at a mirror, but hoping to be dazzled and blind. It may seem that he is painting a self-portrait to be seen by whoever faces the final image, but in fact this is a self-referent and paradoxical situation: "seeing-oneself-being-seen-without-being-seen" (Derrida 1991: 84).

---

[8] It is difficult to agree with Podro's contention that those pieces are ephemera (Podro 1988:438). They stand as Derrida's alternative to traditional philosophical concerns with truth in painting: something that Heidegger could not do.

If Derrida is right, truth-values are pointless considerations. Disregarding that, Heidegger could never be the undertaker of mimesis as correspondence, thus missing the chance of closing down the longest-standing tradition in the history of our representational arts. Heidegger should have known better.

PART 3

Extreme Visions

CHAPTER 6

Tell Me What You See, Rrose Sélavy Retina Denied

THE QUEST for Marcel Duchamp (1887–1968) is endless. We are still learning how to cope with his provocative example. What to do with an artist indifferent to art, a painter who not only searched for painting beyond retinal solutions, but took pride in abandoning the Fine Arts? Of all possible emblems of artistic activity none is more intriguing than Marcel Duchamp. As early as 1934, in "Phare de La Mariée", André Breton (1965: 86) saw Duchamp's work as a result of a methodical denial leading to a rare kind of production, both in the sense of inventiveness and scarcity. With Duchamp, art should come to a necessary end. Nevertheless, there we are, talking of him as nothing more, nothing less than an artist.

Aloof to the point of being compared to a Bizet character, adored but never seen (Waldberg 1976: 99), Duchamp is the object of Thierry de Duve's (1991) *Pictorial Nominalism*, a dense and challenging book to be approached with care. Is it possible to interpret Duchamp with a psychoanalytic concepts? At first sight this is a difficult task: Marcel Duchamp refused the idea of art as a personal stylistic expression. Even his mechanical drawings, paintings of precision, could be tactics of concealment.

As if to remind us of the clear enigma of stars up above, Duchamp is prone to countless interpretations. There is a reason for this. The end product of his actions was astonishing. Not even the tag of avant-garde is sufficient to describe what he did. Art would be denial and denial would be art: How about making a reciprocal readymade, using a Rembrandt as an ironing-board (Sanouillet and Peterson 1975: 32)? A urinal signed by Duchamp as R. Mutt was turned upside down and then titled *Fountain*. In 1919, Duchamp drew a goat beard and handle-bar moustaches on a reproduction of Leonardo's Mona Lisa, writing at the bottom of the picture L.H.O.O.Q. These letters are read phonetically as *elle a chaud au cul* (literally "she has a hot ass," meaning she is a horny piece of ass.)

Readymades are not crafted works of art, but objects elected to be effects of omnipotence. Art would be an act of choice. To choose implied a decisive extension of authorship, a logical consequence of designating. Those gratuitous act of choice brought with them a critical stamp. The readymade is a refusal. An industrialized object is chosen to be a work of art. We cannot relate this object to any criteria of skill, taste or even style (De Duve 1994: 110). In one of his notes, Duchamp asked: "Can one make works of art which are not works of art?" (Sanouillet and Peterson 1975: 74).

Duchamp was not safe from his own ironical squads. He was not even himself. At a certain moment, he became Rrose Sélavy. Authorship inevitably faded away. In the same way he chose objects that were then ranked as works of art, Duchamp assumed a new identity to be kept throughout his productive life. No more fixed identity but simultaneous becoming, without limits, growing beyond his proper name, existing freely. There is an analogy between the change of identity and his previous *oeuvre*. He was transforming and changing himself in a way analogous to his pictorial concern with movement.

Movement was not restricted anymore to painting as Duchamp did in *Nude Descending the Staircase*. In the series of *Nudes*, the movement was already represented conceptually. The transition of the body, or bodies, moving was expressed semiotically as a line. A body dislodged itself from one place to another. And the space was crossed by lines indicating simultaneous expression of the movement. Duchamp saw clearly that movement resulted from signs in action that the viewers would convene in their mind. Dressed up as Rrose Sélavy, Duchamp could display indices that would transform him into a suppressed self.

In 1920, Marcel Duchamp adopted the identity of Rrose Sélavy, a feminine entity derived from Udnie, imagined by his friend Francis Picabia (Lebel 1959: 46). Picabia had asked his pals to sign one of his paintings, including Marcel. Duchamp remembers that he wrote *Pi Qu'habilla Rrose* (Cabanne 1972: 101). Then, Duchamp was photographed by Man Ray, cross-dressed as Rrose Sélavy. Duchamp signed works under the adopted name. He published puns attributed to Rrose Sélavy: "Oh! douche it again... Oh! do shit again!" (Sanouillet and Paterson 1975: 115). In those sentences, like so many of Rrose Sélavy's puns, there is no stable sense. The reader goes backwards and forwards, free from pre-established meanings. Contradictory meanings are displayed. This is what Duchamp created by drawing a beard and moustache in the archetypical feminine figure of Mona Lisa.

If we look at the scholarship on Duchamp, we find a standard critical answer for such puzzling changes of identity. In the end, everything relates to esoteric intentions. This act of impersonating a female role represents the alchemical purpose of reconciling contraries. Archetypes repeat themselves to exhaustion. Arturo Schwarz (1973) presumes that Duchamp developed linearly the themes of esoteric initiation. In the painting entitled *The Bush*, as early as 1910–1911, he represented the initiation of a neophyte. Hands are placed over the novice's head. This is a residue of Hindu iconography. In the background, we can see The Tree, The Apple Tree, with the mystical charge always presented in religious systems all over the world.

Considering another work made in 1911, *Young Man and Girl in Spring*, Schwarz (1973: 7) again recognizes esoteric iconology in Duchamp's paintings. The figures in the foreground are a couple, Hero and Virgin, united by the effort of reaching the Tree. The effort shows them in a special position where we can identify, in the shape of their arms, the letter *Y*. Undifferentiated physically as a young man and a girl, for we only learn this from the title of the painting, those figures try to reach the bliss of immortality, manifested as the conjunction of contraries, represented as the unity of the androgenous. The letter Y stands for immortality and resurrection. We can see again the recurrence of contraries joined. Rrose Sélavy was just another step in this direction.

Esoteric sources could be the real answer to Duchamp's enigma. Then, Schwarz takes a bold new step. He figures the persistence of this theme as a sublimation of Marcel's incestuous passion towards his sister Suzanne. *Young Man and Girl in Spring* was a wedding present to her. In the back of the painting, Duchamp wrote: "To you, my dear Suzanne."

Arturo Schwarz uses a blend of esoterism and quack psychoanalysis to interpret a fact mentioned before by Robert Lebel (1959): Duchamp and his sister were very close in their youth. The psychological power of the incestuous matrix is responsible for a constant repetition in Duchamp's oeuvre. By 1919, Marcel Duchamp sends instructions to his sister to make the *Readymade malhereux*, a wedding gift. She, as The Bride, must hang in her balcony a geometry book, a memento of school days, that would then suffer the action of the weather. The geometry book stayed outdoors until its complete destruction. Schwarz stresses that several of Duchamp's readymade were all presented as hanged.

The passage from archetypes to individual traits of Marcel Duchamp was searched with diligence and delirium. For instance, Calas (1969) remembers that Ulf Lind saw the word *même* (even) in the title of Duchamp's magnum opus, *The Large Glass*, *La Mariée mise à nu par ses célibataires, même* (The Bride stripped bare by her bachelors, even), as a reference to another homophonous words *m'aime* (loves me). Duchamp could be one of the Bachelors.

The Large Glass should be considered a by-product of an image to be found in a book known by Duchamp during his work at the Saint Geneviève Library. The book was *Alchimie* by Eugène Conseliet. It displayed an illustration of a text by Solidonius. The illustration showed an analogy between the stripping of the Bride by her attendants and the Sage stripping the philosophical stone. Duchamp's Large *Glass* is, therefore, the revelation of the precious knowledge. The picture keeps the admirable colors of the philosophical stone in the Glass's splendid transparency.

Esoteric interpretation keeps going on without refrain. Calas also finds keys for the interpretation of *The Glass* in the Tarot. The Bride, the hanged form in the upper part of Duchamp's *Glass*, refers to a Tarot card, The Hanged One, *Le Pendu*. The card suggests something unbearable that cannot persist and must change. Was Duchamp once again representing cryptically the incestuous passion for his sister? Can we know such personal secret from archetypical esoteric contents?

Arturo Schwarz (1974) claims that it is possible. Let us consider three pseudonyms adopted by Duchamp: *Marchand du Sel* (Salt Seller), Rrose Sélavy and Belle Haleine. Marchand du Sel and Marcel Duchamp stand one another as mirror-images: opposites reflecting each other. We will find the same structural thought in the remaining pseudonyms. Belle Haleine (Beautiful Breath) is a mirror transformation of homophonous words: Belle Hélène (Beautiful Helen), the Trojan mythological character. Schwarz indicates that Hélène has some striking similarities to The Bride. Hélène maintained an incestuous relationship with Deiphobus, brother of her first husband. Also, Hélène met a tragic end; she was hanged from a tree. Esoteric symbols appear once more. Duchamp produced a readymade called Belle Haleine, Eau de Voilette (Beautiful Breath, Veil Water), a label for a perfume bottle, which showed his picture dressed up in Rrose Sélavy's attires. Are we, therefore, authorized to detect in Duchamp living a female role an identification with The Bride?

Arturo Schwarz traces further associations. On the label of the perfume bottle it is written Eau de Voilette (Veil Water), instead of Eau de Violette (Violet Water), referring to both The Veil, characteristic of The Bride, and to the process of reaching Truth as unveiling. This Truth is only for esoteric novices initiated into Alchemical secrets. In that case, Truth is transparency, the very substance of the *Glass*. The act of taking up a feminine entity implies the conciliation of contraries. The Bride and the Bachelor are a unity (Schwarz 1974: 32). Rrose Sélavy and The *Glass* are developed from an alchemist's conception of Truth.

Thierry de Duve is hard on esoteric interpreters of Duchamp. All of them, from Schwarz to Calvesi (1975 and 1984), are dismissed as mystifying, sterile, and gratuitous (De Duve 1994: 9). However, De Duve sees some grain of truth in Schwarz's indication of the Bride/Bachelor problematic in a repressed incestuous desire of Duchamp for Suzanne (De Duve 1994: 44). Nevertheless, there is no real reason to state that the incest theme must be taken as the central motif of Duchamp's works.

Esoteric interpretations verge on far-fetched abuses. Calvesi (1984) thinks that his spotting of alchemical symbols is more than analogical findings. Duchamp should have been involved with esoteric initiation, even if Duchamp denied any alchemical practice. He said to Lebel (1959: 73): I could only do alchemy in the way that is admissible nowadays, without knowing it. Nothing deters this kind of interpretation. Analogies strike us as sufficient. The conclusions ring both inevitable and necessary, as in syllogisms. It is true, like Breton said, that Duchamp's *oeuvre* prefigures Surrealism. Therefore, Duchamp is a surrealist. If his works are surrealist, they function according to occultist practices, as an expression of alchemy. If his work is alchemy, then Duchamp was initiated into esoteric rites (Clair 1978: 93).

Art and Freudian Psychoanalysis

There is an evident contradiction between esoterism and the kind of disclosure presumed by psychological theories. If occultist interpretations were right in associating Duchamp's works with esoteric practices, then he would have produced art in such a manner as not to reveal anything of his personal life. Duchamp would have created with the intention of concealing.

Freudian tradition considered art as an exclusive symptom of the maker: Depth psychology and its search for archetypes are useless (Lacan 1971: 154). Freud's theory reformulated the conception of biography.[1] From now on, we

[1] Yet Calvin Tomkins's (1996) biography of Duchamp written in a traditional format is much more revealing than any kind of interpretation presented so far.

find in art products the direct expression of mental processes, especially the ones that are part of the Primary Process (*Primärvorgan*) ruling the Unconscious (*Unbewusste*), whose psychic process runs free, moving without constraint from one representation to another. This conception allowed Freud to presume that dreaming is the representative satisfaction of desires. Art and dream representations are different from the Secondary Process (*Sekundärvorgang*) present in the Conscious or Preconscious system of the individual. The Secondary Process elaborates and disguises the flow of the Primary Process.

Similar to the dream, the art object unveils cryptically what should be kept shrouded. The expressive form of art products is directly related to whoever created them, however adjusted to the technical limitations and conventions of the arts. Representation displayed by Freudian aesthetics is exclusively based upon direct substitution. This is the only model that Freud judged appropriate (Baudry 1968: 82). Unfortunately, Freudianism presumed that in semiotic processes there is no other conception of representation other than symptom. Art is considered a text to be deciphered. Art works and dream works are translations of childhood memories and fantasies (Koffman 1973: 48). And myths are collective daydreams (Bakhtine 1980: 49).

Dreaming and artworks can appear to be senseless. In them something is lost. The very idea of the Unconscious implies the search for restoring the fragments of a lost text. The life of an artist haunts the work of art. The work of art is like a personal dream (Kaufmann 1974: 62). The genesis of any creation is its maker engendering the created world as a coherent and unique experience. A work by Leonardo is a key to Leonardo. In a letter to Carl Jung, in October 1909, after writing his essay on Leonardo Da Vinci, Freud boasts that Leonardo is not an enigma anymore (Gay 1989: 252).

After Freud's essay on Leonardo, psychoanalysis decided to examine artistic expressions as an artist's personal statements. Psychoanalysis enlarged its range of subjects. Cultural products, especially art and literature, became illustrations of psychoanalytic concepts and techniques of interpretations. The idea emerged that art is a non-neurotic, non-obsessive, non-pathological form of satisfying desires (Ricoeur 1969: 196). Art mediated the tense relationship between desire and reality.

The act of seeing a work of art serves as a satisfying complement in itself. The viewer identifies himself with the sign configuration produced by the artist. Creation and reception refer directly to each other. A new ground is open to psychoanalytic interpretations.

Nevertheless, we must keep in mind that Freudian concepts did not offer an original interpretation of art. Freudianism had very little to say about formal problems outlining Art as a semiotic activity. Freud thought his mission was to clarify psychological impulses, such as the reasons for Leonardo's sexual and artistic restrain (Freud 1973: 68).

In his essay on the Moses of Michelangelo, Freud admitted that he had no interest for formal and technical analysis. He lacked the necessary understanding (Freud 1973: 75). Freud's concern was to capture the intention of Michelangelo. As an intellectual objective, there is no real difference between this and explaining any other fact of psychic life. Moses is treated as a living person. How should we comprehend Moses's position holding the Tables of the Law? Is it the moment before an outburst of rage against the idol-worshipping crowd? Freud disagrees with this interpretation. Moses wanted to raise and express his anger. In fact, Moses restrains himself. He remains seated, holding in his fury, feeling hurt and despising the crowd (Freud 1973: 96). Moses holds the Tables. His rage is inhibited. Even statues could be perceived in biographical terms.

Freud did the same with Leonardo. Why did Leonardo pursue so many different interests? Why did he crave knowledge to the point of abandoning and neglecting the visual arts in which he excelled? Freud presumed that Leonardo's desire for knowledge was a sublimated derivation of a sexual drive. In our childhood, we are fated to experience anxiety and crave answers explaining the forces at work in our sexual drives. Leonardo realized this tendency to an extreme. The transformation of sexual curiosity into a generalized yearning for knowledge is a safe conduct that drives us away from reproaches and repression. Without the experience of restraint that a father figure would certainly impose on him as a child, Leonardo felt free to pursue knowledge intensely, with no limits.

Freud started his interpretation of Leonardo with the record of a childhood memory. In one of his notes, Leonardo probes the flight of birds. Then, a surprising revelation: Leonardo remembers that a vulture comes to his cradle. The bird opens Leonardo's mouth and hit inside his lips with its tail several times. Freud could not believe this. It was certainly a belated fantasy that Leonardo misplaced in his childhood (Freud 1973: 25). The meaning of this fantasy could be found in Leonardo's later life.

The logic of symptom relies too heavily on substitution. The vulture's tail stands for *phallus*. The puzzling scene requires translation. The vulture's tail hitting Leonardo's mouth is both an act of fellatio and a replacement for the child's contact with his mother's beast. That could be the clue for the supposed homosexuality of Leonardo.

Freud indicates a series of substitutions around the themes of homosexuality and vultures. Egyptians represented Mother through the signs of vultures. *Mut*, a maternal divinity, was depicted with a vulture's head or with several heads, one of them being a vulture. Freud associated *Mut* with the German word *Mutter* (mother). All of these bonds were completely remote from Leonardo. Nevertheless, Freud (1973: 29) wanders: Why did the Egyptians chose the vulture to represent motherhood? Among vultures, there were more females than males. Vultures were a species where males, and therefore fathers, played a minor role. And, at a certain time of the year, female vultures opened their vaginas to be fertilized by the wind. Vultures were a strictly feminine representation.

Now, Freud changes his mind and supposes that Leonardo knew the bundle of representations associating vultures and motherhood. Living in Milan under the paternal protection of Ludovico Sforza, a patron of arts and sciences, Leonardo must have read natural history treatises describing vultures. And also, the Catholic Church disseminated, with glee, the idea of vultures as fatherless birds, natural counterparts of Christ's virgin birth.

From vultures and motherhood, how could homosexual representations be forged? Most of Mut's images are shown with a penis: a figure with breasts having an erection (Freud 1973: 35). Male and female merge. If Leonardo was not acquainted with Egyptian mythology, he surely held in his early days the child's tendency of presuming that everyone has the same bodily constitution as his, namely having a penis. This fantasy included all female figures, therefore his mother. The factual perception that female had no penis brings a strong voyeuristic desire. It is both a longing to see naked bodies and the intense expectation of finding penis in a woman.

This experience should be common to all men. Then, what made of Leonardo a homosexual? Why did he take more pleasure in those that were the same as him than in others that are women? The predominance of the same is the reason for his auto-eroticism and narcissism. Leonardo was satisfied with reduced sexual activities. This would justify the hypothesis of auto-eroticism to be transformed into narcissism, from which homosexuality would have sprung. Leonardo took motherly care of his pupils. He acted as his own mother would have. It is through the identification (*Identifizierung*) with his mother that Leonardo becomes a passive homosexual. He appropriated and assimilated her feminine traits.

In his vulture fantasy, Leonardo underlined the intense role played by the mouth. The mouth was a residue of breast feeding. It evoked in Leonardo passionate kisses from his mother. Freud glimpsed in this revelation the testimony of Leonardo's pictorial depiction of enigmatic smiles and delicate lips. Leonardo's personality projected itself in both *Mona Lisa* and his painting of *The Virgin, and Child, with Saint Anne*.

As his father had no legitimate son, young Leonardo, an illegitimate child, was taken to live in Ser Piero Da Vinci's house. There, Leonardo was surrounded by women. His stepmother, Donna Albiera, and his paternal grandmother, Nònna Lucia, covered Leonardo with intense affection and hugging. The duplicity of mother figures returned to Leonardo at a later meeting with his presumed real mother, Catalina. As a direct reflection of his childhood experience, Leonardo paints the child together with a mother and a grandmother. The excessive presence of female figures in Leonardo's life coincides with his progressive estrangement from Ser Piero. The joy of being one with women is there in every painted detail of the ageless bodies of Saint Anne and The Virgin. Only Leonardo could have produced this painting. Therefore, Leonardo's personal life should be the access to understand why the painting was composed as such.

A Critique of Freudian Aesthetics

Before reviewing some blunders of Freudian analysis of Leonardo, we should make some general theoretical comments. The semiotics of Freudian aesthetics suffers from a fateful misconception. In it, the notion of representation is never something productive but substitutive. For psychoanalysis, an image is a replacement. So, the semiotics of symptomatology believes in the act of direct and immediate reflection that reconstitutes unconscious psychic processes.

Representations are chained to each other by similarity and linked alternation. Primitive sexual drives are transformed into a desire for sexual investigation. It converts the wish to see into the wish to know. Further on, there is an act of repression (*Verdrängung*) keeping the representation unconscious, and resulting in sublimation (*Sublimierung*). The sexual wish is sublimated by the wish to imitate nature or to search for their secrets. Leonardo shifted from painting to obsessive investigation of nature that would help him in his inventions (Bonne 1973: 729).

Can replacement alone account for the meaning of a sign? Let us presume for a moment that the statement "the snow is white" is a direct and descriptive rendering of an experience. This conjunction of signs would substitute the actual property of white snow. The statement "the snow is white" can be decomposed into indexical expressions singling out their referents. "The snow is white" was produced by the conjunction of two demonstrative propositions: "This is snow" and "this is white." A descriptive representation is reached through indexical propositions that substitute experience. Nevertheless we must say that something more was made. A connective element was added to the demonstrative propositions. The conjunction and joined "this is snow" and "this is white" in a new proposition: "The snow is white." We must also be aware that the conjunction and acts according to formal restrictions. We cannot bring about the conjunction of true statements such as "the snow is white" and "this is green." The conjunction and does not substitute anything; it follows principles belonging to the structure of logical representations and their constitutive rules of reference. Representations not only substitute referents, but mainly act upon each other. Representation and experience are linked by more than substitution. Signs act upon experience, transforming it. Substitution results from the mediation of a repertoire of solutions driving the beholder towards reality. Only then reality is assimilated to the sign scheme. The main trace of signs is to be an action, an addition, something more than a subrogation.

We are taking a critical stand against psychoanalytic semiotics of symptoms. An image is more than a creative substitution.The very reason for producing an image can be something else than the subrogation of unconscious biographical conflict.

Freud's idea that works of art are products of the artist's unconscious fantasy is an updated version of the conception that art expresses a spiritual content (Gombrich 1966). This was a common opinion in the German classical tradition. Perfection and artistic greatness shined through psychological subtleties shown in paintings. Deciphering was an act of interpretation in a way similar to the treatment of patients. In the end, Freud always took it for granted that what we must see in art is the maximum psychological contents of the painted figures themselves (Gombrich 1966: 33). Must we then rewrite the lives of artists? Freud's main contribution was reduced to the reform of biographies and not to any significant thought on the semiotics of images.

Yet the psychoanalytic interpretation of art should be removed from the limits of biographies written in admiration of artists. Until Freud's attempts, the biographer was a charmed admirer, seduced by his object. The real biography should transcend this barrier. Without understanding that psychic forces are at work as constraints and determinations of artistic production, biographers would just produce a literary narrative. Biographies would then be a collection of tales, presenting institutionalized stereotypes (Kris 1964: 64), mere moral examples. Either this, or narratives would be historical, going from beginning to end. Just like Vasari's *Lives of Artists*, they would present a linear interpretation of artistic accomplishments, ranging from Cimabue to Michelangelo. Freud restricted his analysis to psychological description. He never attempted any historical analysis of images.

There are some striking coincidences between traditional biographies and Freudian psychoanalytic revolution. Traditional biographies also underlined childhood and early youth as the time for the emergence of artistic talent. This is exactly what had happened with Cimabue and Giotto. The old master sees Giotto's drawings in the sand and takes the young artist under his fatherly protection. The dexterity of the young artist is evident to people around him. For psychoanalysis, genius also has an origin in childhood. The difference is that a narcissistic injury is always at the birth of artistic production. From then on, we find pathological descriptions and not heroic tales. Freudian biographies can be seen as variations of traditional narratives.

Early talent is a symptom of genius and to be self-taught gives to the artist the status of a cultural hero (Kris and Kurz 1979: 20). Traditional biographies revolve around the themes of hazard and miracle as conditions for the discovery of talent. All themes refer to the idea that forces are always conducting the maker, either under the form of inspiration or as the divine nature of creation. The artist is a cultural hero under an unpremeditated spell. Once again we have the notion of forces unknown and beyond the control of the artist.

Unfortunately, Freud did not live up to his promise of an ultimate interpretation of Leonardo. Some facts contradict Freud's analysis. It is not true that only female figures played a dominant role in Leonardo's early life, therefore influencing the composition of *The Virgin and Child, with Saint Anne*. Leonardo was, from the very beginning, socially recognized as a son by his father. Meyer Schapiro (1982: 141) observed that the record of Leonardo's baptism indicated the presence of ten godfathers all of them neighbors of Ser Piero. It is probably not precise that only three years later Leonardo was taken under his father's protection. Freud knew this (Gay 1989: 257), but he decided not to take it into account.

However original the composition of *The Virgin with Child, and Saint Anne* could be, we must underline Leonardo dependence on schemes and visual solutions that were part of pictorial tradition. The representation of Saint Anne and the Virgin as figures of nearly equal age, a feature that Freud mistakenly attributed to the uniqueness of Leonardo's unconscious childhood memory, was in fact quite common (Schapiro 1956: 161). Leonardo followed the iconography inherited by the Renaissance.

Renaissance paintings represented Saint Anne, a revered saint ever since 1485, as a double of the Virgin Mary. Schapiro also alluded to an announcement of a prayer to the Immaculate Conception of the Virgin Mary to be recited in front of an image of Saint Anne. The woodcut pasted all over walls and church doors depicted Mary sitting on the lap of Saint Anne with the Child on Mary's lap. It was the representation of a familial trinity. This was the year of 1494, before Leonardo drew his cartoon of Saint Anne, the Virgin and the Child.

The iconographic tradition was an important source for Leonardo. Long before Leonardo, saints were depicted as young virgins. They were not sublimated representations of beautiful ephebes. The difference of age was conventionally shown through the difference in size, not through wrinkles in the faces.

As early as 1923, Freud's interpretation suffered a serious set-back. Eric Maclagan (1923) pointed out that Freud's association of the vulture with a symbolic substitute for a fatherless experience, and therefore as the basis for Leonardo's homosexuality, was simply absurd. Everything rested upon a wrong translation of Leonardo's notes by Freud. The word *nibbio*, used by Leonardo, could not be translated as vulture. It designated kite. The consequence of such mistake is disastrous for Freud's interpretation. The whole hypothesis falls apart. Its strength came from the representation of the vulture. With the kite, it made no sense at all, in term of Freud's links between Egyptian Goddess and hieroglyphs, the virgin mother and the fatherless birth. The silhouette of a vulture concealed in Mary's clothes and detected by Oskar Pfister is either wishful thinking or arbitrary attribution.

If natural history treatises conceived vultures as compassionate, tender and caring mothers, kites were the opposite. In that case,does Freud's explanation of homosexual tendencies as a result of Leonardo' attachment to his mother still hold true?

Apparently there is no problem in recognizing that the kite's tail inside a mouth can stand for a phallic representation. Again, Meyer Schapiro (1956) advances an intriguing alternative. Leonardo's note referred to the flight of birds. He was recording observations on the pilot movement of a kite's tail to find clues for the invention of a flying machine. At first, the kite's tail was similar to a ship's rudder. It may be that Leonardo was not talking of a childhood reminiscence. The kite's tail could well be something else than an act of *fellatio*. It could be a literary reference meaning a wishful representation of an omen. The mouth had been traditionally considered the locus where the future is revealed, as in oracles. Schapiro (1956: 152–153) singles out several traditional narratives that mentioned childhood events as omens of future success. Nightingales, bees or grains of wheat in an infants's mouth should be taken as the expression of a special destiny, either as sign of excellence in lyrical poetry, in the case of nightingales, or rhetorical talent, when bees bring sweetness to the lips, or wealth, when ants brought grains of wheat to the mouth of Midas. Leonardo was not telling an actual event of his early life. He was weaving a tale based on a contemporary literary convention.

Freud's interpretation of Leonardo and his works rests on the ignorance of the role played by collective representations in images. If Leonardo designed his visual compositions from patterns donated by tradition, then the whole idea of a private and unconscious fantasy determining pictorial representation does not make sense. If meaning in visual representations has a definite public nature, then there is no direct and unmediated relationship between representations and the psychological conditions of whoever uses them. Private dimension stands on the sign possibilities offered by the age (Gombrich 1954: 411); and only then individual expression can be articulated.Iconographic patterns are appropriated and transformed by the artist, and this is the condition for sharing their meaning. Unconscious constraints are a secondary element in creating visual patterns. Meaning is foremost public; it exists also through institutionalized symbols. Why define visual configurations just as symptoms of a bounded ego? Unconscious drives would have always to adjust themselves to prevailing pictorial conventions.

Some Freudian devotees, like Pontalis (1991: 175) justify all of Freud's problems arguing that he appealed to the best sources available during his lifetime. We could not we blame Freud. But this is not the point. The problem with Freud's interpretation of Leonardo is his overall conception of image making.

Can Freudianism Go Beyond the Fine Arts?

Pictorial Nominalism attempts to rescue psychoanalytic approach to the plastic arts from all the problems in Freud's aesthetics. There are evident obstacles in applying Freudian doctrine to visual images. Nevertheless, we should not give it up so easily.

First, we must admit that Freud's treatment of visual arts was dated. Antique notions of representation sneaked themselves into Freud's theoretical frame. Then, lured by contemporary ideas, Freud adopted a symptomatic reading when dealing with art. Is that true? When Freud wrote assessing Oskar Pfister's psychoanalytic interpretation of expressionist art, his words were harsh. The paintings were just ghastly. Expressionists were people with severe inborn defects of vision who become painters or draftsmen (Gombrich 1966: 34). Freud's overall taste in art was positively conservative, decisively reactionary. Even if Freud were enthusiastic about modern art, we would find a definite problem in his general theoretical frame. Symptomatic theories of representation are doomed to fail with modern art. Modern art does not hide anything. The visual pattern is there, in interaction. Can one interpret modern art with such conception? Thierry de Duve admits that through a symptomatic reading we cannot deal effectively with modern art (De Duve 1994: 3).

The solution is elsewhere and yet very near. De Duve tries to spell out an aesthetic theory to explain the creative dimension of the artist and also the conditions for the reception of the object produced. So we should probe the biographical evidence of the artist and investigate the historical reach of his creation. Everything is under the guise of a subjective dimension of art practice (De Duve 1994: 166). Therefore, psychoanalysis can still be useful, but changed. Freud never knew exactly what he was doing (Lacan 1966: 272).

The kind of psychoanalytic interpretation put forward by Thierry de Duve should resist any form of deterministic standpoint. His critique attacks Marxism in its conception of art as a direct expression of economic conflicts. De Duve also criticizes applied psychoanalysis as a form of determinism. Then, the work of art could not be a direct expression of unconscious fantasies. Should we safely assume that a work of art is a direct symptom of the artist's biographic incidents? For Thierry De Duve, artistic determinations are not causes, but delimitations. A work of art affirms its own *a priori* possibilities (De Duve 1994: 60).

How can we pass from psychoanalytic interest in biographic data to a historical horizon? How can we conciliate history, so very near to the

Secondary Process, with the Unconscious and the Primary Process? History is incompatible with one of the attributes of the Unconscious, i.e., to be non-historical. Psychoanalysis would be useful to art history if one could establish a parallelism between the life of an individual and his age, understood as a kind of collective spirit.

If all the requirements were but biographic, we would still have a lot of trouble. Thierry De Duve is aware that interpreting a work of art can be dangerously retroactive. In this case, we have only hints and guesses. At the very most, we can weave hypothesis from threadbare clues to deal with the artist's unconscious drive (*Trieb*). This should be no real problem. Thierry De Duve is an ardent follower of Jacques Lacan's credo, in which there is no room for objectivity anywhere, in science, in psychoanalysis (Roustang 1988: 23), or even in art.

Truth in art depends only on imaginative processes. Its truth-function is the same as dreaming, fantasy, or daydreaming. Free from the pressures of reality, a work of art is qualified to transform culture. In Neo-Freudian jargon, art is a transition from the Imaginary to the Symbolic. Even if it is a product of the Unconscious, a work of art can change the historical principles where it bursts.

Lacan's conceptual jungle can be somewhat comforting for whoever reached the dead end of Freud's aesthetics. Lacan refuses to rely on contents expressing sexual conflicts; for him, psychological life is attained though formal operations: condensation (*Verdichtung*) and displacement (*Verschiebung*). From a semiotic perspective, condensation and displacement must be renamed metaphor and metonymy. The Unconscious is revealed through semiotic action: Someone is doing of something a sign.

With Lacan, there is no final cause brought by any content. Representations branch out into each other, in multiple determination (*Überdeterminierung*). Symptoms require analysis but there is no complete and definite interpretation. An endless speech flow is what defines the individual. The stuff of psychoanalysis is nothing but speech. Psychoanalysis should be linked to linguistics. Psychoanalysis is linguisterie (Lacan 1975: 20).

We are subjected to language. Languages rules. To change speech is to change reason. Language is therefore waiting for us, ready to concede us an identity. The Unconscious is similar to language, and language is a condition for the Unconscious.

The Saussurian algorithm (S/s) expresses the splitting of the ego (*Ichspaltung*). Two attitudes coexist in the ego, dividing it. Reality Principle commands the delay of desire and Pleasure Principle wants to fulfill it. For us, there is no unity. It is all there in Saussure's graphic draft of the sign; between signifier and signified we can see a bar (barre) that cannot be breached. The signifier is morphologically autonomous.

Lacan stuck faithfully to this conception of sign. In one of his latest seminars, he defined sign as a disjunction of two substances with no common part (Lacan 1975: 21). Signs do not refer directly to objects. The nature of signs is nominalistic and points to the split ego. Signifiers come as a chain sliding endlessly parallel to the signified. Signifiers float and signified flows (Lacan 1977: 30). Signifiers produce the effect signified. One can make sense of this chain recognizing a formal repetition, an insistence in the chain of signifiers.

The subject is a subject of the signifier, in the sense of being determined by it (Lacan 1975: 3065). Therefore, we must recognize that signifiers refer to other signifiers. Only then we can inquire what role a signifier plays as a privileged representation structuring the subject. The phallic attribution is a signifier with the active function of producing for the subject his unconscious dimension. Representations are barred from consciousness. The phallus is an imaginary threat bestowed as the signifier of a possible absence (Lacan 1971: 104). We are talking about castration and the primeval Law prohibiting incest.

Castration and desire are directly related. To become a social being, the subject suffers the action of cultural negativity. He learns to postpone and deny desire. He is subjected to the structure of the fundamental Law, whose rule is rigidly binary. The Law is absolute: Its principle is determined by a logical relation of the kind either/or. There are no middle terms. The social support must remain unchallenged. The discrimination of incest refuses doubt or ambiguity. This rule is the Rule constituting culture. Then, the subject participates in the Symbolic.

On the fringe of the Symbolic, the infant experiences the primordial signifier. We must call it *The Name of The Father*. Lacan's tendency to theorize through puns demands an explanation. The Name-of-the-Father, *Le-Nom-du-Père*, means the identification of the Symbolic father through knowing his name. And also *Nom* (Name) in French is homophonous to *Non* (no), a signifier of denial. So, when the Name-of-the-Father is recognized, the child enters the Order of Culture, the Symbolic Order, through the denial of desire.

Duchamp Revisited

After all the problems in Freud's analysis of Leonardo can we still insist in psychoanalyzing artists and their work? Can one of the most elusive artist of all times, Duchamp, be treated according to a biographic perspective? How can we interpret someone that preferred to hide than to reveal his secrets? Did he really? For instance, in the *Large Glass*, the main term is obviously The Bride: La Mariée. We start with the expression Mariée and then transform it into its counterpart: M'art y est, meaning my art is here (De Duve 1994: 36). Let us take the sound Mar as an abbreviation of Marcel and then associate it with Mariée. We discover a hidden meaning: *Mar y est*-Mar(cel) is here (De Duve 1994: 130).

When signifiers are at play, a revelation is at hand. We just have to look at the surface of signifiers gliding, drifting like puns. We can see that Duchamp was referring to himself, in a cryptic but evident manner.

Thierry De Duve's interpretation of Marcel Duchamp is strictly Freudian. Duchamp's creations are a product of unconscious forces at work within himself. This is not a particular feature of Duchamp. Any artistic creation is an accomplishment of imaginary desires. Visual solutions are the figurative counterpart of unconscious drives. To interpret an artist means to rewrite his life as a description of the conditions from which art works came forth.

De Duve places a turning point in Marcel Duchamp's biography around 1911. The feeling of being a painter was plaguing him. His elder brothers, Jacques Villon (1875–1963) and Raymond Duchamp-Villon (1876–1918), were established artists, members of Puteaux Cubist group. Duchamp used to visit his elder brothers; he was influenced by their intellectual and pictorial concerns. *Duchamp's Nude Descending a Staircase No.1* can be directly related to Cubist compositions. The nude in motion embodies the Cubist concept of simultaneity. A dynamic flow is captured by the painting (Golding 1973: 12). Duchamp presented *The Nude* at the Salon des Indépendants, the place for cubists. Cubist orthodoxy could not bear a picture entitled *The Nude*. Albert Gleizes (1881–1953) asked Jacques Villon and Raymond Duchamp-Villon to convince their younger brother, Marcel, to withdraw the painting from the show.

In his later years, Duchamp refused identification with Cubism. He had experimented with most pictorial styles. Duchamp would refute the idea that Cézanne, the inspiration of Cubism, had any impact over him. We must remember that Gleizes and Metzinger proclaimed that the future of painting came from Cézanne (Fry 1968: 104). On the other hand, Duchamp would say that his real pictorial discovery was Matisse (Cabanne 1972: 25).

Any Freudian interpreter would remark that this is a typical case of denegation (*Verneinung*). A denegation is a defense from uncomfortable and repressed representations. In the end, denegation implies a devious admission. *Verneinung* is a *yes* disguised as *no*. De Duve thinks we have reason to believe that Cézanne was a major figure in Duchamp's development as an artist. Ever since his *Church at Blainville* (1902) we can recognize Duchamp slowly approaching Cézanne. *The Church* was made under the ascendancy of Toulouse Lautrec, a friend of his brother Jacques. Flat colors were surrounded by black contours. Later *The Chess Game* (1910) depicted his two elder brothers over a chessboard and at the front of the painting his brothers's wives, an anticipation of so many brides to be painted. The pose of the brothers was distinctly derived from Cézanne's *Card Players* (De Duve 1994: 47).

It is significative both artistically and psychologically the way Duchamp painted his father in *Le portrait de M. Duchamp pére* (1910). In terms of style, the painting is very Cézannean. It represented Monsieur Duchamp gazing from a superior position. As an efficient notary, Duchamp père kept a record of all the allowances he gave to his children, to deduct the sum from his final inheritance (Cabanne 1972: 48). In Marcel Duchamp's painting, his father is looking from above in a gesture of presumed tolerance. This must have been the expression of his attitude towards his artists sons.

Pictorial Nominalism asserts that, with Duchamp, painting and family life became a mixed affair. When he was recording the preparatory notes for The *Large Glass*, Duchamp wrote: Sign all the glasses, property of Marcel Duchamp son (Duchamp 1983: note 76). *Le portrait de M. Duchamp père* offers a clue: "This painting is an intersection of paternal identification" (De Duve 1994: 46). In this picture, we accept Duchamp's father and Cézanne as paternal figures. Using Lacan's terminology, Cézanne was the pictorial *Name-of-the Father*.

The denial of Cézanne's importance only underlines the unconscious urge to overcome him. Rejected by Gleizes and under the complacency of his own brothers, Duchamp looked for a new ideal-of-ego. Duchamp realized that he would never be a major painter such as Gris, Bracque, Picasso or even his brother Jacques. He would have to be radically different from any painter close to tradition. He was ousted from Cubist circles.

Duchamp left for Munich and stayed there from June 18 to September 10, 1912. Munich is a blank in the interpretation of Duchamp. What was he doing in Munich? Of all places, why did he go there? No one can tell for sure. Why did he come back? What happened there? We cannot know. Was Duchamp searching for solace away from the Parisian art scene that refused to acknowledge his achievements? And why did he go to Munich and not some place else? Had it something to do with Kupka's presence near his brothers's house at Puteaux?

Cubism was an art movement where too many substitute father figures—Cézanne, Jacques Villon, and Raymond Duchamp-Villon—were present. Contemporary common sense considered Cubism as as foreign as Munich itself (Lebel 1959: 5). The assumption is that Duchamp was searching, consciously or not, for deep origins, out of which he could ransom himself from destructive feelings against father-figures. Again, we do not know for sure. Duchamp's sojourn is scarcely documented.

The Munich trip left faint clues. "Beyond the two paintings and the four drawings, all that we have of Duchamp's activities is pure conjecture" (De Duve 1994: 96). The theme of his pictorial production is still movement, but now increasingly mechanical. De Duve thinks the most important work of Duchamp during the Munich days is *The Passage of the Virgin to the Bride*. This painting is considered a sum of all that has concerned Duchamp.

The Passage is the transition from where the Virgin comes from, the family home, to the outside world, where the Virgin will mature into the Bride. The *Virgin No.1* and *The Virgin No.2* are drawings that can be related to The Bride, an oil on canvas also produced in Munich. The Passage dramatizes the change of the Virgin into the Bride. Is The Passage a figurative thought about Duchamp's pertinence to his Cubist family? Is it the expression of Duchamp's extreme homelessness?

There is scant evidence of what Duchamp did or saw in Munich. Then how can this interpretation of *The Passage* as a family romance ever be verified? De Duve takes an audacious step recognizing several tracks that could point to Duchamp's family. If we examine the title of the painting in French, *Le Passage*, we find hints leading to Suzanne, Duchamp's sister. How do we name in French the person crossing a passage? It is "passeur" that can be easily converted into "pas soeur," meaning "sister, no." As a projection of the *Name-of-the-Father*, incestuous desires must be denied. Yet this could be more than just the indication of Duchamp's desire for his favorite sister. It could also indicate Duchamp's attitude toward art.

In the *1914 Box*, a collection of notes published as a complement to *The Large Glass*, Duchamp established a personal algorithm: "Arrhe is to art as shitte is to shit; grammatically: the arrhe of painting is feminine in gender" (Sanouillet and Peterson 1975: 24). We are facing a new equation: Cézanne/Suzanne is a symptom of the relation man/woman = painter/painting. For De Duve, Duchamp's interest in Seurat also reveals an insistence of signifiers indicating pictorial father figures and his sister: Cézanne/Suzanne, Seurat/soeur (De Duve 1994: 171). Duchamp experienced a whirlwind sweeping over family conflicts and artistic problems: kill the father (Cézanne) and marry the mother (painting as it will be after Cézanne) (De Duve 1994: 49).

The trip to Munich brought about a new consciousness to Duchamp. There, he discovered that another history of painting was possible,and with it another Cézanne. Cézanne was not a father figure anymore, a threat, or even a bond to be untied (De Duve 1994: 104). In Munich, avant-garde art was in secession from prevailing Academicians. There was a different kind of rupture from the one that was favored in Paris. Avant-garde was a resolution that redefined art practices.

During his stay at Munich, Duchamp must have been caught in this climate of opinion. It was the foundation of a new heritage, a search of budding historical conventions leading to a ceaseless make it new. An artistic career would be a constant triumph over prejudices (Kandinsky 1990: 201). Under the possible but unverified influence of Kandinsky's writings, Duchamp found role of a rebellious son committed to extreme innovation.

Duchamp did not adopt any pictorial solution that he might have seen in Munich. The Munich art milieu thrived on discussions about abstraction and the future role of non-figurative art. This was the lesson to be learnt. Color was being revaluated as a major pictorial issue. Perhaps that is the reason Duchamp would refer to Matisse and Seurat as artistic landmarks and not Cézanne, at least not the Cézanne of the Cubist credo.

It is difficult to see any colorist tendency in the paintings Duchamp produced during the Munich trip. Nevertheless, Thierry De Duve maintains that color opened a whole new range of possibilities for Duchamp. Duchamp was reacting to the Puteaux group's disregard for color. Now, it was compatible with the nexus between Cézanne and the refusal of realism proposed by abstraction and its stress on pure color.

Abstraction cannot be reduced to traditional painting and Duchamp's readymades cannot be called painting either. This is the extraneous experience of limits that became the history of avant-garde art. Malevitch's *Black Square or White on White* and the abandonment of figurative art are the same abandonment of painting as a craft that we find in Duchamp's readymades (De Duve 1994: 155). When Duchamp made the decision of producing readymades, he was rebelling and simultaneously finding comfort in Cézannean shadows. Cézanne also abandoned perspective as an element of pictorial craft but Duchamp abandoned painting altogether. The link with tradition was kept (De Duve 1994: 178). Thierry De Duve presumes to have found the psychological answer for Duchamp's creation of readymades.

Freudian Aesthetics Criticized Once Again

Thierry de Duve conciliates ingeniously psychological interpretations and a historical perspective. The main problem with this theoretical construction is how unconfirmable his conclusions are. It is very difficult to accept with ease so many crucial and undecidable contentions. Such is the case with the insistency of the signifiers Cézanne/Suzanne and also the lack of record concerning Duchamp's trip to Munich. Even the evidence of a copy of Kandinsky's *Über das Geistige der Kunst*, bought in Munich, in 1912, and supposedly found in Duchamp's library was challenged by Teeny, Marcel Duchamp's wife. The book was really from Jacques Villon's library and the handwritten notes were made by Raymond and not Marcel (De Duve 1994: 204).

It is not enough to force on us the acceptance of unconfirmable data with the argument that this is the nature of readymades. Readymades are suspended between art and painting. They bear the name of undecidability itself (De Duve 1994: 187). How can we distinguish undecidability and sheer gratuitousness? Unfortunately, De Duve does not answer this question.[2]

---

[2] Lacan scholasticism is responsible for this. The Real that would ascribe truthfulness to a statement is conceived by Lacan as an impossibility. Therefore, if only the Symbolic can be apprehended, there is no way to go beyond it. A signifier refers just to another signifier and any hypothesis is as good as any other. Who is right Thierry de Duve interpreting the Munich trip or Anne D'Harnnoncourt (1984)? D'Harnnoncourt also believes in the importance of the Munich experience to Duchamp, but thinks that the central influence on Duchamp was his visit to the Museum of Science and Technology, where he must have seen didactic displays on gas and machinery that inspired *The Large Glass*. Another book on Duchamp, Lyotard's *Le Transformateur Duchamp* (1977) makes a similar claim to de Duve's. Interpretation is considered futile (Lyotard 1977:61). It is impossible to speak the truth, no one can speak it. This a puzzling statement. Why should anyone take the trouble to write anything about anything else, including Duchamp, if even the faintest possibility of speaking the truth is ruled out? Truth is a condition to any

Even an anachronist affiliation between Lacanian psychoanalysis and Duchampian art can be subtly suggested. Lacan read Freud in a revolutionary perspective. The theory of the subject was reformulated as the rhetoric of the subjection to the signifier. Duchamp did the same with Cezannean tradition; he subverted the practice of the subject-artist (De Duve 1994: 166). If anything goes, why not speculate that, without knowing, Duchamp reinterpreted psychoanalysis?

Now, undecidability reaches indifference. We cannot place on the same level the theoretical frame that analyzes an object with the object itself. Only wishful thinking can account for Thierry De Duve's statements: "Painting is its own theory and its own theoricist" (De Duve 1994: 75) and "the work of art is self-analytic" (De Duve 1994: 57). This is just a rhetorical claim. What can one mean by that? Has it something to do with Freud's transferential relationship to Fliess that helped him create psychoanalysis? And how about Duchamp? He thought himself beyond the revelation of unconscious drives; Duchamp is persistently elusive.

An immoderate complacency with analogical bonds is responsible for a flight of imagination such as this. The famous cliche of Duchamp transforming art into life does not attest to the soundness of psychoanalytic interpretations, whose effect is to impoverish Duchamp's work. Duchamp's action is more a reflection on the nature of artistic making than a direct product of unconscious drives that express subjective conflicts. Whatever Duchamp did in his life as an artist was a reflection on how artistic creation was arbitrary (Celant 1984: 69).

Psychoanalytic categories are not really useful when applied to Marcel Duchamp. They lead to exaggerations such as comparing Duchamp with Da Vinci and finding him an unintended impostor. For Charpy (1976: 154) Duchamp is seen as a debased image of Leonardo. Duchamp's attitude of radical criticism to artistic practices is reduced to obsessive pathologies. The positive side of Duchamp's creations is played down.

When Duchamp condemns retinal painting, it is just a defense mechanism on his part. The abandonment of painting spells out an aggressive tendency that responds for Duchamp's switch from art to chess, during the period of 1929–1946. Narcissism accounts for the readymades. Selfish choice was

---

critical utterance whatsoever. It is not a spectral metaphysical entity that scares the wits out of us all.

enough to elevate an object to the heights of art (Charpy 1976: 149). Blunt pathology overcame the intelligence of Duchamp's art.

Readymades are cunning strategies of meaning. Octavio Paz (1977) labeled them non-created creations. Readymades belong to everybody and to nobody (Paz 1977: 62). They are beyond the reach of psychoanalysis. Readymades force us to see common objects in a new light. The object comes to the foreground, renewed through titling or through inscriptions. The viewer builds up the readymade, performing an identification. Seeing is not enough. One must understand what was seen and then recognize the object no longer as an industrial entity, but as a readymade.

The readymade is and is not the original object chosen to be an artistic creation. A sly syllogism is at work. If art is making, and if making is choosing, then art is choosing (De Duve 1994: 169).This choice is not restricted to a personal and selfish election, or even a narcissistic tendency. There are no strict personal dimensions in the readymade. Here, psychoanalysis is impotent. The psychoanalytic weaving of biographical threads is in confrontation with Duchamp's intentions (Krauss 1977: 80). The readymade is a collective action, transcending the creator and actively involving the viewer.

Signs, Self, and Something Else

What is the *raison d'être* of a readymade? All of its magic derives from semiotic inscriptions. Readymade are titling taken to exasperation. Titling a painting The Nude descending a staircase was the source of dispute between Duchamp and Parisian Cubists. From then on, Duchamp's production became an effect of inscribing titles and other signs. Titles ripened into more than names as reference for identification. They were not restricted to providing a description of the work. Titles framed contours that organized the details to be perceived. Speech developed a global structure, a harmonizing representation (Thom 1983b: 87). Verbal signs took over. In the form of instructions, titles furnished guidelines for the perception of images. A title became simultaneously a description and an identification.

Duchamp reached a limit. He finally chose painting as a discourse, in detriment of painting as a craft (De Duve 1994: 44). Titling allowed a discourse about artworks. Only after receiving a title a work could be interpreted (Fischer 1984: 292). A title was more than an evident tag. Titling turned out to be a performance similar to the election that made the readymade.

Words themselves bred visual art. Duchamp claimed that even a dictionary could be an artistic medium. Let's buy a dictionary and then scratch out all the "undesirable" words. Perhaps add a few; sometimes replace the scratched out words with another. He reminds himself: Use the dictionary for the preliminary notes of *The Glass* (Sanouillet and Peterson 1975: 78). Duchamp was also saying that a major work like The Glass was a product of verbal instructions.

The nature of artistic activity should then be named pictorial nominalism, and it states a deep truth about the visual arts. Notes, texts, and words reduce the arbitrary. Close to words, images usher the resolute presence of actual existence. Texts create a world. Without written notes, working as dispersive axioms, a world does not have continuity and harmony. The definite title for *The Large Glass*, The Bride Stripped Bare By Her Bachelors, Even, lends continuity to the picture (Duchamp 1983: note 104). In that case, visual configurations are not undetermined. Titles and texts in general establish the necessary conditions for knowing what the picture is all about. There is no indeterminacy, for indeterminacy is just the measure of our ignorance.

Seeing and saying are complementary experiences. The visual configuration of *The Large Glass* was to be crowned by the publication of a set of notes, a catalogue, written to explain and depict verbally the visual details of the picture (Jouffroy 1964: 115). It was a conscious redefinition of painting, not the result of an unconscious drive.

The role played by words in Duchamp's *oeuvre* yields a further refutation of psychoanalytic speculations. Visual forms confront us as a residue of a verbal flux. Text and image are not just joined as different and equivalent sources of inspiration: They are a new kind of relationship. The image depends on words and the word on images. Words and images cannot manage on their own (Gombrich 1985: 215) The traditional supremacy of visual configuration is at stake. Duchamp's method of composition is "phrasefull." Titles attached to industrialized objects structure readymades. They fulfill an anti-retinal goal. Objects in their material configuration are then undone (Venâncio 1986: 62). The dematerialization of art objects reviews the tasks and the priority of the creator. Biographical inquisition belongs to a vanished world.

Is there a link between the instantaneous election of a readymade and the meticulous weaving of notes that build up *The Large Glass*? Both the *Glass* and the readymades reject all forms of subjectivity, starting with the notion of taste. The choice of industrialized objects to be art objects is the sacralization of banality. Lebel (1959: 35) sees the selection of an object to be a readymade as a protest about the excessive importance conferred historically to art, creation and individual craftsmanship. The arbitrary valuation of a common object is a counteraction against the sacred aura of artistic achievement.

Duchamp clearly perceives the threat of banality. He wonders if he should restrict the number of readymades to be produced yearly (Sanouillet and Peterson 1975: 33). Even his strategy of using industrialized objects can be seen as a discussion of the artist as an author (Carvalho 1991: 357). The repetition of industrialized products takes over the whole act of creating.

Everything is doubled. *The Large Glass* has two dominions: the one where the Bride reigns and the other one of her Bachelors. And furthermore, the object elected to be a readymade is doubled and transformed by its title. The construction *Fresh Widow* (192O) has polished black leather pieces behind each glass in the window that in their turn reflect the museum. The echoes of french window are at work in the title that is in fact signed by Duchamp's double, his travesty self: Rrose Sélavy. The search for a unifying force unconsciously driving the author is pointless.

How can a readymade be an unconscious and positive expression of a personality if, as invention, they are negations. With readymades, identity is dissolved. Nothing is. All is becoming. An object is transfigured by a title. Readymades are impoverished acts of creation. Severing the object from its regular context, a readymade is underlaid by a hive of meaning (Paz 1977: 51). It is difficult to accept the Freudian dogma that each man brings to artistic creation his imaginary world, and inevitably expresses his life story (This 1972: 298). By becoming a conscious hieroglyph, readymades deny communication. They cannot correspond to dreaming as Freudians would suggest. In readymades there is no subjectivity. Beyond good or bad taste, they are a complete anesthesia (Sanouillet and Peterson 1975: 140).

Readymades proclaim visual indifference. Around the same time that Duchamp was producing readymades such as *Bicycle Wheel* (1913), and *Pharmacy* (1914), he was coming out with *Chocolate Grinder* (1914). The chocolate grinder would find a salient place in *The Large Glass*: It represented the Bachelor that ground his chocolate alone, a supposed reference to masturbation. *The Chocolate Grinder* was the culmination of a pictorial method that would expose the logic of appearance. The chocolate grinder meant the abandonment of retinal aesthetics. Duchamp was looking for a precision painting (Lebel 1959: 32).

In Duchamp's theoretical terms, there is a difference between appearance and apparition. The logic of appearance asserts that each decision in the composition of a picture has the status of an axiom. It either results from or functions as an axiomatic principle (Duchamp 1983: note 69). The logic of appearance is independent from visual style. There is no overall guide to unify pictorial constructions. The unity is not anymore in the locus of the viewer from where perspective representation is assembled. Then, the question becomes how to read images precisely.

The readability of images depends on the history they tell. Duchamp's notes and textual references fill the narrative gaps. For instance, *Jeune homme triste dans un train* (1911), *Sad Young Man in a Train*, depicts mechanical forms in the same spirit as *The Passage from the Virgin to the Bride*. Duchamp admitted that it is an autobiographical painting (Cabanne 1972: 48), but the title of this painting results from the charm of the phonetic analogy of *triste* (sad) and train. Nothing else is alluded to. The refusal of retinal painting contemplates also a refutation of explicit biographical roots.

Pictorial methods walk hand in hand with a philosophy of visual forms. The visual indifference that Duchamp cherished and looked for with ardent determination is a belated modernist revival of Neo-Platonic tenets. Intentionally or not, a precise system of ideas justifies the devaluation of visual forms. So the kinship of avant-garde and Neo-Platonic philosophy of symbolism is just waiting to be singled out.

Much to Thierry De Duve's disagreement and criticism (De Duve 1994: 198), Jean Clair (1975: 98) talked about the influence of Platonism in Duchamp's *oeuvre*. Neo-Platonic notions presume ideas as more imperative to art than visual craftsmanship. When we contemplate an image, its efficacy requires more than the senses. We need intelligence to decipher images. Visual representation is purified by writing, so works of art rank with hieroglyphs. The abandonment of visuality is the refusal of the senses. This is similar to the Neo-Platonic opposition of the ideal and the intelligible to what is physical and belongs to the senses.

If we acknowledge love—or even cynical love, as Breton (1965: 94) says—as a paramount theme in Duchamp's pictures, it is tempting to see in them an endorsement of Neo-Platonic conceptions of love as a driving force, unifying diversity. According to Neo-Platonism, love is a continuous flow that bonds God to the world. Marsilio Ficino (1433–1499) argues that love is a special desire. It is a cognition and not a blind sensuous force. Love is real love when conducted by a *virtù cognitiva*.

Sight can be a valuable element in love, but to keep oneself tied to visual manifestations of beauty is a serious setback. In that case, we are condemned to a lower form of love: human love (Panofsky 1972: 202). Visuality cannot be the only aim of art. Art offers ciphered symbols for our intellect. Art can also be a *virtù cognitiva*. Exaltation of a sublime love deters us not only from the strictures of carnal intercourse but establishes an effeminate goal of the purification of the senses. It is possible to admit a tie between Duchamp's purification of nudes through mechanical representations, his excessive intellectual use of literary titles, and his dressing up as a travesty, as another self: Rrose Sélavy. Traces of identity are always to be defaced.

Machine, Duchamp

In one of his writings, Marcel Duchamp finally reaches a conclusion about the title for *The Large Glass*. The proposed title organizes the composition. With the title, the picture evolves into something more than a representation of mechanical dolls fighting. It is now The Bride possesses her partners and the Bachelors strip bare their Bride (Duchamp 1983: note 104).

The incongruent regions of the *Glass* (Lyotard 1977: 124) are blended in the subtitle. In the upper part of the *Glass*, The Bride's region, chance rules. The Bride floats high above, among shifting and indeterminate clouds. The organic depiction of the Bride is premechanic. The forms verge on the biologically amorphous. On the other hand, the lower part of the painting is unified according to mechanical depiction and perspective.

From top to bottom, *The Large Glass* tosses a history of forms (Clair 1975: 117). So, agricultural machine indicates not only natural forms but mechanisms. Machines are in fact perpetual transformations of energy, a work without fatigue, ceaseless movement. Agricultural machine is more than a subtitle; it hinges those two regions.

The movement in the lower part of *The Glass* is strictly mechanical. Whatever the Bachelors do, it will end in the splash of water-mill wheel of *The Large Glass*. From this fall, the illuminating gas provides the energy for the Bride's abiding clockwork. It is the conjunction of the diversity of nature and the constancy of mechanisms.

Machines are artifices. They are additions to nature. This is not all. Agricultural machines are machines to work in fields. In French, *machines du champ*. Du champ? Yes, Duchamp, Marcel Duchamp. At first we felt comfortable that this is a biographical clue linking Duchamp to his *magnum opus*. Then, again, why not conclude the other way round; that biography is a minor residue to be left out in the consideration of art products? Machines are impersonal by definition. They disown formal beauty. The beauty of our age is ironically indifferent,[3] and we came to it slowly.

The social values that allowed Marcel Duchamp to opt for mechanical representations are an exacting historical offspring. In antiquity, machines were just formal compositions. Technical intelligence just investigated possibilities with no concern for the acquisition of their effects. A mechanical project was an end in itself. Their object was cognition. Machines were not planned to be constructed (Schuhl 1938: 12). They did not bear any relation to experience.

Experience had no cognitive status. The position of a concept in theoretical system was enough. Knowledge was fundamentally theoretical: Theory and experience inhabited different worlds. The Dutch opticians that discovered the lunette could not point it above to scrutinize the movement of celestial bodies. A change occured when Galileo pointed the lunette to the sky, therefore trnasforming it into a cognitive tool. At first, empirical research and interpretation of natural events were not a matter for intellectual concern. Only later machines were applied to nature. And then, mechanical devices could defy nature; they could also create objects. In the Modern Age, machines are more than techniques. They embody technology. As technology, machines execute material objects: They result from immediate empirical problems. The construction of machines affirms technological thought (Koyré 1971a: 361).

Out of all this, mechanical experience shuns classical beauty. Modernity is an age of uncertainties. Nothing is stable. Even René Descartes's dream that

---

[3] After Duchamp's death in 1968, it was discovered that he had been laboring on a secret project. It was an installation entitled *Etant Donées — Given —* (1946–66). Previously, in the set of notes issued as *The Green Box*, Duchamp had written a cryptic text under the heading "Preface: Given 1st the waterfall, 2nd the illuminating gas." The rest of the note referred to the accordance of the conditions for the instantaneous state of Rest with a choice of Possibilities authorized by these laws that would also determine them (Sanouillet & Peterson 1975:27). Now the viewer approaches this installation and looks through a hole on an old wooden door to see a naked woman laying down with open legs and hairless vagina, holding a gas lamp; at the background, we can see water running across a landscape. The naked woman in *Etant Donées* is directly related to The Bride in *The Large Glass*. The disregard for taste (Tono 1984:53) is a common feature of both works.

the association of craft and philosophy would redeem mankind of its backwardness went sour. The golden age of enthusiastic hopes for reform ended in disillusion, or resigned desperation (Koyré 1971a: 305). By the nineteenth century, the result was bondage. Machines brought not prosperity but misery. The products of the industrial revolution were not to be considered beautiful. Plenty produced poverty and famine. William Blake (1757–1827) described industry as a loud furnace with anvils of death thundering incessantly, and moved by satanic wheels (Bronowski 1972).

Duchamp's depiction of mechanisms is equally despairing. His machines can move fast, but they get nowhere. At their very best, mechanical experience is indifferent. Indifference is the twin sister of hybridism. Art is reduced more and more to the status of a sign (Cabanne 1972: 105).

A work of art that aspires permanence is made on the fragile surface of a glass. *The Large Glass*, this odd shop window, was in the end shattered and its cracks were absorbed as part of the final picture. Developed from the schematic depiction of *Moulin à café* (a painting made in 1911 from diagrams and arrows to be hanged at his brothers's kitchen at Puteaux), an utmost mechanical image such as *The Chocolate Grinder* should be mounted on Louis XV nickled chassis (Sanouillet and Peterson 1975: 68). Machines can make even music.[4] Creation is unity of the arbitrary and the diverse. In Modern Age, there are no clear-cut boundaries separating the beautiful and the useful.

At least in certain areas, ever since the beginning of the seventeenth century, doubt prevailed. For Descartes, doubt was a radical method of exclusion. Through the exclusion of representations with the slightest doubt,

---

[4] Duchamp's musical compositions were recorded in 1976 by the S.E.M Ensemble for Multipla Records as *The Entire Musical Works of Marcel Duchamp*. Chance and machines are the two major elements in Duchamp's pieces. In *Erratum Musical*, notes are picked up haphazardly from a hat. *Musical Sculpture* uses player piano and mechanical organ. And in another piece named *The Bride Stripped Bare by her Bachelors, even. Erratum Musical*, a funnel, a toy train with open cars (without locomotive) and balls, to be put in the funnel, are part of a random system of composition. "Each ball presents a number which represents one note of a chosen instrument. The amount of balls is determined by the range of the instrument. The balls fall through the funnel into the cars as they pass underneath. Then, the balls are taken out of the cars and the numbers are transformed into notes — each number represents one note." The quote is on the record cover, in which Petr Kotik describes Duchamp's musical instructions.

we reach certainty. Descartes demonstrated that doubt thrived on sensorial perceptions, in our dreams and in mathematics. In fact, Descartes's postulation of a malin génie forced him to recognize doubt in non-contingent knowledge such as mathematics and its fundament. The only representation without a grain of doubt is provided by the experience of the cogito. The act of thinking—cogitare—delivers the certainty of my existence as a self. The thinking subject cannot be sure of the truthfulness of any representation. His very act of thinking is the condition for the certainty of his being. This reveals the existence of two substances, separated from each other: *mind*, and, a form of extension, *matter*.

Mind does not depend on the senses. Thinking is by nature intelligible and autonomous in relation to matter. Mathematical representations are not abstracted from the senses. Mathematical truths are evident: They are eternally present in our minds. Ideas are inborn, and geometrical representations order the experience of the senses. Matter is intellectually deducted from clear and evident principles that inhabit the spirit, even before our contact with the material world. Mathematics holds the secret key to nature. Arithmetical and geometrical representations interpret and underline natural movements. With the Cartesian philosophy, we are on the threshold of modern mechanical representations.

Mechanical representations redefine natural forms. Nature is transfigured into a machinery. It is sheer illusion that our perception of natural forms is an agglomeration of qualities. Now we have to understand nature as numerical quantities. Human knowledge is converted into mechanical metaphors whose parts operate in interaction to each other. Then, cognitive hierarchy is subverted. Authoritative knowledge could blossom equally from scholars, mining engineers, textile inventors, potters, instrument makers, or iron masters. It is an advanced concept of cognition as the joint work of superior craftsmen, engineers and, less so, scholarly people. Learning can come from anywhere. Therefore, there can be no distinction between artifacts and artistic products.

Nature is a mechanical clockwork. Machines are symbols for creation; God himself is the clockmaker (Rossi 1989: 19). Jean Clair (1975: 142) would say that, for Duchamp, the machine is the divine principle. From art, it will come the demiurge of modern life (Le Bot 1973: 87). It is a revolutionary aesthetic program, akin to the claim that industrial age ought to reorganize daily life.

So, in another extreme, artists could even be small manufacturers (Compagnon 1990: 127). Duchamp is the example of this. He created objects with no function, dislodged from their regular usage. Readymades do not respond to a social demand. With them, creation is supreme. It transcends the frontiers of production, consumption, and marketing. Duchamp offers the chosen object elected from the sameness of industrial production, but made new. Compagnon (1990) argues that this feat confers to the artist a role similar to any industrialist.

Nevertheless being outside of the productive milieu, the artist embodies the dilemmas of industrial society. The artist absorbs the rules of modern technical thought. The artistic work develops into a collective enterprise; it is not anymore the expression of a single mind. The artist aims at ceaseless progress and perfection, expressed as constant invention driving his thoughts. Avant-garde, its concern in rewriting the history of art, and industrial age share the same goals.

Machines are apparatuses cleaved from the self and its demand of symptomatic representation. Machines cannot stand for anything else. Machines produce intensive quantities (Deleuze and Guattari 1972: 26). Absent and missing elements play no part in machineries. Their principle of causality is intensely material. The causality of cogwheels and pulleys badly fits Freudian models. It is difficult to be at ease with Jacques Derrida's interpretation that, in Freud, the structure of the psychic apparatus should be represented as a machine for writing, a machine d'écriture (Derrida 1967: 297). To talk of psychic events as if they were mechanisms is nothing more than an imprecise metaphor. Machines have another model; their model of signs is production. There is nothing hidden. Machines fill the void; they are a plenitude.

A productive model of signs is inconsonant with Freudian reductionism. We can see this referring critically to Freud's analysis of Dr. Daniel Schereber's paranoid delirium. Freud ascribed to Dr. Schereber's sexual conflicts the motives for his hallucinations. In Schreber's delirium there is a crowd morphology that offers a precise political model of interrelationships that derives its substance from crowd agglomerations (Canetti 1981: 512).

The self is left well behind. We are facing something more than the expression of a personal pathology. We can see this in the social formation of industrial society, where the crowd morphology is at work. The aim of technical rationality in industrialized communities is to produce in greater quantities. Quantity is an absolute value. So, the accumulative effect is extended inevitably to the sphere of consumption. As consumption is an individualistic action, industrial societies do not encourage all sorts of renunciation. We must accumulate more and more.

The accumulation of crowds arises from smaller gatherings, from packs. A pack surrounds the paranoic. Company and all forms of otherness turns out to be unbearable. Everyone must be absorbed by the deluded self. The hostile pack grows and spread itself to the smallest of signs. Pebbles, or stains, or sun flecks form patterns representing in some awful way messages of doom. Schreber thought that a conspiracy against him would take the shape of a plot to blend him into a woman. Paranoia is not derived from homosexuality. Power is productive. Homosexual representations are products of power.

The morphology of intense individualism demands a power that denies the right of existence to figures of otherness. In Duchamp's travesty into Rrose Sélavy and Schreber's feminine transformation there is something more than mere homosexual hints. They have in common the seed of the same power experience. If it is so, we meet Michel Carrouges's argument suggesting a link between Duchamp's machineries with political experiences that pervaded the twentieth century.

In fact, besides Marcel Duchamp and Raymond Roussel (1877–1933), in 1914, Franz Kafka (1833–1924) also created a strange machine in his story "In The Penal Colony." Kafka minutely describes a mechanism that painfully inscribes a label of guilt over the submissive culprit's skin. This instrument of death is all chains attached to each other. An officer of the penal colony hosts a visiting explorer. He takes the explorer to see the machine designed by the old Commandant of the penal colony. The Commandant did more than design the machine. The whole island—the penal colony—is in itself a machine where every bit fits. In the island "it is impossible to alter anything, at least for years to come" (Kafka 1976: 141). Guilt is not doubted. Trial procedures are not required. Machines embody the trial and the execution, with no intermediate levels. The guilty act ought to be immediately written upon the body of the accused.

Kafka, Roussel, and Duchamp experienced the scientific barbarism and the power concentration in a world on the brink of totalitarian regimes (Carrouges 1976: 24). Carrouges just shows analogical affinities between Roussel, Duchamp, and Kafka.

With Duchamp, we are a step nearer to Kafka's nightmarish tale of Gregor Samsa's transformation into a monstrous insect. Just look carefully. The Bride (*La Mariée*) is the name of an insect: *la nocturnelle*. Its wings are flapping against The Glass; The Bride's Garment almost grasp the scissors of *The Chocolate Grinder* in the Bachelor's region. Another kind of winged insect, Gregor Samsa could have flown through the opened window of his room. And out of The Bride it comes The Milky Way, larvae of nocturnal butterfly (Carrouges 1976: 33).

Duchamp's oeuvre and Kafka's mythologies match each other in the same way that Thierry De Duve discovered analogies between Duchamp's family life and his artistic choices. And that is the weak point. The mere juxtaposition of analogies is no real explanation.

Psychoanalytic dogma asserts that we can unravel dream-like ciphered images in artworks. Psychoanalysis translates the dream-work (*Traumbeit*) into a speech expressing the latent desires of the artist. The latent is then the masked motive generating images. Between latent and manifest contents, there is convergence and transcription. The two series—latent and manifest—are in a state of permanent shift. The meaning of a work of art is a residue drifting along with the formal constitution of an image. It is the role of psychoanalytic commentaries to endow pictures with meaning (Lyotard 1973: 55). Thus, meaning comes from without. There should be a lack, an absence, making the two series, conscious and unconscious, slide endlessly. Nevertheless, with machines, latent levels are a mirage. Nothing is ever deeper than surfaces. That is why Kafka's death machine inscribes sentences upon the skin of the condemned. Revelation arrives from material occurrences.

An exclusive emphasis on surface occurrences denies identity. Processes are ongoing. If there is not the other to identify with, then there is no possible identity. What we have is a steady going forward, a pure and infinite becoming, with no limits, measureless, joining contraries, mingling the more and the less, the growth and the shrinkage, the cause and the effect, the promise of dawn and the morning after, the excess and the insufficiency, the active and the passive, the male and the female. Thus, Marcel Duchamp and Rrose Sélavy have become like one. More than identity, gossamer processes enthrall Duchamp

This is obvious from reading a set of Duchamp's posthumous notes on what he called the infrathin (*le inframince*). In them, we discover the systematic project of a corporeal ontology that André Breton noticed previously. Breton (1972: 329) had discerned that Duchamp's ironical humor, labeled as *ironisme d'affirmation*, came about as the upshot of his lifting the natural laws. His puns and paradoxes are an affair of signs striding on signs, not something causal but the avowal of a funny physics, both reasonable and incorporeal. It makes sense to calculate the volume displaced by a clean shirt and compare it with the one of a dirty shirt (Breton 1972: 333). Or then to reinterpret the interaction of rigidity and hazard, as in the *3 Standard Stoppages* (1913–1914); where a straight horizontal thread one meter long falls from the height of one meter on a horizontal plane, distorting itself as it pleases, creating a new shape of the meter (Sanouillet and Peterson 1975: 22), being still a meter and also not anymore.

Whatever we can convey in words demands existence. Yet existence and words are fluid. When we say that an entity moves are we thinking of the same being? During the process, did it change? Are changes particular forms of existence? Is the becoming something real in itself? Can existence be only corporeal? Are changes substances or qualities? Or are they, like the Ancient Stoics used to say, a mixture of bodies interacting in their intimacy, but having a common extension (Bréhier 1970: 11)? Becoming does not have the regular condition of existence. It is just the faint trace of actuality.

Infrathin has fleeting properties and infinitive attributes. Such is the case with "the warmth of a seat which has just been left" (Duchamp 1983: note 4); or the whistling sound of two velvet trousers brushing against each other (Duchamp 1983: note 9). Infrathin can be both a mixture and a separation. The same can be distinguished from the same and differences can be conjugated. Infrathin oscillates between frailty and fugacity. The mixture happens, for instance, when the tobacco smoke smells of the mouth which exhales it. The two odors marry by infrathin (Duchamp 1983: note 11). Elsewhere, Duchamp (1983: note 12) wrote about infrathin disjunction, otherwise fixed as the "infrathin separation between the detonation noise of a gun (very close) and the apparition of the bullet hole in target (maximum distance 3 to 4 meters) gallery at a fair."

Without being evoked from ideas of essence, timeless, immutable, and necessary, thoughts on infrathin are well beyond the criterion of contradiction. In Thierry De Duve's terms, infrathin has an undecidable nomination (De Duve 1994: 159). If all of Duchamp's aesthetical program is presumed undecidable, Duchamp's meditations on the infrathin are at the core of his *oeuvre*.

Infrathin has no definite logical identity. If it belongs to the realm of possibility, it is not contradictory or illogical. As possibility, infrathin cannot be true or false. Just like Duchamp's early paintings concerned with the representation of moving bodies, infrathin experiences are always on the move. The limits of identity are dissolved in the process of becoming. No object has permanent boundaries; it suffers complete mutation, as the proper destiny of any corporeal nature. What is hot becomes cold, what is young becomes older, and one both is and is becoming. The next sentence illustrates the bonds of possibility and infrathin: "The possibility of several tubes of color becoming a Seurat is the concrete explanation of the possible as infrathin" (Duchamp 1983: note 1).

In this slapstick ontology, we detect a metaphor of total creation. The artist looks at the tubes of paint that he could use. At this moment, painting is modulated into an immanent language. It cannot be a copy or a servile simulation of the outside world. Painting refers autonomously to itself. Even if Kandinsky cannot be effectively associated with Duchamp, we can affiliate their artistic concerns. Kandinsky talked about the name of color as its inner sound, referring to nothing but the metaphor of its being and also its metaphorical being (De Duve 1994: 124); and Duchamp wrote a taxonomy of colors in the hope of achieving "pure tone" (Sanouillet and Peterson 1975: 79). The common origin of both Kandinsky and Duchamp is Cézanne's lesson that pictorial realism cannot be achieved. Thus, the readymade deserves to be considered part of the modern pictorial tradition, but it cannot be under the rules that fathered painting.[5]

Is it mandatory to have had Duchamp's life story to work out his pictorial solutions for what was certainly a problem to anyone painting at the beginning of the century? The effort of psychoanalyzing Duchamp can be very elaborate, intriguing but of little value. It is better to see his work as a reflection on how the material qualities of representation grew into an absolute value for modernist tradition.

---

[5] More than the expression of events in Duchamp's life, this is a pictorial problem shared by so many modern painters. Discussing abstractionism and the readymade, *Pictorial Nominalism* is at its best, even if Thierry de Duve insists on unverifiable hypothesis such as the improbable coincidence of Duchamp's phrase that "the bachelor grinds his chocolate alone" with Max Doerner's advice for painters in his book on the material of the artist: "it is recommended that the painter grind his own colors, not merely for the sake of economy, but also because he needs to become better acquainted with its material, and, furthermore, because color ground by hand possesses a charm which factory-made products frequently lacks" (Doerner 1969:143). It is engaging also to see a resonance of Doerner's advice in the craftsmanship of *The Large Glass*, countered by Duchamp's idea of creating from factory-made objects, the readymades. But there is one problem. We have no concrete evidence that Duchamp ever attended Doerner's lectures in Munich on the craft of art; and Doerner only published his book when the *Glass* was already abandoned unfinished.

We should not take lightly Duchamp's comic thoughts on possibility and infrathin, as in Seurat's coming out of tubes of paint: a readymade pictorial surprise. Duchamp is talking about the virtual instability of the possible prowling behind actual and mass-produced objects. All forms of possibility, including artistic creation, are made out of what actuality furnishes but under another combination. The different qualities of the corporeal world are recombined. We start with one version of actuality and end up with another. Thus, artistic creation can be the construction of a whole new world, with no one-to-one correspondence to whatever rules our immediate sensorial perception.

Duchamp is a worldmaker. He is free to shift common objects from their regular context; and show them in a radically new light, as if they were foreign to our everyday experience. From scratch Duchamp invents alternative and inconceivable modes of creation. His freedom allows him even to abandon painting; or then, determine a set moment and day to create a readymade (Sanouillet and Peterson 1975: 32). If the overall modernist tradition implies a constant overcome of pictorial solutions, then Duchamp takes this convention to the edge of an abyss. Even modernist tradition could be buried as a personal decision on his part.

However much Thierry De Duve has tried to clean out deterministic precepts from psychoanalysis, all kinds of Freudianism are in fact immersed in historical and biographical determinism. Lacan's structuralist emphasis on the Symbolic Order just reinterprets the forces at work in early childhood. Determinism remains the same. In fact, genesis and structure can be now intertwined in an even more deterministic frame. *Pictorial Nominalism* yelds no evidence that could reduce the autonomy between psychological disposition to act and the creations of the human mind. Freudianism only provides unconfirmed and unjustifiable explanations for an artist so taken by the condition of freedom. Psychoanalysis made a ghost of Marcel Duchamp.

CHAPTER 7

The Photographic Paradox
Retina Everywhere

THINGS APPEAR upside down. *Photography: A Middle-Brow Art* could not really be called the English translation of *Un art moyen: Essai sur les usages sociaux de la photographie*. Let us start considering the titles of those editions. There is no *photography* in the original main title and, in the French edition, a *middle-brow art* is not a secondary and qualifying element but the main title. More than a little happened on the way through translation. Just time? Well, twenty-five years elapsed since the original publication, but not just that. A whole array of nuances was toned down in this new English language edition. A minor section called "chronologie des recherches utilisées" (Bourdieu 1965: 333–335) disappeared. The consequence is that it is now fair to presume that an average reader will not suspect that this book originated at the Centre de la Sociologie Européene, where a seminar on the image in the industrial society was held in the academic year of 1961, under the direction of Raymond Aaron. This book was also a response to a commission made by Kodak-Pathé.

Photography, which was so well situated in the original edition, hovers abstractly above our heads and we can only guess or refer to the original publication to know under what circumstances those essays (now apparently autonomous) were produced. It is particularly regrettable that the "appendice" (Bourdieu 1965: 337–355) was excised; in it we could see and assess the statistical frame-work that guided the research. The conclusion "Images et phantasmes," by Robert Castel (Bourdieu 1965: 290–331); Luc Boltanski's brilliant contribution "La réthorique de la figure" (Bourdieu 1965: 174–198); and Gerard Lagneau's "Trompe l'oeil et faux-semblant"(Bourdieu 1965: 210–217) are also missing with the excuse that they are not directly related to photography as such.

This is more than a real pity. If we have any intention of putting this book into a historical perspective, this is quite misleading. Which title to be referred to: *Un art moyen* or *Photography*? What appeared to be the same book in translation is, in fact, a quite different one. An evidence of this is that a name that appears in "l'index des thèmes et noms" of the French edition is wholly absent in the index of this *Photography*: Roland Barthes (1915–1980).

Barthes's Lesson

However critical we may be of Barthes's instigative but flimsy arguments, his seminal work lurks in the background of anyone writing about photography in the mid-sixties. Barthes had taught us that such an apparently minor and debased subject as photography could be analyzed with wit and acuity.

It is also true that Barthes was not talking exclusively of photography. At the beginning of the 1960s, he had started to sketch his project of "sémiologie." As fashion and advertising, photography was one of a set of non-verbal messages that could provide the definite proof that semiology, the science dealing with signs in social life (Saussure 1983: 15), was achievable. It is a strange but pleasant symmetry that in *La chambre claire*, and just before his death, Barthes would face photography again, but then "l'écriture," or rather "le plaisir du texte," and not semiology, was his main concern.

Semiology is a possibility derived directly from Émile Durkheim's influence on Saussure's *Course in General Linguistics* which can be recognized even if we skip through the Saussurean text.[1] Durkheimean notions and terminology crop up repeatedly: Institution and social fact define language, which results from a social contract. There is in linguistic facts the same relationship between what is social and what is individual that occupies sociology. Social life was conceived in both authors as an all-encompassing environment where messages are exchanged. All messages contribute to

---

[1] At the beginning of the 30s, Doroszewski (1933) discussed the theoretical consequences of Saussure's adoption of the Durkheimean conceptual framework. When Saussure defined *langue* as a collectively accepted set of rules, itself more important than individual acts of speech (*parole*), he echoed Durkheim's distinction of *représentations individuelles* and *représentations collectives*. Collective representations are imposed *a priori* to individual conscience, constraining it. Collective representations create social facts. Language-structure (*langue*) are also within collective conscience; its social nature places it beyond individuals. *Langue* is a a set of rules bestowed on the social actors. The essential trace of any language-structure is "its imposition upon the individual through collective usage" (Doroszewski 1933: 90). Dorowszewski also sees Saussure's opposition of langue and parole as a form of conciliating Durkheim's debate with Gabriel de Tarde's conception that language is essentially an individual performance.

keep social experience together; there is no difference between the linguistic emission of signs, “la cuisine,” pantomime, convention of politeness, whatever.

Anyone who followed the historical fluctuations of the social sciences would figure out a very curious inversion. Saussure could be using the terminology and the conceptual framework of *l'école sociologique française* to avoid ties with the nineteenth-century historicism. Sociology would function as a paradigm of the now so much criticized Saussurean paradigm (Percival 1981). Saussure's early and vital dream of a theory of signs could only be possible through Durkheimean notions. One cannot hear the proposal of a science of signs in the midst of social life without recognizing semiology as a new tag for classical problems and deadlocks that pertained traditionally to sociology. Linguistics was soon standing on its own feet, with distinctive contribution and a high degree of scientificity; and this was going to echo along the divide between sociological and anthropological inquiry. Among others, Claude Lévi-Strauss thought that social life could no longer conceived according to organic and biological models. The notion came into being that social life is a vast communication system where each exchange is a message constructed according to rules agreed upon.

This *structure* translates and codifies simultaneously the exogamic order of society (whence kinship systems were derived), the economic values, the exchange of messages, and the circulation of mates (Lévi-Strauss 1975b). Everything could be understood as language, whose role is to integrate social life as a whole not necessarily harmonious. Societies exist through conventions. Structure harbored the basic duality of alliance and rivalry. Each social phenomenon should then be interpreted as a communicative form; society is made by individuals who communicate with each other (Lévi-Strauss 1975a: 336). Lévi-Strauss was then thinking of a sociological question formulated by French Sociology based on the assumption that society has a character that allows us to understand it in its own terms and therefore to search for a sociocentric explanation for the concrete attitudes of individuals within a particular social group. What is the universal rule that acts upon society forming a succession of distinct totalities as well as producing similar formal orders in different geographic areas that had no direct contact with each other? The prohibition of incest and existence of language among human beings were apparently undisputed universals. The universality of incest has been questioned on occasion (Hopkins 1980: 303–335) but Lévi-Strauss was hitting another key. The system of languages articulates material speech patterns with conceptual entities in the same way that the prohibition of incest fuses a biological practice, such as copulation, with another order properly human that intends to transcend natural drives: culture. Systems of kinship would offer us rules for the ordered exchange of mates among social segments.

The ideas presented in Marcel Mauss's *Essai sur le don* were distinct presences in Lévi-Strauss's arguments. Exchange is but an aspect of the global structure of reciprocity, considered as an object of immediate and intuitive apprehension on the part of social human beings (Lévi-Strauss 1976: 176–177). As a manifestation of the cultural order, the circulation of alliance driven by kinship rules would depend, in its logic, on Mauss's principle of reciprocity which rules the gift (*le don*). Lévi-Strauss was pointing to something well beyond strictly anthropological and sociological questions. He was suggesting the possibility of one single discipline dealing with the formerly distinct domains of anthropology, economics, and linguistics.

Goods and services, words and mates are part of what could be defined as the *symbolic order*, and not only these phenomena. Everything is permeated by the symbolic order. Natural and human sciences are both condemned to face symbols produced by the limitations of human sensorial order, "l'ésprit humain." The main difference of natural and human sciences is that natural sciences deal with the symbol of things, while human sciences deal with the symbols of things that are, in themselves, symbols (Lévi-Strauss 1971: 574).

Roman Jakobson's lectures on sound and meaning constituted a decisive influence on Lévi-Strauss. Jakobson would point out that different disciplines could potentially be dealing with a unified object. According to Jakobson, Tallcott Parsons would say that money was a specialized form of language; economic exchanges were modes of conversation; the circulation of notes and coins would follow a *code* in the grammatical and syntactical sense. Jakobson (1971: 666) concluded that the linguistic model was certainly useful for the understanding of economic activities. Linguistics could claim the role of the queen-bee of social sciences. This is not just a new set of ideas: We are on the brink of an intellectual revolution (Benoist 1978).

Barthes was to play a major role in "l'aventure sémiologique." There was something new to be done. Lévi-Strauss's coupling of Saussure and Rousseau was befitting to the study of the *savage mind*. What about industrial societies? The Saussurean notion of linguistic value, an antique economic terminology perfusing linguistic inquiry, brought with it the conception of language as a form rather than a substance (Saussure 1983: 201). So, when we thought of the oppositional binary form, considering the original social contract suggested by Rousseau, we would come to a basic anthropological dichotomy expressed as Nature and Culture. From then on, other formal relations could be derived following transformational rules: man/jaguar, raw/cooked, high/low, and other similar pairs. In a series of books that started with *Le cru et le cuit*, Lévi-Strauss tackled a major project, impressive in its demonstration that social events, not disregarding proper contextualization, could be reduced to an algebra of forms in clear-cut binary opposition.

Nowadays, there are explicit objections to Lévi-Strauss's treatment of the savage mind. British anthropologists, like Edmund Leach (1970), would say that Lévi-Strauss's sauvages were really idealized and romantic version of human beings seen from afar. Lévi-Strauss's *oeuvre* was not in fact anthropology but a kind of philosophical discussion. It is a truism that nothing is as old as the most recent past, but we should remember how exciting and refreshing Levi-Strauss's cold and beautiful prose was, however bad-tempered sometimes, probing algorithms of thought in what was up to then a murky and obscure area: *la pensée sauvage*. When Barthes took on himself the task of dealing with contemporary mythologies, he was trying to cover a residual zone left by Lévi-Strauss's inquiries. The myths analyzed by structural anthropology had a distinct linguistic basis; they were primordially narratives. It was necessary to take a step ahead. Social life is not just expressed and maintained solely by linguistic narrative performances: What about non-verbal phenomena?

In the *Elements of Semiology* (Barthes 1968), we can find no substantial reflection on non-verbal phenomena, rather we see Barthes making merely analogical connections between linguistic concepts and non-verbal forms of communication. The *Elements of Semiology* also had a very smart but questionable contention. It had been Saussure's idea that linguistics was supposed to be part of a yet to be formed general theory of signs, "la sémiologie," but history showed that linguistics developed an impressive theoretical framework. We should therefore surrender to this historical lesson. Sémiologie is to be part of linguistics, not the other way round. What was left to Roland Barthes but to try to prove this hasty remark?

When we look back at these heroic times, we can recognize some ironies. Barthes's scientificism, so fully expressed in his *Système de la mode* was to fade away, but he sustained a stylistic talent worthy of the great French essayists of the past. Barthes continued to have brilliant insights, though supported by rather unstable epistemological pillars. Yet, there is always something interesting to be learned even in his errors. Another irony was that the College de France created the chair of "sémiologie littéraire" for Barthes when he thought of "sémiologie" as a stray adjective.

In 1961, when Barthes wrote "The photographic message," he took "le project sémiologique" seriously. Analogical reasoning would be a strong argument to justify "la sémiologie." If we could recognize linguistic concepts in non-linguistics events, everything would be all right, for the world and its objects have meaning because of the action of a structure that is linguistic in its basic form. Following Jakobson's analogy between "langue" and code, Barthes used as a starting point a classic informational model; there is a message going through a channel that connects a source of emission and a medium of reception. Now come some analogies: The newsroom and the editorial staff of the newspaper are sources of emission of a photographic message, the channel of transmission is the newspaper, and the medium of reception is the public that reads the newspaper. A semiological analysis of the press photograph would be possible if a clear frontier with sociology were kept in mind. Sociology would take care of the investigation of the emission and the reception of the newspaper, but if we treat the photographic image as a structurally autonomous object, then we will be in the domain of semiology. "Sémiologie" and "sociologie" are to be friendly neighbors.

The reference to the press photograph as a structurally autonomous object ought not to be understood as a defence of an untenable isolated analysis. In the consideration of the photographic message, the newspaper text will come into consideration, but as a contiguous and separate element. We can already envisage how linguistic structures are to be insinuated into non-verbal trenches.

An inappropriate idea of Barthes' is the notion of photographic paradox. Photographs represent the literal reality: Everything that comes from external reality is registered on the photographic emulsion. Photographs do not have a code; they are perfect analogons. This hackneyed notion is sufficient for Barthes (1985: 5). But this blunder is not made by Bourdieu. The commitment to the idea of a literal reality is to Bourdieu (1990: 23) no more than a false evidence produced by a vulgar representation of photography. Photography is not a direct record of perception. It is a mode of representation stemming from other representations. Through the relationship between the appearance of reality and the impression made by visual images, the final representation is built. The principle of photography is the same as in the paintings in perspective; the point of view is cyclopean and fixed, from where the image shall be registered. The fixed eye is the place where the vertex of a triangle of light is formed whose base is the perceived object. In earlier times, a painter would trace the projected image on the interior of a camera obscura. In photography, the light sensitive paper registers the projection that comes from external reality. All this is not mere mechanical registration, but the historical development of a long standing tradition in Western visual images. Bourdieu learned from Pierre Francastel (1960: 46) that a historical convention is somewhat at work in photographs. Barthes is in fact so tied up with the misleading conception of literal reality as a basic feature of photography that his next argumentative step is to transfer the meaning and deciphering of those images to another level, to connotation, to the way society represents literal reality (Barthes 1985: 6). The real paradox of photography is shown not in the denotative/connotative duality, but in the way it presents the coexistence of history and instant.

After the invention of photography, the mimetic ideal takes a radical turn. It is quite true that, at first, with photography the mimetic accomplishment seems unsurpassable. No hand-made drawing could ever aspire to what photographs obtain. But, strangely enough, if photographs simulates reality, it is never matchable to reality itself. Not even mechanical devices can achieve the impossible mimetic ideal. Photographs make reality eerie. Photographs are the negative of a presence: Everyone knows that inside the camera, the photographic object was initially perceived as upside down. The photographic image results from formal decisions made through the handling of photographic equipment, therefore determined by the use of a certain lens, as well as the aperture of the camera's diaphragm, and the time required for exposing the film.[2] The decisions are what establish the appearance of the photographed object: They are the image.

Photography inaugurates a new age in image making. It is something altogether revolutionary. Photographs may still import their compositions from the traditional solutions of the Fine Arts. But, with photography, images are now defined in mechanical terms. Photography does more than mutate the idea of skill and craftsmanship inherited from the fine arts. The mechanization of image making is a truly democratic achievement. Anyone can take pictures.

---

[2] Not far from now, the chemical technologies that were indispensable to photographs maybe extinct. Digital cameras still receive light coming from the outside world through lenses, but the radical difference is the digital mutation of light into *bits*, into information. Like never before, the transformation of chemical reaction into bits releases photographs from the strictures of representing what is a presence in nature. The possibilities of representations through images have become virtually without boundaries. Elements originally hauled from reality can be transformed to an unthinkable degree. Photographs will transcend the rigid role of witnesses and providers of evidence. Photographs recast and subvert what was once regarded as reality.

The mechanical nature of photography brings with it the idea of a precise and instant representation. Nevertheless, this is not enough to define a photographic representation. The *photographable* also plays an important role in images as such. Otherwise the result would be the same thing that surprised the viewers of early photographs: a cold, impoverished and trivial image (Freund 1974: 17). The representation just did not look right; it was not considered spontaneous. This really meant that it did not follow the model of a recognizable posture.

Photographs show that the plain reproduction of the conditions of vision cannot suffice. A picture is effective when it borrows from other visual solutions. Then, one discerns how images depend upon other images. Nude pictures echo the poses of Ingres (1780–1867). Photographic images of Che Guevara dead on a table, surrounded by his captors, reflect Rembrandt's (1606–1669) *Anatomy Lesson*. In these cases, and in many others, the reference of an image is not its referent, but other representations. The effect of naturality is never given by the mechanical nature of photography, as we might think, rather it is a result of visual expectations derived from the thesaurus of representative forms learnt by the viewers.

Photography simultaneously projects and hides the phantasmal silhouette of tradition. For the viewer there is no past in photography; only the present is shown under the guise of an instant. History is irrelevant. Photography's most immediate commitment is to an extreme registration of actuality. An analogy with the sensorial experience of touch could initially define photography. First we have some form of track left on the film by the photographed object; only then can images reveal themselves.

Nicephore Niepce's (1765–1833) famous photograph of a set table, made in 1822, took several hours of exposure to leave us subtle marks of a *nature morte*. In 1839, the necessary photographic exposure was 15 minutes. Two years later, it was reduced to 2 minutes. In 1842, 20 or 40 seconds was enough. Thanks to technical progress the instant was slowly conquered as something to be represented.

The shorter the time needed to fix an exposure, the more immediate the representation of this moment. This platitude brings to mind the notion that photography faces a discontinuous world, made of discrete instants. Each photographed instant presumes the discovery of correspondences between representation and actuality. In a photograph, then, an instant is just what is required. When we pose for a photograph, everything appears to be self-sufficient; there should be no need for any further explanation. If someone notices that a lens is fixed on his direction, there is a brisk change: One starts to pose, transforming oneself into another body, offering oneself as image (Barthes 1984a: 22). Barthes's brilliant insight must be countered with the historical evidence that the first photographic portraits were taken according to visual models extracted from classical paintings. The gestures of French noblemen were multiplied vulgarly by photographs and made accessible to the public which was now seeing bourgeois actors. "La bourgeoisie" and "la nobilité" merge, in pictures at least.

Images can be made entirely of images. The naked woman between two dressed men in Edouard Manet's *Déjeneur sur l'herbe* (1863) re-presents a composition feature of Marcantonio Rimondi, a pupil of Raphael. The nineteenth-century sense of immorality is a product of the ignorance of viewers, blind to an erudite iconographical quotation.

Images can direct us to referents. When Claude Monet (1840–1926) painted his *Le déjeuner sur l'herbe* (1865–66), his intention was to offer a visual criticism of Manet's Déjeuner; it was an urgency to bring observation back to nature. Monet was driven to nature by an image. Apparently, the source of his inspiration was not an antique image, but, in fact, Monet's *Déjeneur*. The painted women were taken from fashion images and groups of people strolling in open air (Isaacson 1972: 45–51) pictured in popular magazines. The main reference is again not a referent, but an iconography chosen to represent.

Everything can be transformed into a scene. Reality is reduced to representation. We can carry out our lives under the spell of representations. The photographic record is mandatory at marriage ceremonies, baptisms, birthday parties and when we travel we keep our lover's photograph in wallets, or we hide it, depending on the situation. All the events that are important deserve to be photographed. Photographs underline the importance of the instant. We do not just live; we pose, and there are shadows lurking behind us.

The shadow of connotation is thrown over the denoted literal reality. The coding of this perfect analogon is made by something that is not a photographic structure. Barthes's conception of the photographic paradox forces him to rely on something external to photography. This is one of the prices he must pay for the misleading notion that photography can be a message without a code. Another price is methodological. If there is no code in photography and if the meaning of a photograph comes as a second instance from the newspaper reader's cultural situation (Barthes 1985: 17), the task of providing an interpretation to photography should be essentially an affair for sociology. That consequence is particularly reinforced when Barthes (1985: 20) talks of photographic connotation as an institutional activity. The ghost of Durkheimean terminology continues to haunt “la sémiologie.” Photography, as something to be taken in itself, evaporates. We are left only with society. Barthes’s arguments in favor of “la sémiologie” act as a boomerang, hitting their force back on semiology.

It is therefore fair to mention that the meaningful form of press photographs derives from historical conventions and social stereotypes of realism as an aesthetic idea. The press photograph presents itself as a slice of life. Its nature is defined by the relationship between the photographer and the photographed event. The idea that the press could in any way be taken as an autonomous object is a daydream. As a message intended to address the reader of a newspaper, that kind of photography extracts its meaning from the instantaneous nature of the event. Photos have a confirmational function. The instant registered on a photographic plate implies also that its character as a fleeting moment is irretrievably lost. As a peculiar form of compensation, if the nature of photography is dependent upon conventions historically and socially inherited, then a photographic print is a warranty that the fact really happened. For photographic aesthetics everyday life is moving. On the other hand, everyday life is contemplated through the gaze of collective representations. To illustrate the notion that photography should be considered in social Pierre Bourdieu mentions a study of the reactions of peasants to a photograph of an old woman's hands creased with wrinkles. The peasants would comment, admiringly, on the days spent at the kitchen or the field. They did not see the old woman's hand: What they saw was old age, work and honesty (Bourdieu 1990: 93). That is why Luc Boltanski, in his article “La rhétorique de la figure” suppressed in this new English language edition of *Un Art Moyen*, affirms that Barthes confers upon himself the untenable privilege of an abstract sociology under the tenuous excuse of an immanent analysis. To understand photography it is necessary to study the group of professionals that produce those images (Bourdieu 1965: 195). Photography is inseparable from the craft that generates it.

Any More Questions to Sociology?

Some methodological principles are to be learnt when we take into account the relationship of photography, semiotics, and sociology. Most of Barthes’s failure is due to the fact that his conception of history and society was too far removed from any concrete situation. Bordieu’s analysis does not suffer from this flaw. Every consideration in Bourdieu's book either relates to or springs from an actual social relationship. Photography is a primordial sociological object not because it is anything like being an abstract analogon, but because it is a fact permeating an immense variety of social experiences; and this quasi-universal trait is then redivided according to social fragmentation and concrete power relationships. The general presence of cameras in households, for instance, is then subtly transformed into an index of the differences in the standards of living (Bourdieu 1990: 14). The camera is a sign to be taken in reference to economic distinctions and social constraints.

When we are dealing with a problem like that it is a good rule of thumb to remember three methodological principles: 1) do not separate collective representations from the material reality of the sign; 2) do not dissociate the sign from the concrete forms of social communication; and 3) do not dissociate communication from its forms of material relationship among social strata.

Photography is very efficient in sociological terms not just because it works as a faithful mode of recording social events. Photographs are in fact very forceful social operators: A boy is born, photos of him are taken, letters are sent to other relatives, friends and acquaintances. Social integration is produced in bonds of alliance.

Photography is more than an expression of what is social. The unity of a group does develop around the sign that is the photographic image. It is clearly a two-way thoroughfare. Photography "reinforces the integration of the group, and at the same time, reinforces its inclination to capture the image of its integration, an image which, in turn, seems to reinforce integration" (Bourdieu 1990: 26).

With the dissemination of photography starts a major social trend disregarded both by Barthes and Bourdieu. This trend demands a semiotic approach. Representations refer to representations, in a semiotic process of unending multiplication. Simulation is the main trace of contemporary experience. Photography is a simulation of reality and not its faithful record. Reality is transformed into signs. This obsessive semiotic duplication drives us away from referents, purifying any experience of its material counterpart. Reality comes to be a sign among signs, a secondary element in relation to the image that simulates it. There is a real social revolution at work; we come gradually to prefer the immediate record of an event to its direct experience (Boorstin 1964). What is real ought to be translated into images. Images are metamorphosis, pure metaphors of reality that can present whatever is beyond corporeality, thanks to new techniques of composition. The logic of photography no longer restrict itself to physical permanence, identity and record. Images can insinuate incorporeal processes and even legitimize reality.

REFERENCES

Aarsleff, Hans (1971). Cartesian linguistics: History or fantasy? *Language Sciences* 17, 1–12.

— (1982). *From Locke to Saussure: Essays on the Study of Language and Intellectual History*. Minneapolis: University of Minnesota Press.

Alberti, Leon Battista (1973). *On Painting*. New Haven: Yale University Press.

Alfons, Sven (1987). The musem as image of the world. In *The Arcimboldo Effect: Transformations of the Face from the Sixteenth to the Twentieth Century*, 67–87. Milan: Bompiani.

Alpers, Svetlana (1983). *The Art of Describing; Dutch Art in the Seventeenth Century*. Chicago: The University of Chicago Press.

Alphen, Ernst van (1989). The complicity of the reader. *VS* 52/53, 121–131.

— (1994). Strategies of identification. In *Visual Culture: Images and Interpretations*, Norman Bryson, Michael An Holly, and Keith Moxey, editors, 260–271. Hanover: Wesleyan University Press.

Argan, Giulio Carlo (1986). *Imagine e persuasione*. Milano: Feltrineli.

— (1991). *História da arte como história da cidade*. São Paulo: Martins Fontes.

Aristóteles (1966). *Poética*; tradução, prefácio, introdução, comentários e apêndices de Eudoro Souza. Porto Alegre: Globo.

Aristote (1974). *La métaphysique*; introduction, notes et index par J. Tricot. Paris: J.Vrin. 2v.

Arnauld, Antoine and Nicole, Pierre (1970). *La logique ou l'art de penser*. Paris: Flammarion.

Arnauld, Antoine and Lancelot, Pierre (1992). *A Gramática de Port-Royal ou Gramática geral e razoada*. São Paulo: Martins Fontes.

Bab, Julius (1934). *Rembrandt und Spinoza: Ein Doppelbildnis im Deutsch-Jüdischen Raum*. Berlin: Philo Verlag und Buchhandlung GmbH.

Bakhtine, Mikhaïl (1980). *Écrits sur le Freudisme*. Lausanne: L'Age d'Homme.

— (1984). *Rabelais and his world*. Bloomington: Indiana University Press.

Bal, Mieke (1991). *Reading "Rembrandt": Beyond the Word-Image Opposition*. Cambridge: Cambridge University Press.

— (1994). Dead flesh, or the smell of painting. In *Visual Culture: Images and Interpretations*, Norman Bryson, Michael Ann Holly, and Keith Moxey, editors, 384–412. Hanover: Wesleyan University Press.

Bal, Mieke and Bryson, Norman (1991). Semiotics and art history. *Art Bulletin* 73, 174–208.

Baltrušaitis, Jurgen (1969). *Anamorphoses*. Paris: Olivier Perrin.

— (1989). *Aberrations: An Essay on the Legend of Forms*. Cambridge: The MIT Press.

Banfi, Antonio (1970). *A filosofia da arte*. Rio de Janeiro: Civilização Brasileira.

Barker, Andrew, editor, (1984). *Greek Musical Writings.* Cambridge: Cambridge University Press. 2v.

Barthes, Roland (1968). *Elements of Semiology*. New York: Hill and Wang.

— (1984a). *A câmara clara*. Rio de Janeiro: Nova Fronteira.

— (1984b). *O óbvio e obtuso*. Lisboa: edições 70.

— (1985). *The Responsability of Forms*. New York, Hill and Wang.

Bartky, Sandra Lee (1981). Heidegger's philosophy of art. In *Heidegger: The Man and the Thinker*, Thomas Sheehan, editor, 257–275. Chicago: Precedent.

Baudry, Jean-Louis (1968). Freud et la création littéraire. *Tel Quel* 32, 63–85.

Baxandall, Michael (1991). O olhar renascente: Pintura e experiência social na Itália da Renascença. São Paulo: Paz e Terra.

Benoist, Jean Marie (1978). *The Structural Revolution*. New York, St. Martin's Press.

Bernasconi, Robert (1985). *The Question of Language in Heidegger's History of Being*. Humanities: New Jersey.

Berry, M.V. and Nye, J.F. (1977). Fine structure in caustic junctions. *Nature* 267, 34–36

Blanché, Robert (1985). *História da lógica de Aristóteles a Bertrand Russell.* Lisboa: Edições 70.

Bonne, Jean-Claude (1973). Le travail d'un fantasme. *Critique* 315/316, 725–753.

Boorstin, Daniel J. (1964). *The Image: A Guide to Pseudo-Events in America.* New York: Harper & Row.

Bordes, Phillipe (1983). *Le serment du Jeu de Paume de Jacques-Louis David: Le peintre, son milieu et son temps de 1789 à 1792*. Paris: Ministère de la Culture: Éditions de la Réunion des Musées Nationaux.

Bossart, William H. (1968). Heidegger's theory of art. *Journal of Aesthetics and Art Criticism* 27, 58–61.

Bourdieu, Pierre, Boltanski, Luc, Castel, Robert, and Chamboredon, Jean-Claude (1965). *Un art moyen: Essai sur les usages sociaux de la photographie*. Paris: Minuit.

— (1992). *Photography; A Middle-brow Art*. Stanford: Stanford University Press.

Bourdieu, Pierre (1991). *The Political Ontology of Martin Heidegger*. Stanford: Stanford University Press.

Brandom, Robert (1983). Heidegger's categories in *Being and Time*. *Mind* 60, 386–409.

Brogan, Walter A. (1984). The battle between Art and Truth: A reconsideration. *Philosophy Today* 29, 349–357.

Bréhier, Émile (1970). *La Théorie des incoporels dans l'ancien Stoïcisme*. Paris: J. Vrin.

Breton, André (1965). *Le Surréalisme et la peinture*. Paris: Gallimard.

— (1972). *Anthologie de L'humour noir*. Paris: Jean-Jacques Pauvert.

Brion, Marcel (1952). Le thème de l'entrelacs et du labyrinthe dans l'oeuvre de Léonard de Vinci. *Revue d'esthetique* 5, 18–32.

— (1959). *Léonard de Vinci*. Paris: Livre du club du libraire. 2v.

— (1961). *L'art fantastique*. Paris: Albin Michel.

Bronowski, J. (1972). *William Blake and the Age of Revolution*. London: Routledge & Kegan Paul.

Bryson, Norman (1981). *Word and Image: French Painting of the Ancient Régime*. Cambridge: Cambridge University Press.

— (1983). *Vision and Painting; The Logic of Gaze*. New Haven: Yale University Press.

— (1987). Herméneutique de la perception. *Cahiers du Musée d'Art Moderne* 21, 103–117.

— (1988a). Intertextuality and poetics. *Style* 22 (2), 183–193.

— (1988b). Introduction. In *Calligram: Essays in New Art History from France*, Norman Bryson, editor, xiii–xix. Cambridge: Cambridge University Press.

— (1991). Semiology and visual interpretation. In *Visual Theory: Painting and Interpretation*, Norman Bryson, Michael Ann Holly and Keith Moxey, editors, 61–72. New York: Harper Collins.

— (1992). Art in context. In *Studies in Historical Change*, Ralph Cohen, editor, 18–42. Charlottesville: University Press of Virginia.

— (1994). Géricault and 'Masculinity'. In *Visual Culture: Images and Interpretations*, Norman Bryson, Michael Ann Holly, and Keith Moxey, editors, 228–259. Hanover: Wesleyan University Press. Bryson, Norman, Holly, Michael Ann, and Moxey, Keith, editors, (1994). *Visual Culture: Images and Interpretations*. Hanover: Wesleyan University Press.

Burt, Edwin Arthur (1954). *The Metaphysical Foundations of Modern Physical Science*. New York: Doubleday.

Cabanne, Pierre (1972). *Conversaciones con Marcel Duchamp*. Barcelona: Anagrama.

Calabrese, Omar (1987). *A linguagem da arte*. Rio de Janeiro: Globo.

Calas,Nicolas (1969). The Large Glass. *Art in America* (July/August), 34–35.

Calvesi, Maurizio (1975). *Duchamp invisibile*. Roma: Officina Edizioni.

— (1984). Duchamp y la sabiduria. In *Duchamp*, 59–67. Madrid: Fundación Caja de Pensiones.

Canetti, Elias (1981). *Crowds and Power*. London & Harmondsworth: Penguin.

Cantor, George (1963). *Contributions to the Founding of the Theory of Transfinite Numbers*. New York: Dover.

Carrier, David (1988). The Truth in Painting (book review). *The Journal of Philosophy* 85, 219–223.

Carrouges, Michel (1976). *Les machines célibataires*. Paris: Chêne.

Carvalho, John M. (1991). Repetitions: Appropriating representation in contemporary art. *Philosophy Today* 35 (4), 307–324.

Cassirer, Ernst (1955a). *The Philosophy of Symbolic Forms, vol 1: Language*. New Haven: Yale University Press.

— (1955b). *The Philosophy of Symbolic Forms, vol 2: Mythical Thought*. New Haven: Yale University Press.

Celant, Germano (1984). Marcel Duchamp y la Babel de los lenguages. In *Duchamp*, 68–80. Madrid: Fundación Caja de Pensiones.

Chapman, H. Perry (1990). *Rembrandt's Self-Portraits: A Study in Seventeenth Century Identity*. Princeton: Princeton University Press.

Charpy, Jean-Pierre (1976). *L'Object picturale de Matisse à Duchamp*. Paris: Éditions du Centre National de la Recherche Scientifique.

Chastel, André (1972). *Italian Art*. London: Faber & Faber.

Clair, Jean (1975). *Marcel Duchamp ou le grand fictive*. Paris: Galilée.

— (1976). La fortune critique de Marcel Duchamp: Petite introduction à une herméneutique du Grand Verre. *Revue de l'Art* 34, 92–100.

Clerico, Geneviève (1977). F. Sanctius: Histoire d'une réhabilitation. In *La Grammaire Générale; des modistes aux idéologues*, présenté par André Joly et Jean Stefanni, 125–143. Lille: Publications de L'Université de Lille.

Colie, Rosalie L. (1956). *'Some Thankfulnesse to Constantine': A study of English influence upon the early works of Constantijn Huygens*. The Hague: Martinus Nijhoff.

Compagnon, Antoine (1990). *Cinq paradoxes de la modernité*. Paris: Seuil.

Cooper, Andrew M. (1992). The collapse of the religious hieroglyph: Typology and natural language in Herbert and Bacon. *Renaissance Quarterly* 45, 96–118.

Coppin, André-Charles (1916). Rembrandt et Spinoza. *Revue des Deux Mondes* 31, 160–191.

Crow, Thomas (1986). *Representations of Revolution, Le serment du Jeu de Paume, Word and Image* (Book reviews). Art Bulletin 68 (3), 497–502.

— (1994). Observations on style and history in French painting of the male nude, 1785–1794. In *Visual Culture: Images and Interpretations*, Norman Bryson, Michael Ann Holly, and Keith Moxey, editors, 141–167. Hanover: Wesleyan University Press.

Crowther, Paul (1989). The Truth in Painting (book review). *The British Journal of Aesthetics* 29, 271–3.

Da Vinci, Leonardo (1976). *Tratado de pintura*. Madrid: Nacional.

Damisch, Hubert (1980). L'alphabet des masques. *Nouvelle Revue de Psychanalyse* 21, 123–132.

Davis, Whitney (1994). The renunciation of reaction in Girodet's Sleep of Endymion. In *Visual Culture: Images and Intepretations*, Norman Bryson, Michael Ann Holly, and Keith Moxey, editors, 168–201.

De Dijn, Herman (1986). Conceptions of the philosophical method in Spinoza: Logica and mos geometricus. *The Review of Metaphysics* 40, 55–78.

De Duve, Thiery (1991). *Pictorial Nominalism: On Marcel Duchamp's Passage from Painting to the Readymade*, trans. by Dana Polan with the author, foreword by John Rajchman. Minneapolis: University Press of Minnesota.

Deleuze, Gilles and Guattari, Felix (1972). *El antiedipo: Capitalismo y esquizofrenia*. Barcelona: Barral.

Derrida, Jacques (1967). *L'écriture et la différence*. Paris: Seuil.

— (1978). *La Vérité en peinture*. Paris: Flammarion.

— (1987). *The Truth in Painting*. Chicago: The University of Chicago Press.

— (1989). *Of Spirit: Heidegger and the Question*. Chicago: The University of Chicago Press.

— (1991). Memories of a blind man: The self-portrait and other ruins. *Art International* 14, 82–7.

Descartes, René (1968). *The Philosophical Works of Descartes*; rendered into English by Elizabeth Haldane and G. R. T. Ross, vol 1. Cambridge: Cambridge University Press.

D'Harnoncourt, Anne (1984). Antes del Vidrio: Reflexiones sobre Marcel Duchamp antes de 1915. In *Duchamp*, 130–136. Madrid: Fundación Caja de Pensiones.

Didier-Huberman, Georges (1989). Le Parcours du danseur de corde ou L'histoire de L'art dans les limites de sa simple raison. *Les Cahiers du Musée National d'Art Moderne* 30: 41–58.

Diez, Ernest (1978). Arcimboldo, Giuseppe. In *Allgemeines Lexikon der Bildenden Künstler*, Ulrich Thieme & Felix Becker, editors. Leipzig: E.A. Seemann.

Doerner, Max (1969). *The Materials of the Artist*. London: Rupert Hart-Davis.

Donogan, Alan (1989). *Spinoza*. New York: Harvester/Wheatsheaf.

Dorowszewski, W. (1933). Quelques remarques sur les rapports de la sociologie et de la linguistique: Durkheim et F. de Saussure. *Journal de Psychologie Normal et Pathologique* 30, 82–91.

Dreyfus, Hubert L. (1993). Heidegger on the connection between nihilism, technology and politics. In *The Cambridge Companion to Heidegger*, Charles B. Guignon, editor, 289–316. Cambridge: Cambridge University Press.

Duchamp, Marcel (1983). *Notes*; arrangement and translation: Paul Matisse; preface: Anne D'Harnoncourt. Boston: G.K. Hall.

Duhem, Pierre (1959). *Le système du monde: Histoire des doctrines cosmologiques de Platon a Copernic*, tome X. Paris: Hermann.

Durand, Gilbert (1969). *Les structures anthropologiques de l'imaginaire*. Paris: Bordes.

Eco, Umberto. (1979). *A Theory of Semiotics*. Bloomington: Indiana University Press.

— (1980). *Tratado geral de semiótica*. São Paulo: Perspectiva.

— Edwards, Paul (1979). *Heidegger on Death: A Critical Evaluation*. La Salle: The Hegeler Institute/The Monist.

Elsky, Martin (1984). Bacon's hieroglyph and the separation of words and things. *Philological Quarterly* 63, 449–460.

Eliade, Mircea (1952). *Images et symboles*. Paris: Gallimard.

Ferry, Luc and Renaut, Alain (1990). *Heidegger on Modernity*. Chicago: The University of Chicago Press.

Fink, Eugen (1966). *Le Jeux comme symbole du monde*. Paris: Minuit.

Fisch, Max (1986). *Peirce, Semeiotics, and Pragmatism.* Bloomington: Indiana University Press.

Fischer, John (1984). Entitling. *Critical Inquiry* 11, 286–299.

Foucault, Michel (1966). *Les mots et les choses*. Paris: Gallimard.

— (1973). *The Order of Things: An Archaeology of the Human Sciences*. New York: Vintage Books.

— (1976). *The Archaeology of Knowledge*. New York: Harper.

Francastel, Pierre (1960). *Pintura y sociedad*. Buenos Aires, Emece.

— (1967). *La Figure et le lieu*. Paris, Gallimard.

Frede, Dorothea (1993). The quest of Being:Heidegger's project. In *The Cambridge Companion to Heidegger*, Charles B. Guignon, editor, 42–69. Cambridge: Cambridge University Press.

Freud, Sigmund (1973). *Psiconálisis del arte*. Madrid: Alianza.

Freund, Gisèle (1974). *Photographie et société*. Paris, Seuil.

Fuchs, R. H. (1969). *Rembrandt in Amsterdam*. Greenwich: New York Graphic Society.

Fry, Edward (1968). *Le Cubisme*. Bruxelles: Weber.

Gadamer, Hans-George (1975). *Truth and Method*. New York: Seabury Press.

— (1985). *Philosophical Apprenticeships*. Cambridge: The MIT Press.

Galileu, Galileo (1973). *O ensaiador*. São Paulo: Abril.

Gay, Peter (1989). *Freud: Uma vida para nosso tempo*. São Paulo: Companhia das Letras.

Gebhardt, Carl (1926). Rembrandt und Spinoza. *Chronicon Spinozanum* 4, 160–183.

Gerson, H., editor (1961). *Seven Letters by Rembrandt*. The Hague: Boucher.

Gibson, Walter S. (1971). Hieronymus Bosch and the Dutch Tradition. In *Album Amicorum J. G. Van Gelder*, J. Bruyn, J. A. Emmens, E. De Johgn, D. P. Snoep, editors, 12850132. The Hague: Martinus Nijhoff.

Ginzburg, Carlo (1989). *Clues, Myths, and the Historical Method*. Baltimore: John Hopkins University Press.

— (1991). Checking the evidence: The judge and the historian. *Critical Inquiry* 18:79–92.

Golding, John (1973). *Marcel Duchamp: The Bride Stripped Bare by Her Bachelors, Even*. London: Allen Lane.

Gombrich, E.H. (1954). Psycho-analysis and the History of Art. *The International Journal of Psychoanalysis* 35, 401–411.

— (1960). *Art and Illusion: A Study in the Psychology of Pictorial Representation*. New York: Pantheon Books.

— (1966). Freud's aesthetics. *Encounter* 1, 30–40.

— (1971). *L'art et l'illusion*. Paris, Gallimard.

— (1975). *Symbolic Images: Studies in the Art of the Renaissance*. London: Phaidon.

— (1972). La máscara y la cara: La percepción del parecido fisionómico en la vida y en el arte. In *Arte, percepción y realidad*, Gombrich, E.H. et al., 15–67. Barcelona: Paidós.

— (1985). Image and word in twentieth century art. *Word and Image* 1, 213–241.

— (1990). *Norma e forma*. São Paulo: Martins Fontes.

— (1993). Aditional thoughts on perspective. *The Journal of Aesthetics and Art Criticism* 51: 69.

Goodman, Nelson (1972). *Problems and Projects*. Indianapolis: Bobbs-Merrill.

— (1976). *Languages of Art; An Approach to the Theory of Symbols*. Indianapolis, Hackett.

Guéroult, Martial (1968a). *Spinoza I: Dieu (Éthique, I)*. Paris: Aubier/Montaigne.

— (1968b). *Spinoza II: l'Âme (Éthique, II)*. Paris: Aubier/Montaigne.

Hacking, Ian (1990). *The Taming of Chance*. Cambridge: Cambridge University Press.

Hahan, Hans (1956). Infinity. In *The World of Mathematics*, James R. Newman, editor, 1593–1661. New York: Simon & Schuster.

Hallyn, Fernand (1987). *La structure poétique du monde: Copernic, Kepler*. Paris: Seuil.

Hampshire, Stuart (1978). *Spinoza*. London & Harmondsworth: Penguin. Heidegger, Martin (1957). *Der Satz vom Grund*. Pfullingen: Günther Neske.

— (1962a). *Being and Time*. New York: Harper & Row.

— (1962b). *Chemins qui mènent nulle part*. Paris: Gallimard.

— (1963). *Holzwege*. Frankfurt a. M.: V. Klostermann.

— (1971). *Poetry, Language, Thought*. New York: Harper & Row.

— (1973). The Problem of reality in modern philosophy. *Journal of British Society for Phenomenology* 4 (1), 64–71.

— (1976). *Questions IV*. Paris: Gallimard.

— (1977a). *Basic Writings*. New York: Harper & Row.

— (1977b). *The Question of Technology and other essays*. New York: Harper & Row.

— (1978). *On Time and Being*. New York: Harper & Row.

— (1981). Only a God can save us: The *Spiegel* interview (1966). In *Heidegger: The Man and the Thinker*, Thomas Sheehan, editor, 45–67. Chicago: Precedent.

Hirsch, Jr., E. D. (1983). Beyond convention. *New Literary History* 14, 389–397.

Hocke, Gustav R. (1974). *Maneirismo: O mundo como labirinto*. São Paulo, Perspectiva/Edusp.

Holly, Michael Ann (1984). *Panfosky and the Foundations of Art History*. Ithaca: Cornell University Press.

— (1990). Past looking. *Critical Inquiry* 16, 371–396.

— (1994). Wölfflin and the imagining of the Baroque. In *Visual Culture: Images and Intepretations*, Norman Bryson, Michael Ann Holly, and Keith Moxey, editors, 347–364. Hanover: Wesleyan University Press.

— (1996). *Past Looking: Historial Imagination and the Rhetoric of the mage*. Ithaca: Cornell University Press.

Hopkins, Keith (1980). Brother and sister marriage in Roman Egypt. *Contemporary Studies in Society and History* 22, 305–355.

Huizinga, Johan (1973). *El otoño de la Edad Media*. Madrid: Revista del Ocidente.

Hulten, Pontius (1987). Three different kinds of interpretations. In *The Arcimboldo effect: Transformations of the Face from the Sixteenth to the Twentieth Century*, 19–34. Milan: Bompiani.

Isaacson, Joel (1972). *Monet: Le déjeneur sur l'herbe*. London: Allen Lane.

Iversen, Margaret (1972). Style as structure: Alois Riegl's historiography. *Art History* 2 (1), 62–72.

Jaeger, Hans (1958). Heidegger and the work of art. *Journal of Aesthetics and Art Criticism* 17, 58–71.

Jakobson, Roman (1971). *Selected Writings II: Word and Language*. The Hague: Mouton.

Jouffroy, Alain (1964). *Une révolution du regard*. Paris: Gallimard.

Kahn, Charles H. (1973). *The verb "Be" and its synonyms: Philosophical and Grammar studies, edited by John W. M. Verhar (6): The verb "Be" in Ancient Greek*. Dordrecht: D.Reidel. The Hague: Mouton.

Kafka, Franz (1976). *The Complete Stories*. New York: Schoken.

Kamal, Salim (1986). *Kant and Fine Art: An Essay on Kant and the Philosophy of Fine Art and Culture*. Oxford: Clarendon Press.

Kandinsky, Wassily (1970). *Point, ligne, plan: Contribuition à l'analyse des elements picturaux*. Paris: Denöel/Gonthier.

— (1990). *Regards sur le passé et autres textes: 1912–1922*. Paris: Hermann.

Kant, Immanuel (1952). *Critique of Judgment*, translated, with analytic indexes by James Creed Meredith. Oxford: Clarendon Press.

— (1959a). *Prolegômenos a toda metafísica futura que possa apresentar-se como ciência*. São Paulo: Companhia Editora Nacional.

— (1959b). Ideas of a universal history from a cosmopolitan point of view. In *Theories of History*, Patrick Gardiner, editor, 22–30. Glencoe: The Free Press.

— (1963). An old question raised again: Is the Human race constantly progressing? In *On History*, Leslie White Beck, editor, 137–153. Indianapolis: Bobbs-Merrill.

— (1973). *Critique of Pure Reason*. London: Macmillan.

— (1976). *Critique of Practical Reason, and Other Writings in Moral Philosophy*. New York: Garland Press.

Kaufmann, Pierre (1974). *Psychanalyse et théorie de la culture*. Paris: Denöel/Gonthier.

Kayser, Wolfgang (1986). *O grotesco: Configuração na pintura e na literatura*. São Paulo: Perspectiva.

Kein, Philip J. (1989). Kant's political theory and philosophy of history. *Clio* 18, 325–345.

Kemp, Wolfgang (1994). The theater of the Revolution: A new intepretation of Jean-Louis David's *Tennis Court Oath*. In *Visual Culture: Images and Interpretations*, Norman Bryson, Michael Ann Holly, and Keith Moxey, editors, 202–227. Hanover: Wesleyan University Press.

Kernodle, George K. (1944). *From Art to Theatre: Form and Convention in the Renaissance*. Chicago: University of Chicago Press.

Kisiel, Theodore (1989). Why the first draft of *Being and Time* was never published. *Journal of the British Society for Phenomenology* 20, 3–22.

Klee, Paul (1973). *Theorie de l'art moderne*. Paris: Denöel/Gonthier.

Kockelmans, Joseph J. (1984). *On the Truth of Being: Reflections on Heidegger's Later Philosophy*. Bloomington: Indiana University Press.

— (1985). *Heidegger on Art and Art Works*. Dordrecht: Martinus Nijhoff.

Kofman, Sarah (1973). *El nascimiento del arte: Una interpretación de la estética Freudiana*. Buenos Aires: Siglo XXI.

Knowlson, James (1975). *Universal Language Schemes in England and France 1600–1800*. Toronto: University of Toronto Press.

Kolb, David (1991). Heidegger at 100, in America. *Journal of the History of Ideas* 52, 140–51.

Koyré, Alexandre (1971a). *Études de l'histoire de la pensée philosophique*. Paris: Gallimard.

— (1971b). *Mystiques, spirituels, alchimistes du XVIe. siècle allemand*. Paris: Gallimard.

— (1973). *Études de l'histoire de la pensée scientifique*. Paris: Gallimard.

— (1986). *Do mundo fechado ao universo infinito*. Rio de Janeiro: Forense.

Krauss, Rosalind E. (1977). *Passages in Modern Sculpture*. New York: Viking Press.

Kris, Ernst (1964). *Psychoanalytic Explorations in Art*. New York: Schoken.

Kris, Ernst and Kurz, Otto (1979). *Legend, Myth and Magic in the Image of the Artist*. New Haven & London: Yale University Press.

Lacan, Jacques (1966). *Écrits I*. Paris: Seuil.

— (1971). *Écrits II*. Paris: Seuil.

— (1973). *Le Seminaire, livre XI: Les quatres concepts fondamentaux de la psychanalyse*. Paris: Seuil.

— (1975). *Le Seminaire, livre X: Encore*. Paris: Seuil.

— (1977). *Psiconálisis: Radiofonia y televisión*. Barcelona: Anagrama.

Lakoff, Robin (1969). Review of *Grammaire générale et raisonneé ou La grammaire du Port-Royal*. *Language* 45, 343–364.

Leach, Edmund (1970). *Lévi-Strauss*. London: Fontana/Collins.

Lebel, Robert (1959). *Sur Marcel Duchamp*. Paris: Trianon.

Le Bot, Marc (1973). *Peinture et machinisme*. Paris: Klincksieck.

Levey, Michael (1967). *Early Renaissance*. London & Harmondsworth: Penguin.

Levinas, Emmanuel (1989). As if consenting to horror. *Critical Inquiry* 15, 485–8.

Levisi, Margarita (1968). Las figuras compuestas en Arcimboldo y Quevedo. *Comparative literature* 3, 217–235.

Lévi-Strauss, Claude (1968). *Structural Anthropology*. London & Harmondsworth: Penguin.

— Claude (1971). *Mythologiques 4: L'homme nu*. Paris: Plon.

— (1975a). *Antropologia estrutural*. Rio de Janeiro, Tempo Brasileiro.

— (1975b). *As estruturas elementares do parentesco*. Petrópolis, São Paulo, Vozes/EDUSP.

Lewis, Genviève (1950). Augustinisme et Cartésianisme à Port-Royal. In *Descartes et le Cartésianisme Hollandais*, E.J.Diksterhuis, éditeur, 130–182. Paris: Presses Universitaires de France.

Le Halle, Béatrice (1981). Bilan des méthodes et théories psychanalytiques appliquées à l'art pictural. In *Psychanalyse des arts de l'image*; Colloque de Cerisy, Henriette Bessis et Anne Clancier, éditeurs, 11–19. Paris: Clancier- Guénaud.

Lloyd, Genevieve (1987). Spinoza's version of the eternity of the mind. In *Spinoza and the Sciences*, Marjorie Green and Debra Nails, editors, 211–236. Dordrecht: D. Reidel.

Lovejoy, Arthur O. (1964). *The Great Chain of Being*. Cambridge: Harvard University Press.

Lyotard, Jean-François (1971). *Discours, figure*. Paris: Klincksieck.

— (1973). *Dérive a partir de Marx et Freud*. Paris: Union Générale d'Éditions.

— (1977). *Les transformateurs Duchamp*. Paris: Galilée.

— (1990). *Heidegger and "the jews"*. Minneapolis: Minnesota University Press.

Maclagan, Eric (1923). Leonardo in the consulting room. *Burlington Magazine* 42, 54–57.

Macula (1978), vol. 3/4.

Maiorino, Giancarlo (1991). *The Portrait of Eccentricity: Arcimboldo and the Mannerist Grotesque*. University Park: Pennsylvania State University Press.

Major-Poetzl, Pamela (1983). *Michel Foucault's Archaeology of Western Culture; Toward a New Science of History*. Chapel Hill: University of North Carolina Press.

Marin, Louis (1970). Signe et représentation: Phillipe de Champaigne et Port-Royal. *Annales* 25 (1), 1–29.

— (1975). *La Critique du discours: Sur "La Logique de Port-Royal" et les "Pensées" de Pascal*. Paris: Minuit.

— (1991). The figurability of the visual: The veronica of the question of the portrait at Port-Royal. *New Literary History* 22, 282–296.

Matheron, Alexandre (1969). *Individu et communauté chez Spinoza*. Paris: Minuit.

McKeon, Richard (1952). Literary criticism and the concept of imitation in Antiquity. In *Critics and Criticism*, R. S. Crane, editor, 147–175. Chicago: University of Chicago Press.

Méchoulan, Henri (1992). *Dinheiro e liberdade: Amsterdam no tempo de Spinoza*. Rio de Janeiro: Jorge Zahar Editores.

Merquior J. G. (1987). *Foucault*. Berkeley: University of California Press.

Michel, Paul-Henri (1962). *La cosmologie de Giordano Bruno*. Paris: Hermann.

Montias, J. Michael (1982). *Artists and Artisans in Delft: A Socio-Economic Study of the Seventeenth Century*. Princeton: Princeton University Press.

— (1987). Cost and value in seventeenth-century Dutch art. *Art History* 10, 455–466.

— (1988). Art and economic reasoning. *Art in America* 76, 23–27.

— (1989). *Vermeer and his Milieu: A Web of Social History*. Princeton: Princeton Universty Press.

— (1990). Socio-Economic aspect of Netherlandish Art from the fifteenth to the seventeenth century: A survey. *Art Bulletin* 62 (3), 358–373.

Morrison, James C. (1989). Why Spinoza had no aesthetics. *The Journal of Aesthetics and Art Criticism* 47, 359–365.

Mowhling, Karl A. (1981). Heidegger and the Nazis. In *Heidegger: The Man and the Thinker*, Thomas Sheehan, editor, 31–44. Chicago: Precedent.

Moxey, Keith (1992). The social history of art in the age of deconstruction. *History of the Human Sciences* 5, 37–46.

— (1994a). *The Practice of Theory: Poststructuralism, Cultural Politics and Art History*. Ithaca: Cornell University Press.

— (1994b). Hieronymus Bosch and "The World Upside Down: The case of *The Garden of Earthly Delights*." In *Visual Culture: Images and Intepretations*, Norman Bryson, Michael Ann Holly, and Keith Moxey, editors, 104–139. Hanover: Wesleyan University Press.

— (1995). Perspective, Panofsky, and Art History. *New Literary History* 26, 775–786.

Muller, Joseph-Emile (1968). *Rembrandt*. London: Thames and Hudson.

Murray, Peter and Linda (1972). *A dictionary of Arts and Artists*; revised edition. London & Harmondsworth: Penguin.

Nadler, Steven (1992). Cartesianism and Port-Royal. In *Essays on Early Modern Philosophers; vol. 4: Port-Royal to Bayle*, 1–12. London: Garland.

Nochlin, Linda (1988). *Women, Art, and Power, and Other Essays*. New York: Harper & Row.

Pächt, Otto (1956). Panofsky's *Early Netherlandish Painting* II. *Burlington Magazine* 98, 267–79.

Panofsky, Erwin (1953). *Early Netherlandish Painting: Its Origin and Character*. Cambridge: Cambridge University Press. 2v.

— (1955). *Meaning in the Visual Arts: Papers in and on Art History*. Garden City: Doubleday.

— (1957). *Gothic Architecture and Scholasticism*. New York: Meridian Books.

— (1962). *Studies in Iconology: Humanistic Themes in the Art of the Renaissance*. New York: Harper & Row.

— (1970). *Architecture gothique et pensée scholastique*. Paris: Minuit.

— (1972). *Estudios sobre iconologia*. Madrid: Alianza Editorial.

— (1975). *La perspective comme forme symbolique et autres essais*. Paris: Minuit.

— (1985). *Idea: Contribuición a la historia de la teoria del arte*. Madrid: Catedra.

— (1987). *La vie et l'art de Albrecht Dürer*. Paris: Hezan.

Paracelso (1973). *A chave da alquimia*. São Paulo: Editora Três.

Park, Katherine (1984). Bacon's Enchanted Glass. *Isis* 75, 290–302.

Park, Katharine, Datson, Lorraine J. and Galison, Peter L. (1984). Bacon, Galileo, and Descartes on imagination and analogy. *Isis* 75, 287–326.

Pavlov, Ivan (1974). *Textos escolhidos*. São Paulo: Abril.

Paz, Octavio (1977). *Marcel Duchamp ou O castelo da pureza*. São Paulo: Perspectiva.

Peirce, Charles Sanders (1909). Letter to William James dated December 1925, reprinted in *The Elements of Mathematics*, Volume III/2, Carolyn Eisele, editor, (The Hague: Mouton, 1976), 867–869. Page reference is to the reprint.

— (1931–1933). *Collected Papers of Charles S. Peirce*; Charles Hartshorn and Paul Weiss, editors, vols 2 and 4. Cambridge Harvard University Press.

— (1992). *The Essential Peirce; Selected Philosophical Writings, volume 1* (1867–1893), Nathan Houser and Christian Kloesel, editors. Bloomington: Indiana University Press.

Penley, Constance (1991). Bowerian Motion: Women, Tactics, and Technology. In *Technoculture*, Constance Penley and Andrew Ross, editors, 135–161. Minneapolis: University of Minnesota Press.

— (1994). Feminism, psychoanlaysis, amd the study of popular culture. In *Visual Culture: Images and Interpretations*, Norman Bryson, Michael Ann Holly, and Keith Moxey, 302–324. Hanover: Wesleyan University Press.

Percival, Keith (1981). The Saussurean paradigm: fact or fantasy? *Semiotica* 36 (1/2), 33–49.

Perelman, Chaim and Olbrecht-Tyteca, Lucie (1989). *Tratado de la argumentación*. Madrid: Gredos.

Podro, Michael (1982). *The Critical Historians of Art*. New Haven: Yale University Press.

— (1988). Derrida on Kant and Heidegger. *Art History* 11, 433–438.

Pöggeler, Otto (1967). *La pensée de Martin Heidegger*. Paris: Aubier/Montaigne.

— (1975). Being as appropriation. *Philosophy Today* 19, 152–77.

Polanyi, Karl (1968). *Primitive, Archaic and Modern Economies*, George Dalton, editor. Garden City: Anchor Books-Doubleday.

— (1975). *The Great Transformation*. New York: Octagon.

Pollock, Griselda (1988). *Vision and Difference: Femininity, Feminism and Histories of Art*. London: Routledge.

— (1994). Feminism/Foucault-Surveillance/Sexuality. In *Visual Culture: Images and Interpretations*, Norman Bryson, Michael Ann Holly, and Keith Moxey, editors, 1–41. Hanover: Wesleyan University Press.

Pontalis, J-B. (1991). *Perder de vista: Da fantasia de recuperação do objeto perdido*. Rio de Janeiro: Zahar.

Popkin, Richard H. (1977). *The History of Scepticism from Erasmus to Spinoza*. Berkely: The University of California Press.

Quine, W. V. (1969). Foreword. In *Convention: A Philosophical Study*, David Lewis, xi–xii. Cambridge: Harvard University Press.

Rees, Graham (1975). Francis Bacon's Semi-Paracelsian Cosmology. *Ambix* 22 (2), 81–101.

— (1984). Francis Bacon's biological ideas: A new manuscript source. In *Occult and Scientific Mentalities in the Renaissance*, Brian Vicker, editor, 297–314. Cambridge: Cambridge University Press.

Richardson, William J. (1963). *Heidegger: Through Phenomenology to Thought*. The Hague: Martinus Nijhoff.

Ricoeur, Paul (1969). *Le conflit des interprètations*. Paris: Seuil.

Roger, Alain (1991). Le paysage occidental. *Le Débat* 65, 14–28.

Rorty, Richard (1991). *Essays on Heidegger and Others*. Cambridge: Cambridge University Press.

Rosenberg, Jakob (1948). *Rembrandt*. Cambridge: Harvard University Press. 2v.

Rosenstein, Leon (1976). The ontological integrity of the art object from the ludic point of view. *The Journal of Aesthetics and Art Criticism* 34, 323–36.

Rosenstiehl, Pierre (1988). Labirinto. In *Enciclopédia Einaudi, volume 13: lógica-combinatória*. Lisboa: Imprensa Nacional, 247–273.

Ross, Andrew (1994). The ecology of images. In *Visual Culture: Images and Interpretations*, Norman Bryson, Michael An Holly, and Keith Moxey, 325–346. Hanover: Wesleyan University Press.

Rossi, Paolo (1965). *Clavis Universalis; Arti mnemoniche e logica combinatoria da Lullo a Leibniz*. Milano: Riccardo Ricciardi.

— (1984). *Francis Bacon: De la magia a la ciencia*. Madrid: Alianza.

— (1989). *Os filósofos e as máquinas*. São Paulo: Companhia das Letras.

Roustang, François (1988). *Lacan: Do equívoco ao impasse*. Rio de Janeiro: Campus.

Rousseau, Jean-Jacques (1978). *On the Social Contract, with Geneva Manuscript and Political Economy*, Roger D. Masters, editor. New York: Saint Martin's Press.

Sanchez, Alfonso E, Perez (1987). The Madrid-Prague axis. In *The Arcimboldo effect: Transformations of the Face from the Sixteenth to the Twentieth Century*. Milan: Bompiani. 55–64.

Sanouillet, Michel and Peterson, Elmer (1975). *The Essential Writings of Marcel Duchamp*. London: Thames & Hudson.

Santarcangeli, Paolo (1974). *Le livre des labyrinthes*. Paris: Gallimard.

Saussure, Ferdinand de (1982). *Cours de linguistique générale*. Paris: Payot.

— (1983). *Course in General Linguistics*. London: Duckworth.

Schapiro, Meyer (1956). Leonardo and Freud: An art-historical study. *Journal of the History of Ideas* 17, 147–178.

— (1968). The still life as a personal object: A note on Heidegger and van Gogh. In *The Reach of Mind*, Marianne Simmel, editor, 201–209. New York: Spinger.

— (1969). On some problems in the semiotic of visual arts: Field and vehicle in image-signs. *Semiotica* 1, 223–242.

— (1982). *Style, artiste et societé*. Paris: Gallimard.

Schuhl, Pierre-Maxime (1938). *Machinisme et philosophie*. Paris: Felix Alcan.

Schwarz, Arturo (1973). *Marcel Duchamp*. Paris & Milano: Hachette-Fabbri.

— (1974). Rrose Sélavy, alias Marchand du Sel, alias Belle Haleine. *L'Arc* 59, 29–35.

Schwarz, Gary (1991). *Rembrandt: His Life, his Paintings*. London & Harmondsworth: Penguin.

Sebeok, Tomas A. (1981). Naming in animals, with reference to playing: A hypothesis. *Semiotic Inquiry* 1, 121–135.

— (1986). *I Think I am a Verb*. New York: Plenum.

Selsam, Howard (1935). Spinoza: Art and geometric order. *Studies in the History of Ideas* 3, 255–269.

Silverman, Kaja (1983). *The Subject of Semiotics*. New York: Oxford University Press.

— (1994). Fassbinder and Lacan: A reconsiderattion of gaze, look, and image. In *Visual Culture: Interpretation and Images*, Norman Bryson, Michael Ann Holly, and Keith Moxey, 272–301. Hanover: Wesleyan University Press.

Simmel, George (1950). *Rembrandt; Ensayo de filosofia del arte*. Buenos Aires: Nova.

Simon, Gérard (1991). Le paysage, affaire de temps. *Le Débat* 65, 43–50.

Slive, Seymour (1953). *Rembrandt and His Critics*. The Hague: M. Nijhoof.

Spinoza, Baruch (1963). *Ethics and On the Correction of the Understanding*. New York: Dutton.

Stulberg, Robert B. (1973). Heidegger and the origin of the work of art: An explication. *The Journal of Aesthetics and Art Criticism* 32, 257–65.

Sulzberger, Suzanne (1962). Jérôme Bosch et les maîtres de l'enluminure. *Scriptorium* 16, 46–49.

Summers, David (1981). The "visual arts" and the problem of art historical description. *Art Journal* 42, 301–310.

— (1982). Conventions in the history of art. *New Literary History* 13, 103–125.

— (1986). This is not a sign: Some remarks on art and semiotics. *Art Criticism* 3, 30–45.

— (1987). *The Judgment of Sense: Renaissance Naturalism and the Rise of Aesthetics*. Cambridge: Cambridge University Press.

— (1989). "Form," nineteenth-century metaphysics, and the problem of art historical description. *Critical Inquiry* 15, 372–406.

— (1991). Real metaphor: Towards a redefiniton of the 'conceptual image.' In *Visual Theory: Painting and Interpretation*, Norman Bryson, Michael Ann Holly, and Keith Moxey, editors, 231–259. New York: Harper Collins.

— (1994a). On the histories of artifacts. *The Art Bulletin* 75, 590–592.

— (1994b). Form and gender. In *Visual Culture: Images and Interpretations*, Norman Bryson, Michael An Holly, and Keith Moxey, 384–412. Hanover: Wesleyan University Press.

Tagg, John (1988). The proof of the picture. *Afterimage* 15, 11–13.

— (1994). The discontinous city: Picturing and the discursive field. In *Visual Culture: Images and Intepretations*, Norman Bryson, Michael Ann Holly, and Keith Moxey, editors, 83–103. Hanover: Wesleyan University Press.

This, Claude (1972). Le point de vue Freudien: L'instant de la création. In *Art et science: De la creativité*, Colloque de Cerisy, 289–309. Paris: Union Générale d'Éditions.

Thom, René (1975a). Les mathèmatiques et l'intelligible. *Dialectica* 28, 71–80.

— (1975b). *Structural Stability and Morphogenesis*. Reading: W.A. Benjamin.

— (1983a). *Mathematical Models of Morphogenesis*. New York: Ellis Horwood.

— (1983b). Local et global dans l'oeuvre d'art. *Le Débat* 24, 73–89.

Thurnwald, Richard (1932). *Economics in Primitive Communities*. London: Oxford University Press.

Tickner, Lisa (1994). Men's work? Masculinity and modernism. In *Visual Culture: Images and Interpretations*, Norman Bryson, Michael Ann Holly, and Keith Moxey, editors, 42–82. Hanover: Wesleyan University Press.

Tomkins, Calvin (1996). *Duchamp: A Biography*. New York: Henry Holt & Company.

Tono, Yoshinki (1984). Duchamp y 'Inframince.' In *Duchamp*, 53–56. Madrid: Fundación Caja de Pensiones.

Touttain, Pierre-André (1976). Arcimboldo, Giuseppe. In *Dictionnaire ccritique et docummentaire des peintres, sculpteurs, dessinateurs et graveurs*, Emmanuel Bénézit. éditeur. Paris: Gründ.

Trimp, Wesley (1973). The meaning of Horace's Ut pictura poesis. *Journal of the Warburg and Courtauld Institute* 36, 1–34.

Turley, Peter T. (1977). *Peirce's Cosmology*. New York: Philosophical Library.

Valentiner, W. R. (1957). *Rembrandt and Spinoza*. London: Phaidon Press.

Valéry, Paul (1957). *Introduction à la méthode de Léonard de Vinci*. Paris: Gallimard.

Vasari, Giorgio (1980). *Le vite dí più eccellenti architetti, pittori, et scultori italiani*. New York: Broude International Editions. 2v.

Venâncio Filho, Paulo (1986). *Marcel Duchamp*. São Paulo: Brasiliense.

Venturi, Leonello (1964). *Storia della critica d'arte*. Torino: Einaudi.

Waddington, C. H. (1961). *How animals develop*. New York: Harper & Row.

Waelhens, A. de (1971). *La philosophie de Martin Heidegger*. Louvain/Paris: Éditions Nauwelaerts/Béatrice Nauwelaerts.

Waldberg, Patrick (1976). *Les demeures d'Hypnos*. Paris: Éditions de la Différence.

Wencelius, Leon (1937). *Calvin et Rembrandt*. Paris: Société d'Édition "Les Belles Lettres."

Weyl, Hermann (1952). *Symmetry*. Princeton: Princeton University Press.

— (1963). *Philosophy of Mathematics and Natural Science*. New York: Atheneum.

White, Christopher (1984). *Rembrandt*. London: Thames and Hudson.

White, John (1972). *Birth and Rebirth of Pictorial Space*. London: Faber & Faber.

Williams, Raymond (1973). Base and superstructure in Marxist cultural theory. *The New Left Review* 77, 3–16.

Wilson, Catherine (1993). Constancy, emergency, and illusion: Obstacles to a naturalistic theory of vision. In *Causation in Early Modern Philosophy*, Steven Nadler, editor, 159–178. Pennsylvania: The Pennsylvania University Press.

Yates, Frances A (1971). *Giordano Bruno and Hermetic Tradition*. London: Routledge & Kegan Paul.

Zimmerman, Michael E. Z. (1990). *Heidegger's Confrontation with Modernity, Technology, Politics and Art*. Bloomington: Indiana University Press.

Zumthor, Paul (1989). *A Holanda no tempo de Rembrandt*. São Paulo: Companhia das Letras.

INDEX

I

SEMIOTICS & THE HUMAN SCIENCES

Edited by Roberta Kevelson

This series, Semiotics and the Human Sciences, takes as its leading idea the Peircean assumption that human institutions, in theory and practice, are models and prototypes of the Theory of Signs, or Semiotics. The core of this series is Law, and especially those concepts of the law that are central to all theories of signs, whether Peirce's, Greimasian, or various aspects of structural linguistics, Critical Theory, and similar outgrowths such as Postmodernism, Functionalism, and antipositivism. Included in the special topics developed in this series are Ideological Conflict, Value-making and Aesthetic Functions, Chaos Theory and theories of complex Systems. Just as semiotics presumes an underlying dialogic structure, one of its main focal areas is Legal Contract; others include Public Reason, Comparative Legal Cultures, problems of Paradox; Pluralistic Discourse and International Law. The series is open to proposals in these and other related issues and topics, from many academic and professional perspectives. Collected papers of the Round Tables on Law and Semiotics are a large part of this series, and serve as research tools.

For more information about this series, please contact:

Peter Lang Publishing
Acquisitions Department
275 Seventh Ave., 28th Floor
New York, NY 10001